Afropolitanism: Reboot

This edited collection comprises an original group of contributions on that much maligned figure, the Afropolitan. The contributors do not aim to define or fix the term anew; the reboot is, instead, the beginnings of an activist scholarly agenda in which 'the Afropolitan' is reimagined to include the stealthy figure crossing the Mediterranean by boat, and the Somali shopkeeper in a South African township. In their pieces included here, the authors insist on the need to ask questions about the inclusion of such globally mobile Africans in any theorisations of the transnational circuits we call Afropolitan. This collection, from some of the foremost voices on Afropolitanism, invigorates anew the debate, and reboots understandings of who the Afropolitan is, the many places she calls her origin, and the multiple places he comes to call home in the world.

The chapters in this book were originally published in the *Journal of African Cultural Studies.*

Carli Coetzee is the co-editor of *Negotiating the Past: The Making of Memory in South Africa* (1998) and the author of *Accented Futures: Language Activism and the Ending of Apartheid* (2013). She is the editor of the *Journal of African Cultural Studies* and a research associate at the University of the Witwatersrand, Johannesburg, South Africa.

Afropolitanism: Reboot

Edited by
Carli Coetzee

LONDON AND NEW YORK

First published 2017
by Routledge
2 Park Square, Milton Park, Abingdon, Oxon, OX14 4RN, UK

and by Routledge
711 Third Avenue, New York, NY 10017, USA

Routledge is an imprint of the Taylor & Francis Group, an informa business

British Library Cataloguing in Publication Data
A catalogue record for this book is available from the British Library

ISBN 13: 978-1-138-20856-8

Typeset in Times New Roman
by RefineCatch Limited, Bungay, Suffolk

Publisher's Note
The publisher accepts responsibility for any inconsistencies that may have arisen during the conversion of this book from journal articles to book chapters, namely the possible inclusion of journal terminology.

Contents

Citation Information

The chapters in this book were originally published in various issues of the *Journal of African Cultural Studies*. When citing this material, please use the original page numbering for each article, as follows:

Chapter 1
Rethinking African culture and identity: the Afropolitan model
Chielozona Eze
Journal of African Cultural Studies, volume 26, issue 2 (June 2014), pp. 243–247

Chapter 2
Cosmopolitanism with African roots. Afropolitanism's ambivalent mobilities
Susanne Gehrmann
Journal of African Cultural Studies, volume 28, issue 1 (March 2016), pp. 61–72

Chapter 3
The politics of Afropolitanism
Amatoritsero Ede
Journal of African Cultural Studies, volume 28, issue 1 (March 2016), pp. 88–100

Chapter 4
Afropolitanism as critical consciousness: Chimamanda Ngozi Adichie's and Teju Cole's internet presence
Miriam Pahl
Journal of African Cultural Studies, volume 28, issue 1 (March 2016), pp. 73–87

Chapter 5
Exorcizing the future: Afropolitanism's spectral origins
Stephanie Bosch Santana
Journal of African Cultural Studies, volume 28, issue 1 (March 2016), pp. 120–126

Chapter 6
'Why I am (still) not an Afropolitan'
Emma Dabiri
Journal of African Cultural Studies, volume 28, issue 1 (March 2016), pp. 104–108

Chapter 7
Part-Time Africans, Europolitans and 'Africa lite'
Grace A. Musila
Journal of African Cultural Studies, volume 28, issue 1 (March 2016), pp. 109–113

Chapter 8
'We, Afropolitans'
Chielozona Eze
Journal of African Cultural Studies, volume 28, issue 1 (March 2016), pp. 114–119

Chapter 9
Being-in-the-world*: the Afropolitan Moroccan author's worldview in the new millennium*
Valérie K. Orlando
Journal of African Cultural Studies, volume 25, issue 3 (September 2013), pp. 275–291

Chapter 10
Naija boy remix: Afroexploitation and the new media creative economies of cosmopolitan African youth
Krystal Strong and Shaun Ossei-Owusu
Journal of African Cultural Studies, volume 26, issue 2 (June 2014), pp. 189–205

For any permission-related enquiries please visit:
http://www.tandfonline.com/page/help/permissions

Notes on Contributors

Stephanie Bosch Santana is associate professor in the Department of Comparative Literature at UCLA, USA. Her research focuses on South African, Malawian, Zimbabwean, and Zambian fiction from the 1950s to the present day, moving across national, postcolonial and global frameworks.

Carli Coetzee is the co-editor of *Negotiating the Past: The Making of Memory in South Africa* (1998) and the author *of Accented Futures: Language Activism and the Ending of Apartheid* (2013). She is the editor of the *Journal of African Cultural Studies* and a research associate at the University of the Witwatersrand, Johannesburg, South Africa.

Emma Dabiri is a visual sociology PhD researcher at Goldsmiths, University of London, and a teaching fellow in the African Studies Department at SOAS. She has published in a number of academic journals, as well as the UK national press, and is one of the BBC's Expert Voices.

Amatoritsero Ede is a Nigerian-Canadian poet and independent scholar. He completed a PhD in English Literature from Carleton University, Ottawa, Canada, in 2013, and is now the publisher and managing editor of *Maple Tree Literary Supplement.*

Chielozona Eze is associate professor of English and African American Studies at Northeastern Illinois University, USA. His primary research interests are narrative theory, globalization and culture, and feminism in global contexts. His most recent book is *Ethics and Human Rights in Anglophone African Women's Literature – Feminist Empathy* (2016).

Susanne Gehrmann is professor in the Department of African Studies at Humboldt University, Berlin, Germany. She has published books (in German) on literary configurations of colonial critical discourse, autobiography in Africa, and language experiments.

Grace A. Musila is a senior lecturer in the English Department at Stellenbosch University, South Africa. Her research interests include gender studies, Eastern and Southern African literatures, African popular culture, African intellectual archives, and postcolonial whiteness in Africa. She is the co-editor of *Rethinking Eastern African Intellectual Landscapes* (2012) and the author of *A Death Retold in Truth and Rumour: Kenya, Britain and the Julie Ward Murder* (2015).

Valérie K. Orlando is professor and Head of the Department of French and Italian at the University of Maryland, USA. She writes on Francophone writing from the African diaspora, African Cinema, and French literature and culture, and she has two books forthcoming: *The Algerian Novel* and *New African Cinema* (both 2017).

Shaun Ossei-Owusu is a postdoctoral research scholar and academic fellow at Columbia Law School, USA. He studies social inequality – his work sitting at the intersection of law, history, and sociology. His research is interested in how government provides services to the poor, specifically legal aid and health care.

Miriam Pahl is a PhD student at SOAS, University of London, UK. Her main disciplinary interests are postcolonial theory, political thought, ethics, and cultural production. Her thesis examines the transformation of Anglophone African literature on the 'global stage', post 2005.

Krystal Strong is assistant professor in the Graduate School of Education at the University of Pennsylvania, USA. Her research combines anthropological approaches to formal and non-institutional educational processes, politics, youth, and new media in Africa and the African Diaspora.

Introduction

Carli Coetzee

Scholarly gossip typically repeats two origin stories for the term "Afropolitan", yet both of the people identified as the originators of the term disclaim having invented it. One of these non-originators is Achille Mbembe (his work is always a source that comes with extraordinary weight in any scholarly bibliography, and the citation often preferred in academic papers). Anglophone readers invariably cite his piece "Afropolitanism", published as part of the edited collection *Africa Remix: Contemporary Art of a Continent* that accompanied the touring exhibition of the same name (2005). In their pieces included in this volume, however, Susanne Gehrmann and Stephanie Bosch Santana write of the more nuanced and differently historicized francophone histories of Mbembe's use of the term, in particular as he has expanded his analysis in his *Sortir de la grande nuit* (2013). For those who have not read Mbembe in French, the *Africa Remix* chapter has become something close to an origin myth, its other origin deleted and illegible.

Illegible in other ways is Taiye Selasi's origin text, interpreted often as a festive party piece with a Fela Kuti mix tape as soundtrack, the opaquely named "Bye-Bye Babar". The short piece is often cited as having named a generation (references are too numerous to list here). "Bye-Bye Babar" was published in the now defunct online magazine *Lip* in their issue *LIP#5 AFRICA*, alongside interviews with, and pieces on, writers like Helen Oyeyemi, Chimamanda Ngozi Adichie, film-maker Ousmane Sembène, and a review of a museum exhibition on Afro-beat legend Fela Kuti (http://thelip.robertsharp.co.uk/?cat=14&paged=1). In this original piece, the spelling of the title was "Bye-Bye Babar", perhaps a reference to the collection of essays by Herbert R. Kohl, *Should We Burn Babar*?, in which US based Kohl ("self-styled radical educator" (https://www.kirkusreviews.com/book-reviews/herbert-kohl/should-we-burn-babar/)) derided the series of children's books about the green-suited elephant, Babar, as a celebratory and Eurocentric narrative of assimilation (although Babar is, of course, an elephant not an African individual). When Selasi's piece was picked up by others and widely republished after 2012, the title often slipped and became "Bye-Bye Barbar" (https://gowomenofcolour.wordpress.com/2013/12/21/bye-bye-barbar-or-what-is-an-afropolitan-by-taiye-selasi/). Selasi herself has said that the initial piece has been misunderstood and misinterpreted (and misspelt).

In an interview with *Transition* magazine (with the deliberately un-festive title "From That Stranded Place"), Selasi said: "'Afropolitan' came from [a] stranded place. Not from a utopian vision at all. I was saying, to myself foremost, there are more than six of us. There is an African diaspora, not the original one; there is a *new* one, a smaller one. . . . I wasn't imagining a superhero costume. . . . I think seventeen people read it over the course of five years. Then, because the internet is magic, somebody in South Africa, at the Michael Stevenson gallery, read it and said, "Can we use it in our catalog?" They published it, somebody in Nairobi saw it, published it in a newspaper in Nairobi, and it went viral. But no one read that essay when I wrote it. I wrote it sitting down and shutting up. Really. Really." (http://www.jstor.org/stable/10.2979/transition.117.148?seq=1#page_scan_tab_contents). Here too, it is the inclusion in a catalogue accompanying an art exhibition that brings the piece to a wider public. A piece written "sitting down and shutting up" becomes read, instead, as a celebration and a theorisation of a branded and loud nightclub lifestyle.

In this unmooring of its context, the "stranded" tone of the original piece is deleted, and the tone of "pain" and anger emptied out. Like Mbembe, Selasi does not lay claim to having invented or "coined" the term. Yet the consumerist version of Afropolitanism, in particular that to be found on the many lifestyle web sites that Emma Dabiri has critiqued in her earlier work and again here, has become a main strand in responses to the term and is often linked to "Bye Bye Babar", reading the piece as a programme *for* consumerism and what Dabiri calls the "African hipster experience". Dabiri's "Afro-Rebel (Or Why I am Not an Afropolitan)" piece, published in a number of places between 2013 and 2014, has itself become a foundation text in critiques of the more consumerist versions of Afropolitanism, and in her new piece included here ("Why I am Still not an Afropolitan") Dabiri reflects on the lives and after-lives of the term and on her own positioning as she distances herself from being described by others as having the "look" of an Afropolitan.

Yet another definitive moment in the history of the term was the keynote address by Binyavanga Wainaina, delivered to the African Studies Association UK conference in Leeds, UK, in 2012. The lecture was not recorded, and Wainaina spoke from loose notes only in a genre-defying reflection on autobiography, location and politics. Stephanie Bosch Santana's account of this lost and deleted scene "Exorcising Afropolitanism: Binyavanga Wainaina explains why 'I am a Pan-Africanist, not an Afropolitan'" has become a widely cited resource, standing in for the lost and unrecorded original. Alongside Dabiri's piece, this *Africa in Words* post became part of the growing visibility of the term, by this time increasingly accompanied by a negative qualifier ("*not* an Afropolitan").

In March 2014, an article by Chielozona Eze appeared online in the *Journal of African Cultural Studies*. "Rethinking African Culture and Identity: the Afropolitan Model" rapidly became the "most read" article on the journal's web page and remains so. Typing the term "Afropolitanism" into the search engine "Google trends" mirrors a similar pattern of take-up and circulation in the sources used to compile the citation statistics (http://www.google.com/trends/explore#q=Afropolitan&cmpt=q&tz=Etc%2FGMT-1). While it is not a definitive source, it is instructive to see that "Google trend" cites 0 references of the term Afropolitanism in print and online in February 2012; by April 2012 there is a definite spike with 72 references logged. The important edited collection *Negotiating Afropolitanism: Essays on Borders and Spaces in Contemporary African Literature and Folklore* appeared in 2011, with essays by a range of scholars and a discipline defining foreword by Simon Gikandi. By mid-2014, the Google trends graph shows that uses of the word Afropolitanism reached an all-time peak. It seemed, to many of us, as if the term had reached the end of the road, bankrupted and no longer of any use in discussions with a transformative social agenda. In 2016, Eva Rask Knudsen and Ulla Rahbek's collection of essays on, and interviews with, cultural and literary figures associated with the term even named their project *In Search of the Afropolitan: Encounters, Conversations and Contemporary Diasporic African Literature*, as if the Afropolitan had somehow become an elusive category and person.

In the essays included here in *Afropolitanism: Reboot*, a range of scholars engage with, and respond to, the often contradictory understandings of the Afropolitan and Afropolitanism. Amatoritsero Ede focuses particularly on the contradiction between the culture of Afropolitanism and its politics, through a close reading of some primary texts. Susanne Gehrmann traces the ambivalent lives and afterlives of "Afropolitan characters" in some recent works of literature, while Miriam Pahl investigates the ways in which authors' internet presences give shape to Afropolitanism as a critically engaged practice. These two essays are representative of the growing scholarship through which an Afropolitan canon has become defined: *Ghana Must Go*, *Open City* and *Americanah*. In their essays here, Gehrmann and Pahl show the complexities of the production and circulation of an Afropolitan sensibility, and how the private lives of the authors they discuss often come to be conflated too simply with the Afropolitan characters that people their literary works. Valérie K. Orlando's contribution draws our attention to a geographical location often left out of discussions of the Afropolitan, namely the Moroccan literary and cultural milieu. Her analysis of French-language Moroccan-based Afropolitan discourses shows that what rises to the surface in Afropolitanism conversations is diverse and locally inflected. In Krystal Strong and Shaun Ossei-Owusu's paper, the US-based Naija Boyz's entrepreneurial music-making is analysed as an example of the often counterintuitive ways in which young Africans refashion cultural identities.

This collection of essays does not aim to define or fix the term anew; the reboot is, instead, the beginnings of an activist scholarly agenda in which "the Afropolitan" is reimagined to include the stealthy figure crossing the Mediterranean by boat, and the Somali shopkeeper in a South African township. In their pieces included here, Emma Dabiri and Grace A. Musila insist on the need to ask questions about the inclusion of such globally mobile Africans in any theorisations of the transnational circuits we call Afropolitan. Chielozona Eze articulates a version of Afropolitanism as an "ethics of being in the world" that is the responsibility of all of those he calls "We, Afropolitans". Stephanie Bosch Santana's piece analyses the conflicts and coincidences between Afropolitanism and PanAfricanism, in an argument that seeks to revitalise both. We hope, in this collection, to invigorate anew the debate, and to reboot understandings of who the Afropolitan is, the many places she calls her origin, and the multiple places she comes to call home in the world.

References

ALA Conference: African Futures and Beyond. Bayreuth, June 3–6 2015. http://www.ala2015.com/#/home/

Bosch Santana, Stephanie. 2013. "Exorcizing Afropolitanism: Binyavanga Wainaina explains why "I am a Pan-Africanist, not an Afropolitan" at ASAUK 2012". [Online] Africainwords.com. Available at: http://africainwords.com/2013/02/08/exorcizing-afropolitanism-binyavanga-wainaina-explains-why-i-am-a-pan-africanist-not-an-afropolitan-at-asauk-2012/ [Accessed 10 Aug. 2015].

Dabiri, Emma. 2014. "Why I'm Not An Afropolitan". [Online] *Africa is a Country*. Available at: http://africasacountry.com/2014/01/why-im-not-an-afropolitan/ [Accessed 2 October 2015].

Dabiri, Emma. 2015. "Afro-Rebel (Or Why I am not an Afropolitan)". [Online] http://thediasporadiva.tumblr.com/. Available at: http://thediasporadiva.tumblr.com/post/55036008288/afro-rebel-or-why-i-am-not-an-afropolitan [Accessed 2 October 2015].

Eze, Chielozona. 2014. "Rethinking African culture and identity: the Afropolitan model." *Journal of African Cultural Studies* 26(2): 234–247.

Kohl, Herbert R. 1995. *Should we Burn Babar: Essays on Children's Literature and the Power of Stories*. New York: The New Press.

Mbembe, Achille. 2013. *Sortir de la grande nuit: Essai sur l'Afrique décolonisée*. Paris: La Découverte/Poche.

Mbembe, Achille. 2005. "Afropolitanism." Trans. Laurent Chauvet. *Africa Remix: Contemporary Art of a Continent*. Eds. Njami Simon and Lucy Durán. Ostfildern, Germany: Hatje Cantz Publishers, 26–30.

Rask Knudsen, Eva and Ulla Rahbek (eds.). 2016. *In Search of the Afropolitan Encounters, Conversations and Contemporary Diasporic African Literature*. London: Rowman & Littlefield.

Selasi, Taiye. 2005. "Bye-Bye Babar." *LIP. The LIP Magazine*, 3 Mar. 2005.

Selasi, Taiye. 2013. "Bye-Bye Barbar." (https://gowomenofcolour.wordpress.com/2013/12/21/bye-bye-barbar-or-what-is-an-afropolitan-by-taiye-selasi/).

Selasi, Taiye. Interviewed by Aaron Bady. 2015. "From that Stranded Place". *Transition*, 117, 148–165.

Wawrzinek, Jennifer and J.K.S. Makokha (eds.). 2011. *Negotiating Afropolitanism: Essays on Borders and Spaces in Contemporary African Literature and Folklore*. Brill/Rodopi.

Rethinking African culture and identity: the Afropolitan model

Chielozona Eze

Since the end of the Cold War and, in particular, the demise of apartheid in South Africa, there has been a sustained debate about African identity. There seems to be a consensus among scholars of African culture that the conventional notion of African identity that was conceived in opposition to the West is anachronistic. But what then constitutes the new African? Scholars have suggested concepts such as contamination, cultural hybridity, cultural mutt, conviviality, and most recently Afropolitanism, as means to understand the complex modern African identity. This article takes a critical examination of Afropolitanism and argues that it is an enunciation of the ideas of contamination, hybridity, hyperculturality and other postmodernist terms that disrupt essentialist and oppositional notions of African culture and identity. I hope to achieve two things in this article: situate Afropolitanism within a larger philosophical tradition of cosmopolitanism and examine the moral implications of expanding the notion of African identity beyond the oppositional model.

Introduction

In her famous report on the South African Truth and Reconciliation Commission, *Country Of My Skull*, Antjie Krog (1998) wrote a moving poem in which she asks, as an Afrikaner, the group most responsible for the crimes of apartheid, if the victims can accept her as an African. She asks for 'a new skin'. In her mythopoetic narrative, *Begging to Be Black* (2009), she makes this request even more explicit, arguing for relation rather than opposition, interrelatedness rather than separateness. What exactly does her desire for a new skin imply for our understanding of Africa? Is she committing identity suicide as Max du Preez alleges (2009)? In the same post-apartheid spirit, Thabo Mbeki defined himself as one in whose veins flows African, Asian, and European blood. A few years later, Taiye Selasi, a British-born child of Nigerian and Ghanaian parents, distanced herself from 'African' as a tag of identity; she defined herself instead as 'Afropolitan'. The notions of identity adopted by these and other African writers, authors, and statesmen indicate a subtle but persistent shift in African self-perception. Africa, to be sure, has always been a complex, diverse continent, and Africans have never shared an undifferentiated identity even though the West has sought to impose one on them. It is, however, a welcome development that black Africans increasingly define themselves no longer in opposition to the people of European ancestry, and that the people of European ancestry in Africa – Antjie Krog for one – see themselves as Africans. This shift in self-perceptions is evidently part of the post-Cold War global development in identity construction owing to cultural and economic consequences of globalization. Identity is no longer shaped exclusively by geography or blood, or culture understood in oppositional terms. On the contrary, identity is now relational.

In the recent past, literary works such as Chris Abani's *The Virgin of Flame* (2007), Taiye Selasi's (2013) *Ghana Must Go* and NoViolet Bulawayo's (2013) *We Need New Names*, among others, reveal changes in self-perception within Africa and among peoples of African ancestry outside of Africa. In interviews or memoirs, these writers employ their background to call for a re-examination of the notion of African identity. Their narratives show an intermeshing of relationships across ethnic, religious, and racial lines, thus blurring cheap dichotomous categorizations of persons. Unlike in the age of Achebe, the age that produced *Things Fall Apart*, it is no longer strange to find within Igbo, Yoruba, Zulu, or Shona families persons of European and Asian ancestry. Quite the contrary, many African families are now increasingly multi-ethnic, multi-racial, transcultural; they are now polychromatic. They live in Lagos, Johannesburg, Berlin, New York, Hong Kong ... They are African, or Afri-hyphenated, and because their identities are constituted by relation rather than opposition, they present good examples of Johann Wolfgang von Goethe's concept of 'elective affinities' – (*Wahlverwandtschaften*) – contributing in complex ways to the fluid definition of 'African' in the twenty-first century. In short, African identities, like in most other parts of the world, are now shaped by elective affinities due to cultural and racial intermixing. It is a welcome development that more Africans are acknowledging this fact; they are questioning what it means to be African. To be sure, challenging the operational definition of Africa does not imply rejecting the continent or even the concept; it means calling for a new, more nuanced understanding of identity.

But the intermixing of ethnicities and races, or elective affinities, is just the most obvious form of the negation of the oppositional, rigid identity construction in Africa. Globalization has shrunk the world to the size of one's palms in the forms of cell phones or iPads. It is now possible to experience in most African villages lifestyles hitherto unknown to them thanks to these modern means of mass communication. As Byung-Chul Han (2005) has argued, reality is now hyperlinked and therefore hypercultural. Culture is delocalized. And so is identity. But does this mean that in matters of culture and identity anything goes? Does this imply that there is no longer anything recognizable, or even stable in persons? A quick answer to this doubt, I think, lies in the claim to be African. To claim to be something is to admit that there is something that could be recognized at a certain point in time. What then is that? Is it something immutable, exclusive, or inclusive? What does it mean to be African? In order to examine the complex nature of African identity in a somewhat dialectical form, I will first sketch a conventional notion of African identity. Second, I will explore concepts that ostensibly oppose this initial. Finally, I will take a critical examination of Afropolitanism, highlight its weakness, and suggest its moral potential by situating it within a larger philosophical tradition of cosmopolitanism.

African culture and the oppositional model of identity

For those of us who grew up in Africa in the 1980s and 1990s, and who loved Bob Marley's and Peter Tosh's songs, there was no escaping the Afrocentric ideology of their lyrics. We all sang with Bob Marley, 'Africa unite/Cause we're moving right out of Babylon', and with Peter Tosh, 'Don't care where you come from/As long as you're a black man, you're an African/No mind your nationality/You have got the identity of an African.' We used Marcus Garvey's nativist slogan, 'Africa for Africans', to underscore our pan-African sentiments. Back then, to be truly African was to abjure any obvious cultural identification with the West, which for us embodied oppression against Africans; in contrast, we were trying to imagine a common identity for all people with dark skins.

The idea of Africans being united by a common cause or self-understanding, of course, goes as far back as the mid-nineteenth century when scholars like Alexander Crummell and Edward Wilmot Blyden felt the necessity to conceive of a common African culture and identity in order to combat the racist philosophies of their time (Appiah, 1992; Mudimbe, 1988, 1994). The African American scholar W.E.B. Du Bois revived the idea on a larger political stage when he convened the first Pan African Congress in 1919, in Paris (Adeleke, 1998, 505–536). Resistance against the colonizer and what he stood for was a necessary stage in African liberation.

V.Y. Mudimbe (1988) has argued that Africa is an invention of the West, and Kandiatu Kanneh (1998) has demonstrated that Africa has been reinvented by peoples of African descent. On the African continent, writers and poets such as Leopold Sedar Senghor and Chinua Achebe have greatly contributed to the reinvention of Africa. Simon Gikandi has argued that Achebe invented the postcolonial African culture, which is to say, African culture as discoursed in the institutions of high learning (2001, 3–8). The postcolonial African culture, from an Achebean perspective, is understood as challenging the colonial narrative about Africa and reasserting the *true* African identity. Gikandi's idea is supported by Abiola Irele's observation that *Things Fall Apart* gave form to 'the sense of new beginnings registered' by writers such as Camara Laye and Amos Tutuola, among others (2001, 2). Achebe (2000) has said that he conceived *Things Fall Apart* as a response to the racist images of Africa in Joyce Cary and Joseph Conrad. In his essay, 'An Image of Africa: racism in Conrad's *Heart of Darkness*' (Achebe 1990), he made his attack of Western misrepresentation of the African image more explicit. In an interview granted to Kwame Anthony Appiah, he explained his understanding of African identity thus:

> It is, of course true that the African identity is still in the making. There isn't a final identity that is African. But, at the same time, there *is* an identity coming into existence. And it has a certain context and a certain meaning. If somebody meets me, say, in a shop in Cambridge [England], he says 'Are you African?' Which means that Africa means something to some people. Each of these tags has a meaning, and a penalty and a responsibility. All these tags, unfortunately for the black man, are tags of disability ... I think it is part of the writer's role to encourage the creation of an African identity. (1992, 73–74)

Achebe's primordialist self-identification as a black man in Cambridge is rooted in the history of Africans being perceived as the ultimate Other in the European imagination (Eze 1997; Mills 1998). Africa is a product of the Western political and philosophical imagination. But that product, Achebe argues, is flawed. He saw himself supplying a supposedly authentic African identity, which is understandably a contrast to what the European has constructed.

I bring a sympathetic understanding to the efforts of earlier generations of African and African diaspora thinkers who had to fight their overwhelmingly racist world. Thus their recourse to nativist, relativist, and autochthonous arguments were employed as a means to fight erasure. I understand that nativism has a political relevance as a stage in the liberatory process of a people. Marcus Garvey's 'Africa for Africans', considered to be the theoretical source of African nationalism, was expedient at the time it was propounded. The issue with this ideology, however, is that it does not have within it the means to extend the vision of the world beyond the essentialist enclave of African pristine villages. In most African countries there have been local or tribal versions of 'Africa for Africans'. I think of the many instances of genocide and ethnic cleansing that have taken place after independence in many African countries. But even in our times, the attraction of African nativism for Africans remains strong because it is inextricably linked to heroic sacrifices for African liberation, democracy, and anti-colonial movements. Sabelo J. Ndlovu-Gatsheni has discussed the attraction and dangers of nationalist and nativist movements in Zimbabwe and South Africa; he drew attention to the origins and teleology of the ideology of African nationalism (2009, 61–78). One of the greatest challenges facing African societies is how to go beyond the vestiges of relativism associated with the anticolonial struggles and which have become embedded in parochial ethnic and tribal loyalties. The challenge is to weave a more universal solidarity that can accord individuals anywhere in Africa their rights and dignities regardless of their gender or ancestry.

Much has happened in the world since the conception of Africanness by Achebe and Peter Tosh: The Berlin Wall has fallen; rigid cultural and ideological boundaries between the first, second, and third worlds have been questioned; apartheid is legally defunct. There is an increased movement of people, goods, and ideas between nations. As Anthony Giddens suggests, we now live in a runaway world. By runaway world he means that the world grows smaller every day due to changes brought about by the forces of globalization. These changes affect our culture, our traditions, our families, and our politics. We literally 'live in one world' (2003, 7).

I do not ignore the fact that as much as globalization has shrunk the world it has also increased the gap between the haves and the have-nots. In many instances, it has indirectly encouraged fundamentalist thinking and behaviour as people seek to protect their cultural heritage that is at the risk of being destroyed by external influences. In her book, *Accented Futures: Language Activism and the Ending of Apartheid*, Carli Coetzee argues that apartheid is not truly dead in South Africa, and urges an awareness of how its legacies continue to impact people's lives in ways that are as inimical as apartheid (2013, x).

These, however, do not negate the fact that there has been a profound change in the ways we understand the culture, identity, and citizenship of countries. It would be a mistake to think that there is no difference, in self-reading, between the men of my father's (or Achebe's) generation, who never left their African villages and their grandchildren, some of whom were born in Lagos or Cape Town, but who still identify with their ancestral villages elsewhere. This drastic change is even captured in *Things Fall Apart*, when Nwoye defected from tradition towards the new way of life. While there may not be biological differences between these generations (Okonkwo and Nwoye's generations for example), the same cannot be said of their cultures and worldviews, or even moral topographies.

African culture and the relational model of identity

Jean and John Comaroff observe that the global south is rarely seen as a source of theory and explanation for world historical events; they argue that the enormous historical transformations taking place there provide unique opportunities to theorize about our world. 'In the face of the structural violence perpetrated in the name of neoliberalism, as this suggests, the global south is producing and exporting some ingenious, highly imaginative modes of survival – and more' (Comaroff and Comaroff 2012, 18). By imaginative modes of survival, the Comaroffs are referring to new thoughts and ideas on how to meet the challenges of globalization and modernity. In this regard, they contend that 'the global south is running ahead of the global north' (Comaroff and Comaroff 2012, 19).

New theories, of course, do not automatically translate into better theories. In my judgment, if the global south does not seek to transcend the flaws of the multiple theories from the global north, theories which had largely frozen the world into dichotomies, those new theories would be of little use. Homi Bhabha highlights such potential flaws. In his discussion of 'commitment to theory', he asks whether the only way out of the dualism of Western ideology would imply the 'invention of an originary counter-myth':

> Must the project of our liberationist aesthetics be forever part of a totalizing Utopian vision of Being and History that seeks to transcend the contradictions and ambivalences that constitute the very structure of human subjectivity and its systems of cultural representation? (1994, 19)

I share Bhabha's concerns. It is a fact that the West has inflicted enormous violence on the rest of the non-white world. The worst kind of violence is epistemic, as Frantz Fanon argues in *Black Skin, White Masks* (1967, 109–111). Fanon argues, Western theories about Africa objectified black people everywhere, thus making it possible and, for Europeans, morally justifiable to denigrate black people (1967, 109–112).

I think that the events in South Africa in the past two decades provide some hope that our world is not stuck in oppositionality. I speak of how Nelson Mandela successfully steered South Africa out of potential post-apartheid racial war and subsequently recast the models of identity and solidarity. Despite the enduring legacies of apartheid, South Africa provides ground for the fulfilment of the Comaroffs' dreams of a new theory from the South. I have argued (Eze 2012) that Nelson Mandela's greatest achievement lies in giving South Africa and the world a new moral compass, one that recasts the narrative of postcoloniality into the model of relationality. In that same spirit, Thabo Mbeki defined the African not in an oppositional sense, but in a broader, more encompassing way, as a composite of black, white, and brown bloods. Mbeki writes:

> I owe my being to the Koi and the San whose desolate souls haunt the great expanses of the beautiful Cape ... I am formed of the migrants who left Europe to find a new home on our native land. Whatever their actions, they remain still, part of me. In my veins courses the blood of the Malay slaves who came from the East ... I come of those who were transported from India and China. (1996)

I acknowledge the risk in invoking Thabo Mbeki in a discussion of race- or culture-transcendent ideas given his 1998 speech 'African Renaissance', which hews rather too close to Cheikh Anta Diop's Afrocentric reading of the African past (Mbeki 1998). In other contexts, Mbeki appeared to have yielded to the seductions of nativism that often accompany any liberation struggle or passionate search for justice, as exemplified by his policy positions on HIV infections and disease in Africa. His ideas in this regard did not match the lofty visions of his 'I am an African' speech (Fassin 2007). Mark Gevisser captures the promises and enigmas surrounding the person of Thabo Mbeki in his richly researched biography, *The Dream Deferred: Thabo Mbeki* (2007, 727–794). However, some African thinkers have interpreted Mbeki's African renaissance speech more positively. Elias K. Bongmba, for example, argues that 'it demands a post-nationalist agenda that take the African region seriously, calls for the revitalization of Africa's cultural ideals' (2004, 291).

David Johnson (2012) presents a good synopsis and analysis of the debates that Thabo Mbeki's 'I am an African' speech has generated. My preliminary understanding of the speech is in light of the African National Congress (ANC) vision of non-racialism in South Africa (Ndebele 2002, 133–146). I read the speech as expressing a robust anti-essentialist idea of African identity. The African is no longer understood as being in opposition to the European, but as incorporating Europeans, Asians, and the rest of the world. Being African is no longer anchored in the narratives of autochthony. Against this backdrop, being black in the Cambridge of the twenty-first century does not mean being African. Nor does being white in Johannesburg mean being European. Identity, like culture, is delocalized. Place and origin are no longer exclusive markers of identity, even if they still play vital roles in many people's self-reading.

In the same effort of negating the conventional notion of African identity, Mahmood Mamdani argues for cultural hybridity, and, suggesting that it is the control board of our existence, enjoins African intelligentsias to actively encourage that. For him:

> cultural mixing, whether enforced or voluntary, can arise without a biological mixing. From this point of view, I wonder if we should not consider the postcolonial intelligentsia, with one foot in colonial culture and another in that of their ancestors, as culturally creole. (1999, 129)

The main role of the creolized postcolonial intelligentsias, Mamdani argues, also consists in debunking the 'bipolar identities' which are the core parts of post-apartheid legacies. By bipolar identities, he means the ideology of grouping 'whites as racial and blacks as ethnic beings, welding together its beneficiaries – whether Afrikaners, English, German, Greek – into a single identity called white, while fragmenting its victims into so many ethnic minorities' (1999, 130).

Kwame Anthony Appiah argues that there is no such thing as a pristine culture or identity completely unaffected by another in today's world. In *Cosmopolitanism: Ethics in a World of Strangers*, he argues for more openness towards diversity. He even suggests the idea of 'contamination' as that which best captures the nature of modern culture. By contamination, he means the absence of purity. 'Cultural purity', he states, 'is an oxymoron. The odds are that, culturally speaking, you already live a cosmopolitan life, enriched by literature, art, and film that come from many places, and that contains influences from many more' (2006, 113). Appiah cites the example of Publius Terentius or Terence, an African slave, born in Carthage and taken to Rome in the late second century AD, and who made his name by incorporating Greek plays into a single Latin drama, a style that was dubbed contamination. What Terence did, Appiah argues, is suggestive of the nature of culture and human contact. 'When people speak for an ideal of cultural purity, sustaining the authentic culture of the Asante or the American family farm, I find myself drawn to *contamination* as the name for a counter-ideal' (2006, 111). Appiah's postcolonial culture and identity differ from that of the African nationalists, or that of liberationist aesthetics, which was undoubtedly couched in the write-back rhetoric.

The African is contaminated in the sense that she is not culturally or biologically pure. And this is good. The African is a mutt. To acknowledge her muttness is to concede the presence of the other in her life and to be ready to enter into an I-Thou relationship with this other, to make way for dialogue.

Afropolitanism: theorizing a new African postcolonial identity

In 2005, Taiye Tuakli-Wosornu (later called Taiye Selasi) coined the word Afropolitanism as a means to explain her own complex identity melange. Since then the term has gained some currency in African discourse of culture and politics. Valerie K. Orlando (2013), for example, employed the term in her discussion of contemporary Moroccan literature. Commenting on the 2013 African Union conference, Sospeter Litala (2013) wrote in *Africareview* that the Afropolitan spirit should be inspired and facilitated. In June 2011, the Victoria and Albert Museum hosted a fashion show: 'Friday Late Afropolitans' (Friday Late Afropolitans, 2011). The fashion show was followed by a panel discussion which centred on the meaning of Afropolitanism. On 7 July 2013, the Royal African Society hosted a literature event: 'Fantasy or Reality? Afropolitan Narratives of the Twenty-first Century'. Even though the fashion show was a good means of popularizing the concept of Afropolitanism, it also risked reducing it to a mere capitalist stunt, which is one of the major concerns of the term's critics, such as Binyanvanga Wainaina. He dismissed the term in his keynote speech, 'I am a Pan-Africanist, not an Afropolitan', delivered at the meeting of the African Studies Association UK in 2012 (Santana 2013). With only very few exceptions, which include notable names such as Simon Gikandi and Achille Mbembe, not much attempt has been made to articulate Afropolitanism in a rigorous academic format. In the remaining part of this article, I will argue that Afropolitanism corresponds to what has been called the cultural face of cosmopolitanism; I will also seek to highlight the moral implications of this new African condition.

Afropolitanism has to be primarily understood for what it is: a mere effort to grasp the diverse nature of being African or of African descent in the world today. It is by no means a perfect effort. Indeed, it is plagued by flaws, the most crucial of which is its name. To be sure, it suggests an application of the idea of cosmopolitanism on the African continent or on people of African ancestry. If it is an African way of being cosmopolitan, what do you call a European or Asian way of being cosmopolitan, Europolitanism or Asiapolitanism? Why can an African not just be cosmopolitan?

The more damning weakness of the term, as has been pointed out by many critics, is in its exclusivity and elitism. And this stands out even in the very first paragraphs of the original essay, 'Bye-Bye Barbar' in which Selasi identified herself and those who look like her as Afropolitan: 'You'll know us by our funny blend of London fashion, New York jargon, African ethics, and academic successes. Some of us are ethnic mixes, e.g. Ghanaian and Canadian, Nigerian and Swiss; others merely cultural mutts' (Tuakli-Worsonu 2005). The notion shares the same flaw that has been identified with Selasi's much admired novel, *Ghana Must Go*, a novel whose characters seem to be all products of Oxford, Yale, Harvard, and other elite Western universities.

Yet, these weaknesses should not hinder one from identifying the underlying observation about the nature of African reality as already contaminated, or in Selasi's words, a 'cultural mutt'. While I share the concern that Afropolitanism smacks of elitism, I also admit that one does not need to be an elite or even to live in one of the big cities of Africa or the West to be an Afropolitan. In fact, the genius of Taiye Selasi's idea lies in contesting in an unforgettable way our largely uncritical application of 'Africa' as a tag of identity to any person genetically linked with the continent. In invoking the idea of the cultural mutt, Selasi describes what Ulf Hannerz (2006, 6) has identified as the cultural face of cosmopolitanism, which is an 'intellectual and esthetic openness toward divergent cultural experiences'; it is a way of managing 'meaning in an interconnected but culturally diverse world'. Selasi proposes a transgressive attitude that disrupts static and essentialist notions of identity. An Afropolitan, in my understanding, is that human being on the African continent or of African descent who has realized that her identity can no longer be explained in purist, essentialist, and oppositional terms or by reference only to Africa. Afropolitans claim that they are no longer just X as opposed to Y; rather they are A and B and X. Their realities are already intermixed with the realities of even their erstwhile oppressors. It is not possible to go back to their native place, since they are all mutts, biologically or culturally.

Simon Gikandi reads Afropolitanism sympathetically as an earnest and honest effort to rename and reinterpret the African experience in ways that go beyond the conventional form. For him, Afropolitanism:

> has been prompted by the desire to think of African identities as both rooted in specific local geographies but also transcendental of them. To be Afropolitan is to be connected to knowable African communities, languages and states. It is to embrace and celebrate a state of cultural hybridity – to be of African and other worlds at the same time. (2010, 9)

Gikandi's reading of the African (postcolonial) identity as being rooted in specific geographies, but also as transcending them, is of particular relevance especially in regard to our understanding of cosmopolitanism. Being fixed in specific geographies merely acknowledges the facticity of our being as humans. We all are born into specific places and cultures. But as humans we are not circumscribed by these places; we move, and in moving, we expand our vision and perception of who we are; we incorporate the beings of others the moment we begin to relate to them. I also acknowledge the possibility of people becoming more fundamentalist or essentialist in their attitude to the world. When they leave their original native places, they seek to preserve their roots or heritage, and, in most cases, fall back on authenticity tropes.

For Achille Mbembe, Afropolitanism is a solution to the write-back discourse and its attendant binary identity that implicitly welcomes victimhood as a starting point of discourse and self-perception. He recognizes that Africa's cultural history cannot be discussed without taking into consideration the idea of

> itinerancy, mobility and displacement, [and] recalling the history of itinerancy and mobility means talking about mixing, blending and superimposing. In opposition to the fundamentalists preaching 'custom' and 'autochthony', we can go as far as to assert that, in fact, what we call 'tradition' does not exist. (2007, 26–30)

I do not believe that Mbembe means that traditions, understood as established, organized ways of doing things, no longer exist. However, such traditions are already perforated by hyperlinks. Acknowledging these hyperlinks in every tradition or cultural space implies that such tradition or culture allows for more than is given. Mbembe sharpens his definition of Afropolitanism thus:

> Awareness of the interweaving of the here and there, the presence of the elsewhere in the here and vice versa, the relativisation of primary roots and memberships and the way of embracing, with full knowledge of the facts, strangeness, foreignness and remoteness, the ability to recognise one's face in that of a foreigner and make the most of the traces of remoteness in closeness, to domesticate the unfamiliar, to work with what seem to be opposites – it is this cultural, historical and aesthetic sensitivity that underlies the term 'Afropolitanism'. (2007, 28)

Afropolitanism suggests a reading of the African postcolonial identity as necessarily transcultural, transnational, indeed, cosmopolitan; it must embrace the solidarity that these conditions imply.

Understanding Afropolitanism in a cosmopolitan context

In this section, I will sketch a short history of cosmopolitanism in order to provide an intellectual context for an appreciation of Afropolitanism. It is hoped that by going through the history of cosmopolitanism, I will suggest, if only by association, the potential of the concept of Afropolitanism to expand insight on the emergent discourse of African identity and moral topography.

Like Afropolitanism, cosmopolitanism has been misunderstood; it has been misinterpreted as referring to people without roots and to privileged snobs alike. Bruce Robbins states that the term has been applied spitefully to 'Christians, aristocrats, merchants, Jews, homosexuals, and intellectuals'. It later began to apply to 'North Atlantic merchant sailors, Caribbean au pairs in the United States, Egyptian guest workers in Iraq, Japanese women who take gaijin lovers'. Robins, however, believes that the term could be understood as a 'fundamental devotion to the interests of humanity as a whole', and as a 'detachment from the bonds, commitments, and affiliations that constrain ordinary nation-bound lives' (1998, 1). Robbins has also identified it as a detachment from the bonds of nation-bound, culture-bound lives. To be sure, no human being can exist in complete independence from a nation or a culture. Yet we know that while individuals might be geographically bound within the spaces of their nation, while they might be located within a given culture, their imaginations are not; they can transcend such boundaries, even if in their own limited ways.

We owe much of our understanding of cosmopolitanism to the Greeks. Hugh Harris reminds us that, 'Democritus complains 'I visited Athens and no one knew me.' Yet, as a result of his wanderings farther afield, he could say, 'To the wise man every country is a dwelling-place, for the whole world is the fatherland of a good soul' (1927, 7). Democritus' dictum seems to be close to the core of cosmopolitanism, and Martha C. Nussbaum, relying on Plutarch, argues for just this sort of spiritual expansiveness: The cosmopolitan is 'the person whose allegiance is to the worldwide community of human beings' (1996, 4). I think it is of particular importance that Nussbaum underscores not just the world, which could be abstract, but the *community of human beings*. The emphasis on human beings, obviously of diverse ethnic abstractions, beliefs, and even political persuasions draws attention to what really counts about cosmopolitanism: relation rather than opposition. In being open to relate to diverse people, we form a community whose justification lies in its fundamental openness to all persons, and such a community is 'the source of our moral obligations' (1996, 4). Exploring Plutarch's ideas further, Nussbaum argues that after accepting this wide community of human beings with respect to basic moral values such as justice, 'we should regard all human beings as our fellow citizens and neighbors' (1996, 7). When, for instance, an African defines herself as one in whose veins are German, Chinese, and Zulu bloods, she subscribes to the idea of fundamental openness to a diverse community. She is therefore cosmopolitan, or, Afropolitan.

Being a citizen of the world does not demand that one give up one's history, or one's membership in a particular ethnic abstraction. Stoics, according to Nussbaum, provided us with an excellent model for the exercise of our allegiance to local as well as to universal communities. In the Stoic view, we are surrounded by many concentric circles, which move from the self to the immediate family, on to the extended family, to neighbours, to fellow city dwellers, and to fellow countrymen. 'Outside all these circles is the largest one, humanity as a whole. Our task as citizens of the world will be to "draw the circles somehow toward the center"' (1996, 9).

Nussbaum's mediation between patriotism and cosmopolitanism echoes Mitchell Cohen's idea of rooted cosmopolitanism. Cohen takes issue with 'votaries of multiculturalism', who have become 'unreflective celebrants of particularism', and who fail to mediate between different diversities within a particular geopolitical dispensation (1992, 483). He cites David Ben-Gurion's metaphor of circles. Ben-Gurion understood Israeli society as consisting of circles in which individuals stand. These circles are not independent; they mesh and intermingle with others. Ben-Gurion writes: 'when we stand in two circles it isn't a question of standing in two separate areas, one moment in one and the next in another, but rather in what is common territory to both of them' (1992, 483). For Cohen, then, standing in many circles implies accepting the idea of plural loyalties; this, in turn, has far-reaching 'implications for concepts of citizenship' (1992, 482). He argues that being rooted in a particular place should underline our mutual interdependence rather than excluding others. Cohen's idea of multiple belongings as opposed to unitary identity, is in agreement with Gikandi's interpretation of Afropolitanism as being rooted 'in specific local geographies but also transcendental of them'. By transcending local geographies, the Afropolitan seeks to go beyond the confines of ascribed identities, and makes room for how she feels and perceives herself.

David Hollinger's distinction between cosmopolitanism and pluralism emphasizes Cohen's and Nussbaum's ideas, and helps us understand the apparent moral rewards of cosmopolitanism. 'Cosmopolitanism is more oriented to the individual as a member of a number of different communities simultaneously', whereas pluralism is more oriented to the group, and always understands the individual as a member of a primary community. Pluralism relies on ascribed identity (1995, 86). Thus, the cosmopolitan acknowledges from the outset that he can no longer define himself by an exclusive reference to people from his communities because, as Hollinger argues, the individual or unit has already absorbed 'as much varied experience as it can, while retaining its capacity to advance its aims effectively' (1995, 84). It is against this background that Ulf Hannerz examines cosmopolitanism as a mode of managing meaning in a complex, globalized world characterized by the 'plurality of cultures understood as distinctive entities'. Cosmopolitanism, for him:

> includes a stance towards diversity itself, towards the coexistence of cultures in the individual experience. A more genuine cosmopolitanism is first of all an orientation, a willingness to engage with the Other. It is an intellectual and aesthetic stance of openness toward divergent cultural experience, a search for contrasts rather than uniformity. (1990, 239)

Bruce Robbins, who is interested in engagement based on equality, critiques Hannerz's phrase 'aesthetic stance' as having much in common with traditional aesthetics. In Robbins' view, cosmopolitanism as interpreted by Hannerz:

> becomes an autonomous, unforced appreciation of coherence and novelty among distinct cultural entities ... [it is its] presumption of inequality and its spectatorial absence of commitment to change that

inequality, which disqualifies [Hannerz's understanding] from representing the new transnationality of intellectual work. (1993, 189–190)

In Robbins' view, aesthetic stances with regard to other cultures, as adopted by most elites, amount to no more than touristic voyeurism. This is the indictment of cosmopolitans as snobs. This is also some of the concerns many critics of Afropolitanism have about the concept. However, I am interested in Hannerz's idea of intellectual openness, which is not to be equated with intellectualism, but rather with the desire to understand the other in order, as he puts it, to engage with him. 'It may be one kind of cosmopolitanism where the individual picks from other cultures only those pieces which suit himself' (1990, 240). Hannerz is emphasizing the freedom of the individual to engage with other people from other cultures. Such engagement implies an affirmation of those worlds. However, one is not obliged to accept every aspect of other cultures, much less play the messiah. But does one also accept other people's humanity? I want to assume that this is implicit in Hannerz's idea of engaging with others and in the 'coexistence of cultures in the individual experience'.

Amanda Anderson discusses cosmopolitanism as a moral virtue, noting the difference between exclusionary and inclusionary cosmopolitanism:

In exclusionary cosmopolitanism, little to no weight is given to exploration of disparate culture: all value lies in abstract or 'cosmic' universalism. In inclusionary cosmopolitanism, by contrast, universalism finds expression through sympathetic imagination and intercultural exchange. (2006, 72–73)

Anderson seeks to reclaim the primacy of universalism over essentialism. The new universalism, for her, 'focuses on those ideals and practices that propel individuals and groups beyond the confines of restricted or circumscribed identities' (2006, 70). 'Sympathetic imagination' allows the cosmopolitan to feel with the world of the other. It is against this backdrop that Anderson conceives of cosmopolitanism not just as an intellectual programme, but rather as an ethical ideal 'for cultivating character and negotiating the experience of otherness' (2006, 74). Emphasizing the importance of openness to otherness rather than the adoption of a universal system, Gerard Delanty (2006, 27) proposes the idea of critical cosmopolitanism. In critical cosmopolitanism:

the cosmopolitan imagination occurs when and wherever new relations between self, other and world develop in moments of openness. It is an approach that shifts emphasis to internal developmental process within the social world rather than seeing globalization as the primary mechanism and is also not reducible to the fact of pluralism.

The moral challenges of relational conception of identity

As mentioned above, Achille Mbembe interprets Afropolitanism as the ability to 'recognise one's face in that of a foreigner' (2007, 28). I think that this interpretation agrees with Amanda Anderson's argument about the advantages of cosmopolitanism as a means for cultivating character and negotiating the experience of otherness. In Anderson's understanding, a true cosmopolitan is someone who has already acknowledged the humanity and dignity of others as constituent of his own. Negotiating the experiences of otherness demands that such a person will interact with this other in a Martin Buber I-Thou paradigm. I think, however, that Anderson's 'sympathetic imagination' still smacks of elitism. In my understanding, sympathy issues from a position of power that refuses to acknowledge the coequality of the other with a sympathizer. I would therefore replace that term with 'empathic imagination'. Empathic imagination is the idea of switching perspectives with others; it is the challenge to see the world from the other person's standpoint without any traces of superiority or a position of power or privilege that could be detected in pity. Cosmopolitanism, informed by empathic imagination, is in alignment with the moral attitude of the Golden Rule, the idea of one treating others as one would have others treat one.

I propose that Afropolitanism, explored within a cosmopolitan context, promises some moral re-examination of the world. I understand that morality can be used in a very constricting sense to mean how one conducts one's private life, or in a descriptive sense to refer to a people's tradition or customs. I use the term 'moral' here in a broad sense as the attitude to the world that predisposes us to judge something or to impute value to something or someone and therefore to view it or him as acceptable or not acceptable. In this sense, morality embraces ethics, which is about one's relation to the other. I am interested in how person A relates to person B regardless of person B's gender, ethnic, religious, or cultural background. I work within the context of the normative conception of morality, which stipulates that there are universal codes of conduct that can be justified by a systematic application of reason in all societies. All those who recognize the principles derived from that process can conduct themselves accordingly (Gert, 2012).

Charles Taylor used 'moral topography' to designate the structure of the Western sense of self which evolved over time. He argued that 'what we are as human agents is profoundly interpretation-dependent' and every interpretation is done from a perspective. What we are, that is to say, our individual self, exists 'essentially in moral space by means of a master image, a spatial one [and] this inherent spatiality of the self is essentially linked to a moral topography, a sense of where moral source lies' (Taylor 1988, 299–300). The idea is that our identities are constructed and the constructions are space-dependent. Conversely, how we construct and interpret our identities influences how we relate to others. In this regard, therefore, there can be universal normative codes of conduct arrived at via cosmopolitan (Afropolitan) cultural attitudes. Given that my attitude to the world, indeed, my existence, is shaped by my self-understanding, I raise questions such as: who deserves my solidarity? My relative? My tribesman? A person from my race? How can my understanding of the world help me relate to people in ways that enhance our humanity, our rights and dignities? Thus, the knowledge that in my worldview is European, Asian or Oceanic predisposes me to relate to persons from these and other worlds in more fruitful, life-enhancing ways. Rather than see them as my opposite, I am inclined to negotiate with them. Negotiating with people of diverse ethnic, cultural, and racial backgrounds necessarily challenges any rigid binary construction of my world.

In the introductory part of this article, I wondered whether Antjie Krog was committing identity suicide by begging to be black African. Max Du Preez, who used the term 'identity-suicide' in his review of *Begging to Be Black*, implies that Krog is betraying her roots, and, indeed, her ontology, by seeking to be African rather than Afrikaner. Krog, in my reading, takes to heart the truth that identity is constructed and the construction involves an enduring dialectic. If it was possible for a group of Europeans (Dutch, German, and French) to become Afrikaners in Africa, why would it not be possible for an Afrikaner to become African? Thus Krog reminds us that being is in becoming, and becoming consists in relating. She simply contests the strictures of ascribed identity, and acknowledges her active role in shaping who she is. Put in a historical context, she refuses to define herself in the paradigms of apartheid. Krog (2008) rejects the Socratic-Cartesian notion of the individual moral self, constructed solely by an individual's acts of ratiocination. She welcomes Desmond Tutu's (Tutu, 1999) interpretation of the philosophy of Ubuntu, and argues that Ubuntu captures the essence of 'becoming'. In this case, being African has little to do with blood or skin colour; rather it has much more to do with moral topography, with how one positions oneself vis-à-vis the other people on that continent. The African interconnected moral self that she lays claim to as an African is the self in conversation with the other:

> The conversation that eventually creates the moral entity is not with the self, but with the people around one, the stranger-accommodating community. One's self awareness is not formed by splitting oneself into two, but by becoming one-in-many dispersed as it were among those around one. (2008, 363)

Begging to Be Black is a mythopoetic enunciation of the insights articulated in the above article. In begging to be black, Krog effectively complicates the idea of Africa. For her, being African is not tied to blood or skin colour; it is a choice and attitude.

Antjie Krog's application of the philosophy of Ubuntu to her life can help us to understand Afropolitanism as an individual's effort to contest ascribed identity, and to forge a new, more expansive one by relating to other people. Afropolitanism is the realization that existence is always hyphenated. While in Achebe's time, identity was conceived in terms of opposition, whose justification was rooted in resistance, the present-day definition of African identity is based on complementarity, and its justification is in the flourishing of life for everyone. It acknowledges the necessity to address historical wrongs that have put people in permanent disadvantage. Engaging the crippling legacies of the past, which is one of Antjie Krog's prime philosophic and poetic projects, is a way of being African and living actively in the present. The awareness of historical wrongs is also what Carli Coetzee calls our attention to in her idea of 'accented futures' (2013). Within the Afropolitan context, the colonized is no longer at the periphery. Nor is she to be understood exclusively as a victim. She now has a voice and, in her relation, she adopts a moral attitude that grants her and others in her world agency. Even while individuals of conceive themselves in Afropolitan, hypercultural paradigms, they are still rooted in geographical spaces, and are still 'parts of' a larger community through which they construct meanings. For Afropolitans, community is primary, but this community is polychromatic, polymorphic, diverse, and open.

Acknowledgements

I am greatly indebted to Alfred Frankowski, Carli Coetzee, Ryan Poll, and the anonymous reviewers for their invaluable criticisms and suggestions. I also thank Northeastern Illinois University, Chicago for the 2013 Summer Stipend that allowed me to produce this work.

References

Abani, Chris. 2007. *The Virgin of Flames*. New York: Penguin Books.
Achebe, Chinua. 1958. *Things Fall Apart*. Oxford: Heinemann.
Achebe, Chinua. 1990. *Hopes and Impediments*. New York: Anchor Books.
Achebe, Chinua. 2000. *Home and Exile*. New York: Anchor Books.
Adeleke, Tunde. 1998. "Black Americans and Africa: A Critique of the Pan-African and Identity Paradigms." *The International Journal of African Historical Studies* 31 (3): 505–536.
Anderson, Amanda. 2006. *The Way We Argue Now: A Study in the Culture of Theory*. New Jersey: Princeton University Press.
Appiah, Kwame Anthony. 1992. *In My Father's House: African in the Philosophy of Culture*. New York: Oxford University Press.
Appiah, Kwame Anthony. 2006. *Cosmopolitanism: Ethics in a World of Strangers*. New York: W.W. Norton.
Bhabha, Homi. 1994. *The Location of Culture*. London: Routledge.
Bongmba, Elias K. 2004. "Reflections on Thabo Mbeki's African Renaissance." *Journal of Southern African Studies* 30 (2): 291–316.
Bulawayo, NoViolet. 2013. *We Need New Names*. New York: Reagan Arthur Books.
Coetzee, Carli. 2013. *Accented Futures: Language Activism and the Ending of Apartheid*. Johannesburg: Wits University Press.
Cohen, Mitchel. 1992. "Rooted Cosmopolitanism: Thoughts on the Left, Nationalism, and Multiculturalism." *Dissent* (Fall): 478–483.
Comaroff, Jean, and John L. Comaroff. 2012. *Theory from the South or, How Euro-America Is Evolving Toward Africa*. Boulder, CO: Paradigm Publishers.
Delanty, Gerard. 2006. "The Cosmopolitan Imagination: Critical Cosmopolitanism and Social Theory." *The British Journal of Sociology* 55 (1): 25–47.

Du Preez, Max. 2009. "Identiteit-selfmoord is beslis nie nodig." *Rapport*. Accessed October 14, 2013. www.rapport.co.za
Eze, Emmanuel, ed. 1997. *Race and the Enlightenment: A Reader*. Oxford: Blackwell Publishing.
Eze, Chielozona. 2012. "Nelson Mandela and the Politics of Empathy: Reflections on the Moral Conditions for Conflict Resolutions in Africa." *African Conflict & Peacebuilding Review* 2 (1): 122–135.
Fanon, Frantz. 1967. *Black Skin, White Masks*. New York: Grove Press.
Fassin, Didier. 2007. *When Bodies Remember: Experiences and Politics of Aids in South Africa*. Berkeley: University of California Press.
Friday Late Afropolitans. 2011. Accessed October 14, 2013. www.msafropolitan.com/va-museum-friday-late-afropolitans
Gert, Bernard. 2012. "The Definition of Morality". *The Stanford Encyclopedia of Philosophy* Edward N. Zalta (ed.). Accessed May 20, 2013. http://plato.stanford.edu/archives/fall2012/entries/morality-definition
Gevisser, Mark. 2007. *The Dream Deferred: Thabo Mbeki*. Johannesburg: Jonathan Ball Publishers.
Giddens, Anthony. 2003. *Runaway World: How Globalization Is Reshaping Our World*. New York: Routledge.
Gikandi, Simon. 2001. "Chinua Achebe and the Invention of African Culture." *Research in African Literature* 32 (3): 3–8.
Gikandi, Simon. 2010. "Foreword: On Afropolitanism." *Negotiating Afropolitanism: Essays on Borders and Spaces in Contemporary African Literature and Folklore*, edited by Jennifer Wawrzinek and J. K. S. Makokha, 9–11. Amsterdam: Rodopi.
Han, Byung-Chul. 2005. *Hyperkulturalität: Kultur und Globalisierung*. Berlin: Merve Verlag.
Hannerz, Ulf. 1990. "Cosmopolitans and Locals in World Culture." In *Global Culture: Nationalism, Globalization and Modernity*, edited by Mike Featherstone, 237–251. London: Sage Publications.
Hannerz, Ulf. 2006. "Two Faces of Cosmopolitanism: Culture and Politics." Barcelona Centre for International Affairs (CIDOB), Barcelona, Spain. Accessed November 14, 2013. www.cidob.org
Harris, Hugh. 1927. "The Greek Origins of the Idea of Cosmopolitanism." *The International Journal of Ethics* 38: 1–10.
Hollinger, David. 1995. *Beyond Multiculturalism: Postethnic America*. New York: Basic Books.
Irele, F. Abiola. 2001. "Chinua Achebe at Seventy: Homage to Achebe." *Research in African Literature* 32 (3): 1–2.
Johnson, David. 2012. *Imagining the Cape Colony: History, Literature and the South African Nation*. Edinburgh: Edinburgh University Press.
Kanneh, Kandiatu. 1998. *African Identities: Race, Nation and Culture in Ethnography, Pan-Africanism and Black Literatures*. London: Routledge.
Krog, Antjie. 1998. *Country of My Skull: Guilt, Sorrow, and the Limits of Forgiveness in the New South Africa*. New York: Three Rivers Press.
Krog, Antjie. 2008. "This Thing Called Reconciliation … Forgiveness as Part of an Interconnectedness-Towards-Wholeness." *South African Journal of Philosophy* 27 (4): 353–366.
Krog, Antjie. 2009. *Begging to Be Black*. Cape Town, South Africa: Random Struik.
Litala, Sospeter. 2013. "The 'Afropolitan' Spirit should be Inspired and Facilitated" http://www.africareview.com/Opinion/The-Afropolitan-spirit-should-be-inspired-and-facilitated/-/979188/1865964/-/qghjq8/-/index.html
Mamdani, Mahmood. 1999. "There Can Be No African Renaissance Without an Africa-focused Intelligentsia." In *African Renaissance: The New Struggle*, edited by William Makgoba Malegapuru, 125–134. Cape Town: Mafube/Tafelberg.
Mbeki, Thabo. 1996. "I am an African." 1996. Accessed May 20, 2013. http://soweto.co.za/html/i_iamafrican.htm
Mbeki, Thabo. 1998. "African Renaissance." http://www.dfa.gov.za/docs/speeches/1998/mbek0813.htm
Mbembe, Achille. 2007. "Afropolitanism." In *Africa Remix: Contemporary Art of a Continent*, edited by Njami Simon and Lucy Durán, 26–30. Johannesburg: Johannesburg Art Gallery.
Mills, Charles. 1998. *Blackness Visible: Essays on Philosophy and Race*. Ithaca, NY: Cornell University Press.
Mudimbe, V. Y. 1988. *The Invention of Africa: Gnosis, Philosophy and the Order of Knowledge*. Bloomington: Indiana University Press.
Mudimbe, V. Y. 1994. *The Idea of Africa*. Bloomington: Indiana University Press.
Ndebele, Nhlanla. 2002. "The African National Congress and the Policy of non-racialism: A Study of the membership issue." *Politikon: South African Journal of Political Studies* 29 (2): 133–146.

Ndlovu-Gatsheni, Sabelo J. 2009. "Africa for Africans or Africa for 'Natives' Only? New Nationalism and Nativism in Zimbabwe and South Africa." *Africa Spectrum* 44 (1): 61–78.
Nussbaum, Martha C. 1996. "Patriotism and Cosmopolitanism." In *For Love of Country: Debating the Limits of Patriotism*, edited by Joshua Cohen, 4–17. Boston, MA: Beacon Press.
Orlando, Valerie K. 2013. "Being-in-the-World: The Afropolitan Moroccan Author's Worldview in the New Millennium." *Journal of African Cultural Studies* 25 (3): 275–291.
Robbins, Bruce. 1993. *Secular Vocations: Intellectuals, Professionalism, Culture*. London: Verso.
Robbins, Bruce. 1998. "Introduction." In *Cosmopolitics: Thinking and Feeling Beyond the Nation*, edited by Cheah, Pheng, and Bruce Robbins, 1–14. University of Minnesota Press.
Santana, Stephanie. 2013. "Exorcizing Afropolitanism: Binyavanga Wainaina explains why 'I am a Pan-Africanist, not an Afropolitan' at ASAUK 2012." Accessed November 14, 2013. http://africainwords.com
Selasi, Taiye. 2013. *Ghana Must Go*. London: Penguin Books Ltd.
Taylor, Charles. 1988. "The Moral Topography of Self." In *Hermeneutics and Psychological Theory: Interpretive Perspectives on Personality, Psychology and Psychopathology*, edited by L. Messer, A. Sass and R. L. Woolfolk, 298–320. New Brunswick: Rutgers University Press.
Tuakli-Worsonu, Taiye. 2005. "Bye-Bye Barbar." Accessed May 20, 2013. http://thelip.robertsharp.co.uk/?p=76
Tutu, Desmond. 1999. *No Future Without Forgiveness*. New York: Image Doubleday.

Cosmopolitanism with African roots: Afropolitanism's ambivalent mobilities

Susanne Gehrmann

This paper explores some aspects of the controversy which is now surrounding Afropolitanism, and examines the philosophical and literary output in relation to the concept. Mobility between spaces, in the cosmopolitan tradition, as well as digital mobility and visibility through the use of social media, are considered as key elements of Afropolitanism as a diasporic movement. So Afropolitanism can be described as a form of cosmopolitanism with African roots. However, the commodification of the term as a brand, and the class bias of Afropolitan lifestyle are more problematic. In the second part of the paper, the positions of African intellectuals are shown to convey more philosophical depth and moral relevance to Afropolitanism. In this vision of the concept, as it was initiated by Achille Mbembe, Afropolitanism is relevant for both the diaspora and for Africa. Afropolitanism in this understanding of it decentres, de-essentializes and valorizes the continent. The paper closes with readings of two novels of celebrated writers of the Afropolitan generation, namely Taiye Selasi's *Ghana Must Go* and Teju Cole's *Open City*. These novels feature complex Afropolitan characters and create a dense literary landscape through which to explore contemporary Afro-diasporic identity politics. The spatial and cultural mobilities expressed in this literature confirm Mbembe's repositioning of Africa as a philosophical locus of passage and mobility.

Put in a nutshell, Afropolitanism can be said to be cosmopolitanism with African roots. While the concept came up in 2005 with Taiye Selasi's essay 'Bye bye Babar!' and was further developed by Mbembe (2005, 2007, 2010), the years from 2011 to 2013 marked by the publication of several highly acclaimed literary works by authors considered as Afropolitans can be considered as the climax of Afropolitan enthusiasm, which was then quickly followed by upcoming critical voices. In this paper, I would like to think through some of the aspects of the controversy, which is now surrounding Afropolitanism, and look at the philosophical and literary output with regards to the concept. In doing so, I consider mobility[1] as a key concept for Afropolitanism. Mobility in a cosmopolitan tradition is the ability to move between and to inhabit different places and cultures. However, nowadays it includes also digital mobility which encompasses a quick circulation of ideas and images via the cyberspace that characterizes both the construction and contestation of Afropolitan lifestyles and cultural production.

At the last African Literature Association annual conference, which took place in Bayreuth in 2015, a lengthy panel was dedicated to Afropolitanism. The controversy on the pros and cons of this concept was thus taken from the cyberspace and other popular public debate formats[2] into a deliberate academic setting. While some participants valorized the concept as a positive path into African futures[3] in a globalized world, others criticized the concept for its superficiality, its commodification and its class bias. Yet other participants tried to take the concept beyond its predominant diasporic overseas' context and to apply it to inner-African circulations and cultural attitudes.

The controversy: to be or not to be an Afropolitan

One of the invitees at the Bayreuth panel was Emma Dabiri, an Irish-Nigerian sociologist at Goldsmiths' and School of Oriental and African Studies (SOAS), who is also an occasional model and a dedicated blogger. She raised a complaint that she was herself often taken for an Afropolitan. While as an academic with a conscience about class issues she took her distance to what she considers a largely commodified concept, Dabiri ironically admitted that her looks and family background apparently qualify her as prototypically Afropolitan. In my opinion, her versatile twitter account where she features as 'The DiasporaDiva' in a peculiar mixture of political comment and fancy fashion photographs does even more so. In this respect, Dabiri's cyber-presence is quite similar to that of a self-declared MsAfropolitan, Nigerian-Finnish feminist blogger named Minna Salami. But while Salami defends Afropolitanism as an important move against afropessimism (2013), in her statement 'Why I'm not an Afropolitan' on the online platform 'Africa is a Country', Dabiri writes that:

> The danger of Afropolitanism becoming the voice of Africa can be linked to the criticisms levelled against second wave feminists who failed to identify their privilege as white and middle class while claiming to speak for all women. Because while we may all be Africans, there is a huge gap between my African experience and my father's houseboys. [...]
>
> The problem is not that Afropolitans are privileged *per se* – rather it is that at a time when poverty remains endemic for millions, the narratives of a privileged few telling us how great everything is, how much opportunity and potential is available may drown out the voices of a majority who remain denied basic life chances. (2014)

In fact, three major reproaches are now regularly being addressed as regards Afropolitanism, namely: (1) its elitism/class bias, (2) its a-politicalness and (3) its commodification. But let us return to the origins of the concept and focus on what Taiye Selasi said in her founding essay published in the London based *LIP magazine*. She describes:

> Afropolitans – [as] the newest generation of African emigrants, coming soon or collected already at a law firm/chem. lab/jazz lounge near you. You'll know us by our funny blend of London fashion, New York jargon, African ethics, and academic successes. Some of us are ethnic mixes, e.g. Ghanaian and Canadian, Nigerian and Swiss; others merely cultural mutts: American accent, European affect, African ethos. Most of us are multilingual: in addition to English and a Romantic or two, we understand some indigenous tongue and speak a few urban vernaculars ... There is at least one place on the African Continent to which we tie our sense of self: be it a nation-state (Ethiopia), a city (Ibadan), or an auntie's kitchen. Then there's the G8 city or two (or three) that we know like the backs of our hands. We are Afropolitans: not citizens, but Africans of the world. (Selasi 2005)

Obviously borrowing from cosmopolitan discourse, Selasi describes a diasporic generation with deep, yet fluid relations to Africa (cf. Abebe 2015, 2), addicted to urban hip life as well as international careers. Her now prominent curriculum vitae (CV) illustrates the idea of Afropolitan mobility perfectly: born in London to Ghanain–Nigerian–Scottish parents, raised in Boston, studied in Oxford and Yale, has lived in Accra, New Delhi, Paris, Rome, Berlin; creative output as writer, photographer, fashion icon, cybernaut.

Interestingly, Kwame Appiah's rewriting of cosmopolitanism as a moral philosophy in the age of globalization in *Cosmopolitanism: Ethics in a World of Strangers* (2006) came up at about the same time as Afropolitanism. Appiah's exploration of the major virtues of the cosmopolitan:

curiosity beyond the habitual (57), the capacity for conversation across cultures (85) and the will to respect pluralism (144) is not at odds with what Afropolitanism means and does, rather cosmopolitanism can be said to be an indispensable component of Afropolitanism. Moreover, the cosmopolitan globetrotter's mobility has often just as well been perceived as an elitist type of travelling when compared to the average migrant's peregrinations. What distinguishes the Afropolitan from the 'common cosmopolitan' is his/her privileged bonding with Africa, as pointed out by Selasi:

> What distinguishes this lot (in the West and at home) is a willingness to complicate Africa – namely, to engage with, critique, and celebrate the parts of Africa that mean most to them. Perhaps what most typifies the Afropolitan consciousness is the refusal to oversimplify; the effort to understand what is ailing in Africa alongside the desire to honor what is wonderful, unique. Rather than essentialising the geographical entity, we seek to comprehend the cultural complexity; to honor the intellectual and spiritual legacy; and to sustain our parents' cultures. (2005)

Indeed, Selasi's remark resonates more like a philosophical then a political stance, and yet it is also clearly related to the postcolonial gesture of twisting the simplified colonial image of Africa around and to restore the perception of the continent's cultural diversity, complexity and richness. Therefore, I argue that Kenyan author Binyavanga Wainaina's claim to reject Afropolitanism in favour of a still valid Pan-Africanism, which he pronounced at the African Studies Association (ASAUK) conference in 2012 (cf. Bosch Santana's discussion 2013), is too simplistic. Both concepts clearly do not have the same weight in the political history of Africa's decolonization and other Black liberation struggles and at the same time they are not mutually exclusive (cf. Khonje 2015). It is also noteworthy that Selasi's Afropolitan stance to 'complicate Africa' instead of essentializing it, is in its basic meaning very much related to Wainaina's ironic essay *How to Write about Africa* (2008).

While the Internet is the space in which much of the controversy around Afropolitanism is being carried out now, it is equally the space where it is most celebrated and constantly reinventing itself. Teju Cole, who was one of the key note speakers at the above mentioned African Literature Association gathering, was announced by conference convener Susan Arndt as 'the writer who transformed the tweet into a new literary form' (quote from memory). And during her recent stay in Berlin, Selasi published a website with her photographs where she also comments upon the best coffee, cakes and swimming experience in the city – while not once mentioning the controversy around the refugee movement in Berlin or any social imbalance at all in Germany for that matter.[4]

The point I want to make is that neither the success of the Afropolitan generation nor the controversy around the concept would have been possible without the cyberspace as a new venue for mobility in the sense of the circulation, of ideas, images, and self-celebration. Cybermobility is now just as important as mobility in the real world, a movement in a bid to become a recognized Afropolitan. On the other hand, the glossiness of online lifestyle magazines such as *The Afropolitan* (South Africa)[5] and the commercial endeavours of the *Afropolitan shop* (USA/Kenya)[6] just as the more often than not consumerist orientated tweets by Taiye Selasi, have provoked a serious backlash in the reception of the idea. As blogger Eleanor T. Khonje admits:

> There is a certain 'superficiality' or better yet 'unseriousness' if I can call it that, whereby Afropolitanism is usually associated with elements of pop culture, consumerism, with privileged status, luxury, and carries with it a sense of exclusivity, elitism, as well as some undeniable tones of neoliberalism. It's really an ideology about how us Africans who live in the diaspora choose to relate to an Africa which we have mentally created for ourselves; an Africa of the Afropolitan imaginary. (2015, author's emphasis)

Two provisional conclusions can be drawn from the arguments which are being circulated in the cyberspace:

(a) That Afropolitanism is a useful concept as a tool of identity politics for diasporic middle-class Africans: 'an idea that gives individuals who feel rooted in Africa but live across the world, a sense of belonging' and enables them to maintain 'an "idea of Africa" at the centre of their experiences' (Khonje 2015).
(b) That Afropolitanism is able to promote an image of Africa without actually including permanently Africa-based Africans. Mainstream media have confirmed the preceding statement. For instance, the *African-American Black Experience Television* platform recently published a list of '10 Afropolitan writers you should know'.[7] With the notable exception of the late Kabelo Sello Duiker who lived and worked in South Africa, none of the writers presented in this list is actually based in Africa. Furthermore, there is only one francophone writer who qualifies for the list, Alain Mabanckou, who is also a well-known fashion icon just as Selasi, and who left Paris for the USA, where, to no surprise, the majority of the writers on the mentioned list are based. Given the ambivalence of this somewhat exclusionary social and spatial mobility of the Afropolitan, let us now move out of the cyberspace for a moment and consider more traditional scholarly writing that deals with the concept.

The ethics of Afropolitanism

Achille Mbembe's promotion of Afropolitanism in his (2007) article for the *Africa Remix* exhibition catalogue (first published in French in the online magazine *Africultures* at the end of 2005) and his further elaboration in *Sortir de la grande nuit: Essai sur l'Afrique décolonisée* (2010) have helped immensely to lend more philosophical depth and ethical weight to the concept. The chapter 'Circulation des mondes: l'expérience africaine' that links up with Afropolitanism in Mbembe's (2010) seminal monograph on the unfinished decolonization of Africa is generally less known, because it is so far available only in French. It is the last chapter of Mbembe's book which largely revisits Frantz Fanon's prophecies and analyses the political failures of postcolonial Africa as well as the relations between ex-colonizers and ex-colonized, in particular inside the system of the infamous *Françafrique* political entanglement. However, not entirely pessimistic, Mbembe also looks at the vitality of African urban and globalized cultures, which he valorizes as decisive for a necessary transformation process of the continent. As one of the book's reviewers, Sandeep Bakshi, points out:

> 'Afropolitanism' as Mbembe calls it, holds to scrutinity the earlier movement of 'Négritude' through a redefinition of reality, origins and transnational movement. It subsumes a 'cultural métissage' that arises from an imbrication of the self with the other, and the familiar and the strange. (2013, 567)

Indeed, while Senghor's *Négritude* concept theoretically praised cultural *métissage* and universal civilization (Senghor 1977), it obviously privileged African signs and signifiers and remained stuck in the rhetoric of difference.

Mbembe elevates Afropolitanism to a philosophical concept apt to lead the way towards an integral transformation of identity politics. He sees artists such as the Africa Remix representatives who have a transnational – though not necessarily diasporic – agenda, as forerunners (2005, 2007). Cosmopolitan in scope, anti-essentialist, open to cultural and intellectual hybridization, but endowed with a particular consciousness for Africa's historical wounds, Afropolitanism is praised as an attitude which can contribute to complete the as yet unfinished decolonization process of Africa. Additionally, as Chielozona Eze proposes, Afropolitanism 'promises some moral re-examination of the world' (Eze 2014, 244).

With regards to literature, for Mbembe Afropolitanism does not start with today's diasporic stars of the global cultural scene – that is, those on the list of 'the Afroplitan writers you must know' – but rather with the generation of revolutionary Francophone writers endowed with an aesthetics of transgression (Mbembe 2010, 223), such as Ahmadou Kourouma, Yambo Ouloguem and Sony Labou Tansi, who all debunked myths of a pure African origin as early as the 1960s–1980s (Mbembe 2010, 221f.). Following Mbembe's argument, these writers can be considered Afropolitans *avant la lettre*. Furthermore, he sees a *second* historical moment of Afropolitanism in the contemporary idea of global mobility:

> Le second moment de l'afropolitanisme correspond à l'entrée de l'Afrique dans un nouvel âge de dispersion et de circulation. Ce nouvel âge se caractérise par l'intensification des migrations et l'implantation de nouvelles diasporas africaines dans le monde. Avec l'émergence de ces nouvelles diasporas, l'Afrique ne constitue plus un centre en soi. Elle est désormais faite des pôles entre lesquels il y a constamment *passage*, circulation et frayage. (Mbembe 2010, 224, author's emphasis)
>
> The second wave of Afropolitanism corresponds with Africa's entry into a new age of dispersion and mobility. This new age is characterised by the intensification of migration and the creation of new African Diasporas throughout the world. With the emergence of these new Diasporas, Africa no longer constitutes a centre for itself. Henceforth, it is constructed through poles, between which there is constantly a *passage*, mobility, and facilitation. (my translation)

In this phase, identities and cultural productions are being more radically de-essentialized. Therefore Africa, as part of the world, becomes a place of passage in similar to those other territories through which Africans pass. This conception, notably, goes a step further than postcolonialism, to accentuate that not only is the colonial centre being de-centred, but Africa in its entirety as well. Although Mbembe is one of the few Francophone thinkers who seriously valorizes, but also critically questions postcolonial theory,[8] in my view he clearly pleads for a rupture with the postcolonial obsession of the colonial burden. Put even more bluntly, he coins Afropolitanism as a concept which challenges victimhood discourses attached to Africa and the Black diaspora or, as Eze concurs, '[f]or Achille Mbembe, Afropolitanism is a solution to the write-back discourse and its attendant binary identity that implicitly welcomes victimhood as a starting point of discourse and self-perception' (Eze 2014, 240). Hence, Mbembe coins Afropolitanism as a concept which overthrows victimhood discourses attached to Africa and the Black Diaspora when he claims:

> It is a way of being in the world, refusing any form of victim identity – which does not mean that it is not aware of the injustices and violence inflicted on the continent and its people by the law of the world. (2007, 30)

The arts and literature already fulfil this program, even if political consequences have not yet become visible:

> L'objet de la création artistique n'est plus de décrire une situation où l'on est devenu spectateur ambulant de sa propre vie parce qu'on a été réduit à l'impuissance en conséquence des accidents de l'histoire. Au contraire, il s'agit de témoigner de l'homme brisé qui, lentement, se met debout et s'affranchit se ses origines. (Mbembe 2010, 225)
>
> The object of artistic creation is no longer to describe a situation in which one has become an ambulant spectator of one's life because one has been reduced to powerlessness by historical accidents. On the contrary, it is a question of bearing witness to a bruised human who slowly stands up and emancipates him/herself from their origins. (my translation)

For Cameroonian born, French educated Mbembe who has now firmly established himself in South Africa for many years, Afropolitanism does not only transcend the question of diasporan vs. African-based urban cultures as he explicitly includes both, but it also transcends the question of race. White South Africans, Asian diasporic Africans and so forth could be part of Afropolitanism, as long as they identify with, and do not essentialize Africa. Consequently, with Mbembe the spatial and cultural mobility which characterizes Afropolitanism can never be understood as unidirectional. If there are culturally important and productive African diasporas across the world, Africa has at the same time always been a destination for migrants who contribute to its genuine diversity today (Mbembe 2007, 26, 27, 2010, 226f.).

Simon Gikandi, renowned Kenyan literary scholar based at Princeton, links up with this progressive ethical development of the concept, when he writes in the preface of a (2011) essay collection:

> The idea of Afropolitanism […] constitutes a significant attempt to rethink African knowledge outside the trope of crisis. Initially conceived as a neologism to describe the imaginary of a generation of Africans born outside the continent but connected to it through familial and cultural genealogies, the term Afropolitanism can now be read as a description of a new phenomenology of Africanness – a way of being African in the world. […] To be Afropolitan is to be connected to knowable African communities, nations, and traditions; but it is also to live a life divided across cultures, languages, and states. It is to embrace and celebrate a state of cultural hybridity – to be of Africa and of other worlds at the same time. (Gikandi 2011, 9)[9]

In contrast to the tendencies of the cyberspace contributors who clearly discuss Afropolitanism as a diaspora phenomenon which rather excludes continental Africans, intellectuals such as Mbembe, Gikandi, and Eze (2014) strive to expand the concept through the explicit inclusion of cultural dynamics in Africa itself. While this may be a valuable philosophical project, it is open to question whether this idea will be embraced by a representative number of artists, thinkers and citizens both in and out of Africa and if it can stand against the criticism which comes with the now commodified use of the word as a 'brand'.[10]

The Afropolitan literary boom

As a literary critic, let me also have a quick look at the literary production labelled as Afropolitan before I conclude this essay. From a German point of view, 2013 was the year of an incredible boom of African diasporic literature. Teju Cole's *Open City* was translated into German and won the important *Internationaler Literaturpreis des Hauses der Kulturen der Welt* in Berlin. Taiye Selasi's *Ghana Must Go* and Chimamanda Ngozi Adichie's *Americanah* were published the same year and translated almost immediately. Both authors gave readings in sold out exclusive venues all over Germany and Selasi was even invited to give the opening speech at Berlin's prestigious International Literature Festival.[11] Add to this Mbembe's recent distinction through the Bavarian Geschwister-Scholl-Preis for the German translation *Kritik der schwarzen Vernunft* (2014) of his *Critique de la raison nègre* (2013). Now this is remarkable in as far as the literatures of the African continent as well as literature of the African diaspora based in Germany occupy a rather marginal space on the German book market. I had never seen the face of any African or Afro-diasporic writer on the literature magazine of *Die Zeit*, Germany's leading weekly newspaper, before. But recently Taiye Selasi and Teju Cole both had their covers[12] published in *Die Zeit* and Chimamanda Ngozi Adichie is regularly reviewed and interviewed in the same newspaper's *feuilleton*.[13] The marketability of Afropolitan authors – largely sustained by their American publishing houses' systematic publicity campaigns – points again to its commodification. Yet, books that sell well are not necessarily bad books and I will certainly not question Selasi's, Cole's and Adichie's talents as writers; on the contrary I commend their dexterity. Rather, a closer look at the tropes of mobility and the narratives of un/belonging in their novels reveals the complexity of Afropolitan identities as embedded into literary discourse. My point is that 'Afropolitan literature' – I use the label in inverted commas as its usefulness is still under question – is worth reading because it goes much deeper than some of the cyberspace presences and discussions into the concept of Afropolitanism. Therefore, I shall conclude with a brief reading of *Ghana Must Go* and *Open City*.

Mobility as restlessness in Selasi's *Ghana Must Go*

Taiye Selasi's novel title alludes to the 1983 expulsion of Ghanaian refugees from Nigeria and introduces the cheap market plastic bag for hasty travellers also known as 'Ghana must go' as a central metaphor for mobility, at least for those readers who understand the expression. The 'Ghana must go' bag suggests migrant displacement inside Africa and under difficult social conditions, but it also alludes to the remarkable human capacity to pack, leave home behind and start anew.

The four siblings who are the main characters in the family novel *Ghana Must Go* can certainly count as prototypical Afropolitans. Born and raised in the USA by Ghanaian/Nigerian–Scottish parents, one brother is a successful medical doctor, the other a recognized painter in London, the two sisters are gifted Columbia/Oxford/Yale students: on the surface level they are all proof of the success story of African migrants in America and move, apparently, smoothly between worlds. However, mobility in *Ghana Must Go* is more often than not an answer to conflict, a form of voluntary or forced flight, a form of restlessness – and not of glossy cosmopolitanism *à la The Afropolitan* magazine. The underlying trauma which shapes the complicated family relations in the novel[14] is the sudden rupture of the father's relationship with his wife and children, after he loses his job as a surgeon due to structural discrimination. He flees back to Ghana, cyclically repeating the gesture of his own father who had left his mother when confronted with humiliation during colonial times. The absolute striving for success as much as mobility as a state of unrootedness and restlessness will be the father Kweku's heritage to his children.

Selasi's family novel reminds us that today's Afropolitan success stories are deeply linked to the upward mobility of a generation of parents, many of whom were the first academically educated individuals in their families and the first generation of overseas migrants. As the novel reflects, on the one hand the sacrifices of the parents smooth the way for the next generation, on the other hand their strong commitment to success does not always privilege affection in the family. The father wants his children to be 'well educated, well traveled, well regarded by other adults. Well fed. What he wanted, and what he wasn't, as a child' (Selasi 2013a, 47). When he breaks up with his family, the mother holds on to this ideal success story, despite her limited financial back-up. In order to ensure their education, she sends two of her children to her rich brother in Nigeria, where they will encounter traumatizing abuse. When the youngest daughter, significantly still surnamed 'baby' at 20 and who suffers from bulimia, blames the mother for her over-caring, the centre of the family unit breaks, when the mother hastily leaves the USA to settle down in Ghana on her own.

While Olu, the surgeon, compensates for his childhood losses with an exaggerated sense of order, cleanliness, and unconditional bonding with his Chinese-American wife, the other siblings remain largely uprooted and insecure in their relationships. Mobility, then, becomes more often than not a sign of a struggle of identity and not of glamorous cosmopolitanism. For example we learn about Kehinde, the artist of the family, that he 'won the Fulbright to Mali, waited tables in Paris, started showing in London' (2013a, 176); an Afropolitan CV indeed. The death of the father, which triggers an unexpected family reunion after many years, becomes the occasion to ask '*the question of why he had left after school,* won the Fulbright to Mali, waited tables in Paris, started showing in London, *and never came home*' (2013a, 176, my emphasis), to complete the quote. In the face of the father's death, uncanny questions about the siblings' restlessness and their movement from one place to the other, escaping family burdens, testing identities, come up. Selasi constructs a complex multifocal narrative of two generations and six intertwined stories of six strong characters. She convincingly shows that the ability to take one's 'Ghana must go' and move on is an ambivalent gesture, a mixed bag containing both constraint and freedom. Her personae are frequently caught between rupture, loss and personal progress as well as the reinvention of the worlds to which they strive to belong.

Mobility across space and time in Cole's *Open City*

In contrast to the multivocality of Selasi's family saga, Teju Cole's[15] success novel relies, solely, on the perspective of the first person narrator and protagonist Julius, a young psychiatrist of

Nigerian-German descent who completes an internship in New York. The big apple offers itself as the 'open city' of the novel's title: a space with fluid cultural borders, speedy transport and aesthetic sensations ranging from the cityscape's interplay with natural phenomena such as cloud formations to arts and music from all over the world. *Open City* is basically a novel relying on movement and the stream of consciousness technique. Julius wanders and travels through New York, while his thoughts and reflections prompted by the cityscape make up the text: 'New York City worked itself into my life at walking pace' (Cole 2011, 3).

The particularity of the protagonist-narrator's mobility is that it is not only spatial inside the present time, but that he also wanders back and forth in time and across cultures, as well as from personal memories to collective historical reminiscences. Julius is an extremely well-read intellectual, versed in the culture of at least three continents: Africa, Europe and America (including Latin America). His thinking is made up of a dense network of intertextual and intermedial references[16] to world literature, music and the arts, all of which qualifies him to be regarded as a prototype of the elitist intellectual cosmopolitan (cf. Hallemeier 2013, 240). Through his position as an urban wanderer and detached observer he is at the same time constructed as a twenty-first-century version of the *flaneur*: a postmodern variant in his cultural eclecticism and detachment, but also a postcolonial variant in his political consciousness.[17]

Julius's narrative is 'self-consciously transnational in scope' and frequently reflects on 'experiences of displacement and migration in the context of globalization' (Hallemeier 2013, 214). He is conscious of his own elitist position and pays attention to the plights of less privileged groups, of the Black diasporans in particular: be they African-American (through his visit to the African Burial Ground, a New York memorial for slaves), Caribbean (he has an encounter with a Haitian shoeblack) or African (he visits a centre for refugees without official papers). A meticulous observer who identifies politically as Black, but obstinately refuses any racial group affiliation (cf. Miller 2015, 199), Julius nevertheless tries to keep his emotional distance from social issues.

A shorter visit to Brussels serves as a counterpoint to New York.[18] The history of the exploitation of the Congo is so thoroughly inscribed into Brussels's architectural cityscape that it seems to narrow down the possibilities for the open cosmopolitan life style Julius got used to in New York. He befriends some Moroccan immigrants, intellectuals who are largely overqualified for the jobs they manage to get, although he is taken aback by their fundamentalist tendencies. This anachronistic version of Europe as metonymically represented through the Belgian/European capital is not yet a space for successful Afropolitans. Ironically, once back in New York, Julius sends a copy of Appiah's book *Cosmopolitanism* to his Moroccan friends in Brussels.

Open City is a race and class conscious novel, although this is displayed in a subtle, not openly politically engaged manner for the most part.[19] Julius's transcultural aesthetic engagements often position him in spheres beyond tangible time and space, and yet his African roots bind him back to unsettling experiences, even inside the open space of New York City. I wish to conclude by pausing on the note of this ambivalence between unbound mobility in space and time versus boundaries which must constantly be renegotiated through the example of Julius's passion for Gustav Mahler's music:

> I found myself thinking of Mahler's last years as I sat on the uptown-bound N-train last night. All the darknesses that surrounded him, the various reminders of frailty and mortality, were lit brightly from some unknown source, but even that light was shadowed. I thought about how clouds sometimes race across the sunlit canyons formed by the steep sides of skyscrapers, so that the stark divisions of dark and light are shot through with passing light and dark. Mahler's final works were all first performed posthumously; all are vast, strongly illuminated, and lively works, surrounded by the tragedy that was unfolding in the life. The overwhelming impression they give is of light: the light of a passionate hunger for life, the light of a sorrowful mind contemplating death's implacable approach. (Cole 2011, 250)

This passage is typical for the novel as movement through the city and visual impressions trigger reflections on art, and, in this case on the figure of a tragic migrant, Gustav Mahler, a late Romantic Austrian composer who fled to New York due to the growing Anti-Semitism in Europe. Julius often shares the melancholic mood which also characterizes Mahler's oeuvre. However, when Julius goes to a concert of Mahler's ninth symphony, in spite of the aesthetic pleasure he experiences, he feels trapped in the concert hall as a space of racial boundaries, in contrast to the open city:

> Almost everyone, as almost always at such concerts, was white. It is something that I can't help noticing, I notice it each time, and try to see past it. Part of that is a quick complex series of negotiations: chiding myself for even seeing it, lamenting the reminders of how divided our lives still remain, being annoyed that these thoughts can be counted on to pass through my mind at some point in the evening. Most of the people around me yesterday were middle-aged or old. I am used to it, but it never ceases to surprise me how easy it is to leave the hybridity of the city, and enter into all-white spaces, the homogeneity of which, as far as I can tell, causes no discomfort to the whites in them. The only thing odd, to some of them, is seeing me, young and black, in my seat or at the concession stand. At times, standing in line for the bathroom during intermission, I get looks that make me feel like Ota Benga, the Mbuti man who was on display in the Moneky House at the Bronx zoo in 1906. I am weary of such thoughts, but I am habituated to them. But Mahler's music is not white, or black, not old or young, and whether it is even specifically human, rather than in accordance with more universal vibrations, is open to question. (Cole 2011, 252)

The comparison between today's White gaze and the display of an African on a colonial exhibition show makes a strong point about ongoing racism at present times. At the same time Mahler's music – which we can understand as a superbly dense synecdoche for highly valued cultural achievements in Julius's thinking – clearly transcends human separation through difference constructions. This is exactly the state of mind strived for by the Afropolitan *flaneur* in Cole's novel.

Conclusion

As my brief analysis of Selasi's and Cole's novels indicates, there is more depth in the narratives of the 'Afropolitan generation' than in certain commodified circulations of the concept that resonate with glamorous online images of the authors involved. Taiye Selasi argues that the Afropolitan novel as a genre does not exist when she states that 'Afropolitan is a personal identity. Fiction has no need for such things' (Selasi 2013b, 13). That notwithstanding, her *Ghana Must Go* and Cole's *Open City* are novels which feature complex Afropolitan characters. These novels open up a fruitful literary landscape for the uncovering of contemporary Afro-diasporic identity politics traversing America, Africa and Europe. While every single one of the varied and individually shaped novelistic characters can count as cosmopolitan, their mode of attachment to Africa is different and, it is worth mentioning, never superficial. When the youngest sister in Selasi's family saga visits Ghana for the first time, she discovers that dancing to African rhythms fulfils a part of her being that had previously been disturbed by a void. Yet this romantic vision of a return to African roots remains balanced by the other siblings' more rational or even sceptical connections with Africa. Far from being apolitical, Cole's protagonist negotiates his place in New York City and the world along ambivalent boundaries of race and class while keeping up with his compelling transcultural lifestyle. The spatial and cultural mobilities expressed in the literature of 'the Afropolitan generation' indeed confirm Mbembe's repositioning of Africa as a philosophical locus of passage and mobility.

Disclosure statement

No potential conflict of interest was reported by the author.

Notes

1. A first version of this paper was presented at the Point Sud/Stellenbosch Institute for Advanced Studies workshop on 'Place and Mobility: People and Cultural Practices in Cosmopolitan Networks in Africa, the Atlantic & Indian Ocean' at the University of Stellenbosch in August 2015. I would like to thank the organizers, in particular Shaun Viljoen for inviting me, and the readers and discussants of my paper, in particular Grace A. Musila and Mamadou Diawara, for the stimulating scholarly exchange.
2. The 'Redefining 2015: After Afropolitanism' exhibition and conference organized by the Caribbean Cultural Center African Diaspora Institute in New York must be mentioned here, see http://cccadi.org/01/feb-21-redefining-2015-after-afropolitan/ (accessed 10 September 2015). No report or proceedings are available at the moment.
3. The conference's general theme was 'African Futures and Beyond, Visions in Transition', see http://www.ala2015.com/#/home/ (27 July 2015).
4. For the fancy photographic article see http://www.hundertvierzehn.de/artikel/berlin-im-blitzlichtgewitter_535.html (10 September 2015). Since August 2015, Selasi touches on the topic of refugees on her twitter account *Afripedia*, at least through crosspostings.
5. http://www.afropolitan.co.za/ (26 June 2015)
6. http://www.theafropolitanshop.com/ (26 June 2015).
7. http://www.bet.com/news/global/photos/2014/07/10-afropolitan-writers-you-should-know.html (29 July 2015) features Dinaw Menegstu, Chimamanda Ngozi Adichie, Helen Oyeyemi, NoViolet Bulawayo, Teju Cole, Taiye Selasi, Olufemi Terri, Aminatta Forna, Kabelo 'Sello' Duiker, and Alain Mabanckou.
8. His 2000 essay *De la postcolonie : Essai sur l'imgaination politique dans l'Afrique contemporaine*, translated as *On the postcolony* (2001) offers a thorough analysis of the perpetuation of colonial structures in the postcolonial state and has itself become a classic of postcolonial theory.
9. Simon Gikandi's foreword: 'On Afropolitanism' precedes the essay collection *Negotiating Afropolitanism. Essay on Borders and Spaces in Contemporary African Literature and Folklore* edited by Makhoka/Wawrzinek in 2011 which offers a rather mixed bag of essays on African literatures, put together quite arbitrarily under the label 'Afropolitan'. Like Gikandi, US-based Nigerian born scholar Chielozona Eze is equally in praise of Afropolitanism in his recent essay 'Rethinking African culture and identity: the Afropolitan model', in which he suggests Afropolitanism as a way of reading 'African postcolonial identity as necessarily transcultural, transnational, indeed, cosmopolitan; it must embrace the solidarity that these conditions imply' (2014, 214).
10. For instance, Nigerian born South Africa-based writer Yewande Omoteso's stance 'I'm not an Afropolitan – I'm of the Continent' in her interview with Fasselt (2014) points to the non-acceptance of the term which seems just too heavily charged with the idea of extra-continental diasporic experience.
11. The speech is available as free PDF download at http://www.literaturfestival.com/archiv/eroeffnungsreden/die-festivalprogramme-der-letzten-jahre/Openingspeach2013_English.pdf (14 September 2015). It was published in German in *Süddeutsche Zeitung*. In this text, Selasi defines Afropolitanism as a category of personal identity politics and refutes its validity as a literary category: 'But I am not an African writer. […] Nor am I an Afropolitan writer, disappointing as the news may be. Afropolitan is a personal identity. Fiction has no need for such things' (Selasi 2013b, 13).
12. Cf. Taiye Selasi' portrait on the cover of *Zeit Literatur* No. 12 March 2013, headline: 'Die Weltbürgerin. Taiye Selasi hat unser Bild von Afrika über den Haufen geworfen. Ihr erster Roman zeigt: Der afrikanischen Weltliteratur gehört die Zukunft' and Teju Cole's portrait on the cover of *Zeit Literatur* No. 11 March 2015, headline: 'Amerikas Traum. Teju Cole ist der neue Star unter den jungen Autoren: Ein New Yorker mit nigerianischen Wurzeln. Sein Debüt 'Jeder Tag gehört dem Dieb' erzählt von der Suche nach Herkunft'. Both issues feature richly illustrated interviews of the authors with Afro-German *feuilletonist* Ijoma Mangold.
13. In an interview with Mangold (2014), Adichie distances herself from the label 'Afropolitan'.
14. The author herself proposes to classify the novel in 'the Seriously Dysfunctional Family section' (Selasi 2013b, 14), a suggestive proposal.
15. Born in 1975 as *Obayemi Babajide Adetokunbo Onafuwa* in Michigan from Nigerian parents, bred in Lagos, Art historian with degrees from SOAS, University of London and Columbia University in New York, Teju Cole has successfully americanized his name – while Taiye Tuakli-Wosornu has wittingly turned hers in an internationally more pronounceable African version; Selasi – with an Ethiopian flair.
16. Cf. Jacobs (2014, 94) footnote 9 for a comprehensive list of these references.

17. The *flaneur* trope has already been used in Cole criticism, but has not yet been linked back to Afropolitan discourse. I don't agreed with Pieter Vermeulen's dismissal of the *flaneur* in favour of the 'less glamorous figure of the *fugueur*' (2014, 40), as his reading of Julius as a fundamentally egocentric figure does not convince me.
18. However, ironically Brussels was an open city according to the vocabulary of warfare, meaning it had capitulated in front of the German forces during WW II and thus escaped bombing (cf. Cole 2011, 97; Jacobs 2014, 88).
19. Abebe, one of the young online defenders of Afropolitanism, herself an Oxford-based political scientist with roots in Ethiopia, writes:

> Afropolitan discourse is selective in its politics rather than being apolitical, as it is often charged. It generally masks class differences an iniquities within the African diaspora, but regularly challenges gender roles and representations. The matters of African regime changes and 'ethnic politics' (which preoccupied their parents' generation) are rarely discussed; however, Afropolitans often align themselves with broader emancipatory political projects such as Black activism and postcolonial critique. (2015)

Teju Cole's novel exemplifies the case of a cosmopolitan elitist surface, which has a selective political agenda. In the case of *Open City*, however, race and class layers are more prominent than is gender.

References

Abebe, Alpha. 2015. "Afropolitanism: Global Citizenship with African Roots." April 4. Accessed June 15, 2015. http://blog.qeh.ox.ac.uk/?p=910.

Appiah, Kwame Anthony. 2006. *Cosmopolitanism. Ethics in a World of Strangers*. New York: Norton & Company.

Bakshi, Sandeep. 2010. "Review of Achille Mbembe. *Sortir de la grande nuit: Essai sur l'Afrique décoloniseé*. Paris, La Découverte 2010." *International Feminist Journal of Politics* 15 (4): 565–567.

Bosch Santana, Stephanie . 2013. "Exorcizing Afropolitanism: Binyavanga Wainaina Explains Why 'I am a Pan-Africanist, not an Afropolitan' at ASAUK 2012." February 8. Accessed August 23, 2015. http://africainwords.com/2013/02/08/exorcizing-afropolitanism-binyavanga-wainaina-explains-why-i-am-a-pan-africanist-not-an-afropolitan-at-asauk-2012/.

Cole, Teju. 2011. *Open City*. New York: Random House.

Dabiri, Emma. 2014. "Why I am not an Afropolitan." January 21. Accessed July 3, 2015. http://africaisacountry.com/why-i-am-not-an-afropolitan.

Eze, Chielozona. 2014. "Rethinking African Culture and Identity: The Afropolitan Model." *Journal of African Cultural Studies* 26 (2): 234–247.

Fasselt, Rebecca. 2014. "'I'm not an Afropolitan – I'm of the Continent': A Conversation with Yewande Omotoso." *The Journal of Commonwealth Literature* [online]. Accessed March 15, 2015. http://jcl.sagepub.com/content/early/2014/10/03/0021989414552933.

Gikandi, Simon. 2011. "On Afropolitanism." In *Negotiating Afropolitanism: Essays on Borders and Spaces in Contemporary African Literature and Folklore*, edited by J. Wawrzinek and J. Makokha, 9–11. Amsterdam: Rodopi.

Hallemeier, Katherine. 2013. "Literary Cosmopolitanisms in Teju Cole's *Every Day is for the Thief* and *Open City*." *A Revief of International English Literature* 44 (2–3): 239–250.

Jacobs, Karen. 2014. "Teju Cole's Photographic Afterimages." *Image & Narrative* 15 (2): 87–105.

Khonje, Eleanor T. 2015. "To be both an Afropolitan and a Pan-Africanist: A Response." April 19. Accessed July 22, 2015. http://unravelingthmind.com/2015/04/19/t-be-both-an-afropolitan-an-a-pan-africanist.

Mangold, Ijoma. 2014. "'Ich bin nicht Schwarz.' Auf ein Chicken Curry mit Chimamanda Ngozi Adichie, der international gefeierten nigerianischen Autorin." *Die Zeit* 21, May 15. Accessed October 19, 2015. http://www.zeit.de/2014/21/chimamanda-ngozi-adichie-americanah.

Mbembe, Achille. 2005. "Afropolitanisme." *Africultures*. December 26. Accessed September 24, 2015. http://www.africultures.com/php/?nav=article&no=4248.

Mbembe, Achille. 2007. "Afropolitanism." In *Africa Remix: Contemporary Art of a Continent*, edited by S. Njami and L. Durán, 26–20. Johannesburg: Johannesburg Art Gallery.

Mbembe, Achille. 2010. *Sortir de la grande nuit*. Paris: La Découverte.

Mbembe, Achille. 2013. *Critique de la raison nègre*. Paris: La Découverte.

Mbembe, Achille. 2014. *Kritik der schwarzen Vernunft*. Berlin: Suhrkamp.

Miller, Stephen. 2015. *Walking New York. Reflections of American Writers from Walt Whitman to Teju Cole*. New York: Empire State Editions.

Salami, Minna. 2013. "Can Africans Have Multiple Subcultures? A response to 'Exorcising Afropolitanism'." April 3. Accessed July 24, 2015. http://www.msafropolitan.com/2013/04/can-africans-have-multiple-subcultures-a-response-to-exorcising-afropolitanism.html.

Selasi, Taiye. 2005. "Bye-Bye Babar." *The LIP Magazine*, March 3. Accessed May 10, 2015. http://thelip.robertsharp.co.uk/?p=76.

Selasi, Taiye. 2013a. *Ghana Must Go*. London: Viking.

Selasi, Taiye. 2013b. "Afrikanische Literatur gibt es nicht." *Süddeutsche Zeitung* 205, September 5, 2014. English online version accessed October 1, 2015. http://www.literaturfestival.com/archiv/eroeffnungsreden/die-festivalprogramme-der-letzten-jahre/Openingspeach2013_English.pdf.

Selasi, Taiye. 2015. "Berlin im Blitzlichtgewitter." *Hundertvierzehn. Das literarische Onlinemagazin des S. Fischer Verlag*. Accessed September 10, 2015. http://www.hundertvierzehn.de/artikel/berlin-im-blitzlichtgewitter_535.html.

Senghor, Léopold Senghor. 1977. *Liberté 3. Négritude et civilisation de l'universel*. Paris: Seuil.

Vermeulen, Pieter. 2014. "Flights of Memory: Teju Cole's *Open City* and the Limits of Aesthetic Cosmopolitanism." *Journal of Modern Literature* 73 (1): 40–57.

Wainaina, Binyavanga. 2008. *How to Write about Africa*. Nairobi: Kwani Trust.

Wawrzinek, Jennifer, and Justus Makokha, eds. 2011. *Negotiating Afropolitanism: Essays on Borders and Spaces in Contemporary African Literature and Folklore*. Amsterdam: Rodopi.

The politics of Afropolitanism

Amatoritsero Ede

Afropolitanism has evolved over the past 10 years as a rubric for describing transnational African identity. This piece develops a cultural-materialist analysis of that phenomenon as a metropolitan instrument of self-affirmation, in the first instance. I argue that the phenomenon of Afropolitanism is to some extent a subjective and cultivated condition, and has become a cultural instrument of black political agency in the Metropolis. However, the resultant self-affirmation accrues only to the Afropolitan cultural producer, who acquires symbolic capital towards that goal. A larger black migrant population and diaspora, which does not possess symbolic capital and therefore lacks this same social and class mobility, is still marginalized. This creates a division between the culture of Afropolitanism and the politics it aims to engender. I conclude that a dialectical interaction between culture and politics is necessary and important in order for the condition of Afropolitanism to jettison its elitist tendency and to enable rich theoretical, and more progressive, ideological gains.

Introduction: genealogy, Africa and cosmo-politics

In the past decade 'Afropolitanism' has become a buzzword in the black metropolitan cultural arena and in Western Africanist conference circuits. Taiye Selasi (as Taiye Tuakli-Wosornu [2005]) first deployed it as a neologism to describe globetrotting, mixed-race blacks or migrant and 'newly diasporized' Africans – including herself – whose self-perception transcends geographies, nationalities, languages or time zones. This term has generated heated virtual debates in that public sphere that the Internet has become; a debate that has been without any resolution.

In a theoretically nuanced reformulation of Selasi's initial rumination and the public discussions which followed it, scholars like Achille Mbembe (2007), Gikandi (2011) and Eze (2014) expound on how Afropolitanism captures the complexity of identity in a hybrid, postmodern world where centre/periphery models have become inadequate for analysing global cultural flows, and in which African identity can no longer fit into the neat historical Pan-African uniformity of Edward Blyden's 'African personality' (Eze 235–236). The scholarship that exists so far on Afropolitanism agrees that it is a useful concept for re-thinking or revising transitional or 'ossified' (Mbembe 26) frameworks of transnational processes and realities signalled in such accustomed ideas as Diaspora, Cosmopolitanism, Pan-Africanism or Ethiopianism. I tentatively suggest the plural form, 'Afropolitanisms', to account for the different public apprehensions and possible multiple future theoretical trajectories of this cultural phenomenon (see Bosch Santana 2015; Dabiri 2015; Eze 2015; Gehrmann 2015; Musila 2015 in this same volume).

Here, I wish to appraise Afropolitanism as a transnational material and ideological condition, which leads to an inherent individualism and identity politics when it is confronted by metropolitan racial/class tensions and politics of difference. Although my approach is cultural materialist, I do not emphasize cultural artefacts – specifically, literary products – but focus rather on the social and material conditions leading to their production. This is in keeping with a larger view of culture as a 'constitutive human process' (Williams 1977, 20), *constitutive*, that is, of a complex of social and material processes and their interaction. It is an 'approach to understanding culture that explores its connections with economic activity, social power, and social inequality' (Castree, Kitchin, and Rogers 2013, 88). In other words, I focus on Afropolitanism as an *ideological condition of cultural production* occasioned by metropolitan hierarchies and creating social hierarchies and class formations of its own.

It is important to note from the outset that Afropolitanism is arguably and mostly a metropolitan concept of self-representation and black agency, but only amongst a percentage of the intellectual, creative, artistic and sometimes business and professional sections of a black metropolitan population that is either exiled, migrant or diasporic. My focus here is on the intellectual/artistic and writerly. I should also remark that Afropolitanism as a cultural phenomenon is not necessarily an automatic repository of agency but that it performs black agency and provides an ontological ground for its existence. That means that consecration is a precondition for the effectiveness of agency. And even if there seems to be a critical tendency to universalize Afropolitanism, a blanket application of the term is not supported by actual lived experience and contemporary global and local material realities. As Eze submits in 'Rethinking African Culture and Identity', cosmopolitanism is an overarching phenomenon under which Afropolitanism should be subsumed as merely a 'cultural face' (2014, 239) or phase. Moreover, in a recent self-revision, Selasi maintains that: 'I am Ghanaian, Nigerian and *cosmopolitan*' (emphasis added, *The Guardian* 4 July 2015), giving more weight and purchase to the idea of the cosmopolitan.

I argue that Afropolitanism has devolved in theory and praxis into two seemingly conflicting strands, with one being cultural (as phenomenon) and the other political (in its effects); and that the contradictions and seeming indecisions surrounding the notion derive from, and are closely related to, the discursive bifurcation it has engendered. I discuss each facet of that split and posit that these aspects are imbricated with, and need to dialectically interrogate, one another for the micro-politics of Afropolitanism to have a cultural unity and an ideological balance. This might also enable it, as a theoretical concept, to jettison a tendency towards myopia and the kind of homogenization that will be implicit today in the outdated notion of African Personality.

I conclude that the promise of a redemptive politics that Afropolitanism holds *in theory* can only be fulfilled with respect to lived experience if its two strands (that is, the cultural phenomenon and its political effects) meet as nuanced complements of an ideologically conscious and sophisticated social agency. The philosopher, Michael E. Bratman's, idea of 'individual autonomy, self-governance and agential authority' (2007, 4) informs my understanding of agency as 'human agency'. Consequently, agency here refers to otherwise powerless individuals' ability to have a willed and positive effect on their own existential and material condition. That ability has always meant the difference between freedom and emancipation or oppression – as far as the history of Africans and their diasporas are concerned. It is with this in mind that I remark that, besides the post-traditionalist and transnational insights of her formulation, Selasi's inaugural reflections have as their political unconscious an empowering act of self-writing. This counter-balances the African subject's usual historical 'narratives of loss' (Achille Mbembe 2002, 239) and the 'crushing objecthood' (Fanon 1963, 109) that circumscribes the black Metropolis and negatively inflects social interactions with the Other.

Human agency, as I said above, has always been historically indispensable for black social and political self-definition and, as such, its coincidence with Afropolitanism simply continues that tradition of self-apprehension and -reinvention. This is why Afropolitanism owes a debt to the Black Atlantic and to Black Paris (Jules-Rosette 1998) as original loci of human agency in Africa's insertion into the project of modernity. Pre- and post-abolitionist Black Atlantic (July 1967) and colonial Parisian Black Internationalist literary production from the sixteenth century into the twentieth respectively were instrumental in the New World abolition of slavery, Emancipation in America and decolonization in Africa. Such literary production was energized by political and cultural phenomena such as Abolitionism, Harlem Renaissance, Negritude, Negrismo and indigeneity and anti-colonial movements (Huggins 1973; Jahn 1968; Kesteloot 1974; Fabre 1991).

Olakunle George (2003) references the Black Atlantic origins of human agency in relationship to postcolonial African writing, which continued emancipatory ideals in the twentieth century. He establishes a broad aesthetic and critical discursive category in African modernity, which he refers to as African Letters. This countering epistemology in the form of (foundational) and postcolonial African writing, discourses, political philosophies and cultural criticism – Marxist and otherwise – contested Western misrepresentations of the African self and world. Through this alter/native self-representation of the continent, African Letters created a 'positive [human] Agency' (x). It attempted an 'epistemological decolonization', which served to 'counter-act the epistemic violence of colonialism' and revealed an 'authentic African reality and self' that led to a 'rehabilitation of the African subject' (75). This is why I posit that, in contemporary times, 'black agency' is predicated on the Afropolitan's ability – through aesthetic means – to arrest, in some degree, the residual powerlessness which accompanied global postcolonial modernity. That aesthetic arresting of powerlessness can be achieved through various media. My concern in this instance is with writing as a technology, an aesthetic and an ideological practice. It has a metropolitan history as a repository of human agency, as I have delineated above.

Historically, there is a seminal inter-relationship in Western thinking between the script, aesthetics, otherness and social powerlessness. This is the subject of the historically significant special issue of *Critical Enquiry*, 'Race, Writing and the Difference It Makes' (1985, 1–20). According to Henry Louis Gates Jr. in the introduction to that special issue, 'Blacks were 'reasonable', and hence 'men', [or women] if – and only if – they demonstrated mastery of 'the arts and sciences', the eighteenth century's formula for writing' (8). I posit that traces of that old established relationship between the ability to write and social prestige or class in the Western Metropolis has been sustained to shape a global modern hierarchy of social, aesthetic and class valuation marked by such cultural practices as the inauguration of the Nobel Prize for Literature in 1901 (James' F. English 2005, 28). This underscores the rationale for an historical study of consecration and class that is the subject of J. F. English's *Economy of Prestige: Prizes Awards, and the Circulation of Cultural Value* (2005).

I have dwelt at some length on the genealogy of human agency in black aesthetics because, while its emancipatory goals were Pan-Africanist historically, that universal appeal has developed into an individualistic instinct within the condition of Afropolitanism today. At this juncture, it will be useful to analyse the ways in which an alienated Afropolitanism undermines collective black agency.

Afropolitanism's culture and self-denial

The culture of Afropolitanism, as it is now mostly configured, can be regarded as short-sighted because of its individualistic political effects. This is exhibited through Afropolitan individual self-empowerment that ideologically mutates into an ironic and symbolic collective black self-negation, couched as a celebration of cultural hybridity and transnationalism.

Cultural producers and contemporary African writers like the Anglophone Petinah Gappah, Olufemi Terry and the Francophone Jean-Luc Raharimanana and Kossi Efoui celebrate a nascent Afropolitan cultural mood by publicly rejecting the term, '"African writer" (Adesokan 2014, par. 9; Cazenave and Célérier 2011, 97; 183). Writers, commentators and discussants broadcast the idea of Afropolitanism as a subjective condition on- and offline through interviews, in blogs and in articles – and in novel lifestyles that combine the here, there and the in-between. Finally, metropolitan cultural brokers (artists, curators, musicians, fashion designers and stylists) have caught the mood and interpreted the aura of Afropolitanism. Faddish promotional and marketing strategies have projected a version of Afropolitanism onto cultural products like artworks, music CDs, clothing as well as books. Fashion and music shows, art exhibitions and installations, book readings, literary festivals and other cultural events in Western capitals like London, New York and Frankfurt have provided yet another realm for interpreting and performing the spirit of Afropolitanism (see Hassan 2013, 3–5; also Achille Mbembe 2007).

The cultural mood of Afropolitanism has since been consolidated in academic journals and in a major scholarly anthology on the subject, *Negotiating Afropolitanism* (Wawrzineck and Makokha 2011). That mood announced itself first as an elevated *subjective* reality – and then as a marker of 'commodity fetishism' as some commentators like Binyanvanga Wainaina (see Bosch Santana 2013) have rightly noted and later as an abstracted concept whose globalising significance needs to be theorized. In other words, Afropolitanism began first as an intense artistic self-perception or self-identity, that 'heightened self-awareness' typical of the eighteenth century Romantic artist in England (Eagleton 1983, 20). It was then translated as a highly stylized cultural production and marketing strategy, and more recently as an infectious cultural phenomenon to be theorized.

In 'naming' that cultural politics, Selasi, as a poster woman for Afropolitanism, unifies (in herself as a writer) a class- and age-appropriate specific 'cultural capital', that is, 'forms of cultural knowledge, competences or disposition' (Bourdieu 1993, 5), which position her within the field of cultural production as someone with an ability to produce a work of art – a prose fiction novel in this instance. A public and institutional acknowledgment of that cultural capital through literary consecration empowers the Afropolitan culturally; that is, he or she has symbolic capital as a result of that consecration.

One of the ways in which Afropolitanism becomes political is in its pressing of symbolic capital towards self-empowerment and the enabling of human agency. To appreciate this properly, it will be difficult to imagine a migrant 60-year-old working-class minority with little cultural capital living in London, Brussels, Frankfurt or New York describing or conceiving of himself or herself as Afropolitan. The reason might lie in relative degrees of metropolitan alienation and lack of human agency, depending on whether minorities possess symbolic capital or not. This is because it is remarkable that Afropolitans are, in the first instance, upwardly mobile youth possessing symbolic capital and an unconscious desire to establish an ideological, aesthetic and especially ethical generational distance (Cazenave and Célérier 2011, 15–22) from their predecessors of African writers, artists and intellectuals – hence 'the spectacular ritual rejection of the label of "African writer"' (Adesokan 2014, par. 9).

Nevertheless – and even if this is at variance with a certain measure of ideological undecidedability vis-à-vis ideological commitment in the work of some expatriated African writers (Cazenave and Célérier 2011, 22, 24, 50) – a few Anglophone contemporaries like Chimamanda Ngozi Adichie, Yewande Omotoso,[1] Patrice Nganang and Binyavanga Wainaina do espouse a Pan-African sensibility that is demonstrated in their public lives. While a Pan-African sensibility expresses some form of political allegiance in the Anglophone, Francophone African Literary Studies calibrates the Afropean as a 'natural' and de-politicized result of transnationalism. However, the more radical emotional distance from the idea of Africa suggested by the term Afropean could be understood as political, whether self-negating or self-actualising is debatable. Such radicalism is exemplified in the Francophone writer, Jean Luc Raharimanana's complaint about the burden of commitment (Cazenave and Célérier 2011, 48–49; 50) from the distance of France:

> We were only promising young authors ... filled with revolt, with a desire to abscond from the legacies of our elders, a legacy that was hard to bear, the whole continent's pain in fact. Our only wish was to write, to be good writers, to play with aesthetics or just tell a story, and here we were, twenty years old, and summoned to save Africa! (Cazenave and Célérier 2011, 97)

From the foregoing, it can be argued that while those contemporary Anglophone African writers who self-identify as Afropolitan appear only to vacillate about ideological allegiance to roots, there is a trend among Francophones, as exemplified in the quote above, towards a more 'violent' rejection of the label of 'African writer' (2011, 97–98; 22, 23–24, 50). It seems that this group of writers identifies rather as 'Afropean'[2] (see Van Deventer 2014, 64–65; also Hitchcott and Thomas 2014) – an apparently more radically alienated variation of Afropolitanism which could mean, 'African and European', 'black French' or, by a triumphalist cultural assimilationist progression, 'French rather than African'. The Afropolitan, I argue in comparison, can be typified as rather apologetic and often excuses his/her rejection of the 'African writer' label on its being a typically Western interpellation that is essentialising, reductionist and professionally limiting or a 'pigeonholing' (see Selasi 2015).

Hence John Nimis's assertion about the label Afropean:

> 'Afropean points to a group with dual cultural and political identities without any basis or investment in the national, either as a source of legitimacy or a target of resistance. The absence of a hyphen in the term therefore registers the integrity of human subjects, thus designating a seamless mixture and crossing, across distance and across imagined categories of humans (black and white) (Nimis 2014, 49).

While Nimis is right in principle, it could also be argued that a political disinterestedness in the continent and an aforementioned genealogical self-disavowal is implicit in this vision of the contemporary Francophone writer.

Against the Afropean over-privileging of hybridity and Afropolitan apologetic embrace of the idea of Africa, there is the matter of identity and metropolitan belonging and what it constitutes that Afropolitanism conjures up, along with questions about translocation or race and ethnicity. Where the Afropean feels a sense of belonging due equally to French cultural assimilation as well as to the possession of symbolic capital, the Afropolitan feels a sense of belonging to the metropolitan society only in being seen, in an artistic sense, as 'cultured' and as an ideal citizen. This is why it is mostly cultural-brokers – writers, visual artists, musicians, dancers, and so on, one might say *cultured people* who occupy a venerated social stage because of their *valued* and acquired symbolic capital, – who identify as Afropolitan. Opposed to them are members of larger black migrant populations and diasporas, who feel alienated and lack agency within metropolitan political and social establishments from the USA to the EU or South Africa (which one might consider to be strategically part of the *West* by dint of its long occidental geo-political history and current Westernized socio-economic infrastructure).

Afropolitanism and the metropolitan public sphere

It is worth repeating that, beyond its precipitating cultural contexts, Afropolitanism is, in the main, a recuperative project of socio-political and economic agency. This is in the face of a historical and contemporary malaise, which Jemima Pierre (2006) and Henry Louis Gates Jr. (1985) in different instances have referred to as the 'racing of difference'. That is the political unconscious at work when the (post)colony meets the Metropolis, that originary site of modernity's primal sins – slavery, colonialism, apartheid and their contemporary institutional, material, existential, psycho-social and affective manifestations. Afropolitanism, as cultural politics, can be viewed as a coping mechanism against the nausea of history. That politics occurs, within a postcolonial context, in relationship to the global public realm.

Consequently, there is a primary public sphere in the West, which I refer to as the metropolitan public. Its racial composition and (upper and middle) class allegiance is mostly (but not necessarily only) white and it is privileged and powerful. Parallel to that is an auxiliary social formation, a powerless, under-privileged social configuration, which I will refer to as a 'minority public'. It is mostly black, mixed-race, migrant, exilic and often working class or lower-middle class but can also be middle class. It has a global relationship to local extensions in the formerly colonized global South – Africa in this case. Those local African spatial extensions are similar to what Peter Ekeh (1975) conceptualizes as the 'primordial and civic publics' (92) in a discussion of corresponding amorality and morality respectively in postcolonial public governance and administration.

I argue that the minority public is intersected by, and continuous with, another equally dispossessed public populated by an older black diaspora, an example of which is the African American community in the USA. These Western publics have their own internal class gradations that might mediate social mobility within them. A natural consequence of my thesis about these different publics is that there would be liminal spaces of cultural – that is, social, racial, economic and political – interaction (positive or negative) and of cooperation between these publics in the Metropolis. Access to such spaces, again, depends on social mobility as it is circumscribed by the black individual's possession of symbolic capital or lack thereof.

The Afropolitan artist's symbolic capital – as well as class and spatial mobility – are achieved by the winning of literary prizes or other forms of consecration. Some have suggested that contemporary African writers' narratives can be read as examples of an exertion towards consecration, a trend discernible in their work's appeal to metropolitan taste through sensationalized narrative strategies (Ede 2015; Huggan 2001, 32). In this reading, the Afropolitan's first audience is the powerful metropolitan public. This trend has been theorized by Eileen Julien as 'extroversion' in African literature. It is African writing's '[…] condition of being turned outwards' (2006, 681; also 681–685), she notes, away from a secondary continental audience to target a primary metropolitan readership. This is understandable if global literary consecration is decided by formal and informal metropolitan and transnational literary canonising bodies like awards institutions, publishers, book reviewers, readers, literary critics and, academic institutions through their pedagogic curricula (Gallagher 2001, 54).

The literary power imbalance between the Metropolis and the local suggested above is mirrored when the Nigerian Writer, Tricia Adaobi Nwaubani, asserts that:

> Publishers in New York and London decide which of us to offer contracts, which of our stories to present to the world. American and British judges decide which of us to award accolades, and subsequent sales and fame. […] Literary audiences in many African countries also simply sit and wait until the Western critics crown a new writer, and then begin applauding that person. (Nwaubani 2014, par. 4)

It is, perhaps, easy to corroborate Nwaubani's statements above. Remarkably, and despite a plethora of other literary prizes for publishing in and from Africa like the former Noma Award and the very recent Etisalat Prize in Nigeria, it is only global metropolitan literary prizes established on behalf of Africa, from the outside, that imbues African postcolonial literary production with global consecration and metropolitan agency.

The cultural imperialist ramifications of the inequality in powers of illumination between global and local literary organs of consecration is affirmed in the critical assertion that Western literary patronage has become 'a means of sustaining less overtly and directly the old patterns of imperial control over symbolic economies and hence over [African] cultural practice itself'

(English 298). Considering what is at stake, namely literary fame, it ought not be surprising if the Afropolitan chooses to address the Metropolis as his or her first audience and thereby constitute a cultural interpreter of Africa or an unwitting native informant for the metropolitan public.

It might well be worth wondering why Selasi's novel, *Ghana Must Go* (2013), opens with a glossary of pronunciations and definitions, an item that would usually be reserved for the end matter. Perhaps, that textual detail bespeaks an overt authorial anxiety to be accessible to the metropolitan public when material that should make up part of end-matter, if at all necessary, is strategically placed in the work's prelims. The logic which makes this detail of literary production urgent and necessary is the same anthropological unconscious which Christopher Miller (1990) insists still informs Western reading of African literature. He maintains that 'a fair Western reading of African literature demands engagement with, and even dependence on anthropology' (4). It is arguable that, were the text not orienting itself in the first instance towards the metropolitan public, a glossary of African names or African place names would have been superfluous. This is underscored by the fact that an American or British novel written in the same global English in which African fiction is written, hardly ever comes embellished with glossaries of place names or American and English names. This double standard perhaps only exemplifies the power inequity which Pascale Casanova insists exists between 'dominant' [i.e. British and American] [and] 'dominated (83, 155) or "small literatures" (175) such as those found on the continent of Africa.

It is also noteworthy that the fictional world created in Teju Cole's *Open City* (Cole 2011) – that novel with its most archetypal of literary Afropolitan characters, the self-conscious Julius – addresses the metropolitan public first and foremost. In other words, my 'Afropolitan reading' of this work understands Julius to be a mixed-race cosmopolitan middle-class figure whose membership of the minority public as a 'black man' is guarded and always referenced mostly as an afterthought, as an inevitable detail of his past. In my reading, he is more 'German-Nigerian' than 'Nigerian-German'; he emphasizes a privileged cosmopolitanism and discountenances the possible limitations insinuated by his African-ness. Julius's references to classical music, Western art, philosophy and epistemology, and his display of general erudition, though sprinkled with knowledge of local African art and traditional lore, underscores a civil, genteel front, which foregrounds his possession of symbolic capital as a medical professional and Renaissance man. His fictional persona appears to appeal more to the metropolitan public, with whom he openly aligns himself. That suggestion is notable in his reservation and distance when interacting with other members of the minority public who have no symbolic capital like him or who are placed lower on the social ladder.

The informal politics of representation enacted between the metropolitan public and the Afropolitan results in the social invisibility of a larger and faceless minority public within the scheme of metropolitan power/powerlessness. The metropolitan human agency inherent in Afropolitanism renders itself as merely token – rather than expansive – in automatically confining a larger and increasing minority group to those global spaces of existential trauma and powerlessness in the Metropolis which Frantz Fanon describes as 'zone of occult instability' (1963, 227). As mentioned earlier, the minority public's powerlessness within the metropolitan social life-world can be said to be exacerbated by a privileged Afropolitan individualism and ambivalence towards Africa when the Afropolitan declares 'I am not an African writer' or 'I am Afropean'. This is a symbolic political refusal by the Afropolitan or Afropean to represent a group, of which it is ironically considered by metropolitan civil society as a visible and prominent member, and representative.

Afropolitanism as a phenomenon thus sets itself apart from a pedestrian and often powerless crowd of metropolitan blacks or coloured people. This is because the Afropolitan actually does pander to the white metropolitan gaze in targeting that public as its first literary audience. That fact is underwritten by the title of Nwaubani's essay on the subject above, 'African Books for Western eyes'. It is then understandable if the sum of the Afropolitan's creative work, self-styling and -comportment is choreographed to create an aura of postcolonial exception. Moreover, his or her personal 'story' becomes a paratext to that creativity, increasing its aesthetic and commercial value. In other words, Afropolitans, due to their preoccupation as successful artists, are positioned in the Metropolitan Gaze as exceptional and treated as exempt from an often discriminatory and hostile black interpellation by the Metropolis. Afropolitanism – at least the metropolitan variation of it – is then a marker of elevated class, valued citizenship and relative black prestige and comparative privilege and, human agency.

In *Open City*, Julius possesses human agency by dint of his double, and therefore rich Afropolitan cultural heritage, which makes him a Renaissance man. This is apart from his professional expertise and competence. He is imbued with symbolic capital as a psychiatrist due to the discipline's social prestige and its valued place in the medical profession, especially one that is urgent for the mental health of the society, as it were. Thus we find him – in my reading at least – symbolically trying, in a manner of speaking, to heal America's fragile racialist psyche and violent colonialist past in his effort to treat a traumatized Native American and New York University Professor of History, V, for a depression caused by her scholarly immersion in Native America's tragic history (2011, 25–27).

Julius's privileged social position allows him the leisure of daily walks across class, race and geographical boundaries from one end of a (for him) 'open' New York City to the other. He is widely travelled in Europe too. While he can gravitate between the metropolitan and minority North American and European publics and the primordial and civic publics in Africa – he did spend a part of his privileged high school years in Nigeria – other Blacks or coloured people on the fringes of the metropolitan society are not as socially mobile. This Afropolitan protagonist's walks bring him in contact with the marginalized and powerless. However, Julius displays a cynicism, snobbery and aloofness that is typical of Afropolitan elitism. During one of his peregrinations across New York City, he takes a break to go inside a restaurant, sit at the bar and order a drink. As Julius finishes his drink and pays his bill a black immigrant originally from the Island of Bahbuda, Kenneth, approaches for acknowledgment. Kenneth recognizes Julius from having seen him on a different day at the Folk Art Museum where the former works as a *mere* security guard. Julius withdraws the solidarity and fellow-feeling sort by Kenneth.

'Kenneth was by now starting to wear on me, and I began to wish he would go away. I thought of the cabdriver who had driven me home from the Folk Art Museum – hey, I'm African just like you. Kenneth was making the same claim' (53). Julius has an opportunity to reach down from his privileged position and extend a hand of solidarity to the cabdriver but refuses; he equally denies Kenneth coevalness. Only when it serves his selfish purposes does Julius acknowledge or self-identify with the minority public – this time in class rather than racial terms. On a visit to Brussels he sets out to befriend a Moroccan Internet Café worker, Farouq, referring to him obsequiously as 'my brother' (101). Farouq, a Morrocan, surprised by this ultra-familiarity from a 'black' man and stranger, responds with a 'puzzled smile' (101). Even if Julius's assumption of familiarity echoes and underscores an equally unsuccessful one from Kenneth towards him in a different place and context, what is significant for my reading is the protagonist's snobbish Afropolitan sense of affiliation based on class and privilege, which Kenneth does not have, being a mere Museum guard, but which Farouq has as a scholar. Moreover, the end justifies the means for Julius. His 'aggressive familiarity' (102) served a purpose. 'I would be going into the shop for a few weeks, and it was best to make friends; and that interaction, as it turned out, set the tone for the following day' (103).

Julius is conscious of his own prestige, and his social class; he is not just any 'black' man, but a mixed-race medical practitioner who is probably 'light' enough to pass in a city full of 'nonwhites' (99) and refers to a disbelieving Moroccan as 'brother'. And he was always quick to display his erudition, to announce his class, his ability to criss-cross different publics with ease. When he discovers that Farouq is reading Walter Benjamin, he identifies a kindred spirit and an alter ego and engages the former in long discussions of politics and philosophy (102–107). Julius's 'solidarity' in this exceptional instance only underscores his usual aloofness and distance towards the minority public, especially one that speaks in the idiolect of the two African-American youth who, along with a third one, attack him once on one of his daily walks in New York City. First in passing him and nodding at him, they address each other thus: 'He come up, word? Said one. He come up yo, said the other, I thought you knew that nigga. Shit said the first, I don't know that motherfucker' (211).

That black speech, for the genteel and disconnected Julius, is 'prodigious profanity' (211). However, it is also actually a code of class affiliation and solidarity amongst a lower-class downtrodden and marginalized black minority public with no symbolic capital. For Julius, the street encounter established only 'the most tenuous of connections between us' (212). He has different speech habits and did not speak the street lingo. He considered the young men's eye contact with him as representing 'looks on a street corner by strangers, a gesture of mutual respect based on our being young, black, males; based in other words on our being "brothers"' (212). Julius's cynicism is emphasized in his having the word, brother, in scare quotes. As such the youths, after their initial acknowledgement of Julius in passing him – and intuiting his stiffness, middle class snobbery and social estrangement despite appearing to be a brother or black like them – immediately consider him a legitimate target. They double back and mug, beat up and brutalize Julius. It was the street's revenge against him for flaunting his Afropolitan privilege in its face. 'Somehow it was clear that they did not intend to kill me. There was an ease to their violence [...]. I was being beaten, but it was not severe, certainly not as severe as it could be if they were truly angry' (212–213). The young thugs mocked him with words, with a lazy banter, as they beat him up. 'And the words, fluent, spiking in and out of their laughter, seemed somehow distant from the situation [...] They were intended, now, to humiliate me, and I shrank from them' (212–213).

The youths probably read Julius's aloofness as condescending or considered him as someone who hid his disdain for the streets behind a pretended racial/class affiliation while flaunting his obvious privilege (perhaps discernible in dress and comportment) to claim social superiority. They probably came to the conclusion that he was taunting them – even if this seems to be a misunderstanding. In this way Julius appears to refuse to represent, by way of proper acknowledgment and show of solidarity, the minority public made up of working class or lower class metropolitan blacks with no symbolic capital. This is in spite of the fact that the same minority public is his own immediate representative group in racial and socio-political terms. The Afropolitan protagonist's exchanges with the street youths (before the attack), and with the cabdriver and Kenneth are restrained, taciturn and impatient due to his ambivalence towards roots, perhaps.

If the self-absorbed and individualistic kind of Afropolitanism that I have been discussing has an impact on its immediate publics, it is only in terms of a token and empty representation of them. This is because when the conservative brand of Afropolitanism under consideration rejects the label of African writer, it automatically rejects political or moral responsibilities for its constituency, thereby subverting the interests of those same publics in preference for political self-interest as I have suggested earlier. In this way Afropolitanism's first instinct is to forfeit any form of advocacy on behalf of its historically marginalized constituency, an advocacy that is otherwise possible given the Afropolitan's ability to negotiate, and his or her easy access to, different publics consequent upon accumulated symbolic capital. That access is made possible through the porousness of social boundaries, made fluid by upward class mobility.

Consequent upon the Afropolitan's global upward social mobility, the public momentum from consecrating events in the Metropolis carries into the primordial and civic publics in Africa where each of these local publics respectively lay ethnic or national claims to the new 'celebrity' and where metropolitan consecrating activities are replicated, even if on a lower scale. This puts a more urgent moral burden on the Afropolitan to actually represent his or her constituencies. However, the Afropolitan writer merely globetrots between Africa and the West, his or her primary base, where he or she is viewed by the metropolitan gaze (and acts) as a voice for the minority public within the Metropolis. The same metropolitan gaze also sees the Afropolitan as the 'face' of Africa (that is of the primordial and civic publics) in the metropolitan public. It is then ironic that the Afropolitan rejects the label of African writer, and refuses to 'represent' his or her 'natural' ideological constituency in the minority, primordial and civic publics. The result is a cultural negation of the black group agency that Afropolitanism could have inspired on the political level.

Conclusion: (im)moral agency

It is easy to ascribe the apolitical politics of Afropolitanism as detailed above to a loss of cultural memory (Erll 2011) or to what Leela Gandhi (1998) refers to as 'postcolonial amnesia' (4), in which the formerly colonized represses the colonial past. However, these writers seem to be very much aware of the ideological choices they are making. With specific reference to contemporary Francophone African literature, writers' desire for a break with, or need to elide, the ethical past and political engagement typical of foundational African literature is occasioned by the fact that they are 'weary of the label of "African writer" and dissociate themselves from the notion of [ideologically or politically] engaged writing' (Cazenave and Célérier 2011, 183). They have also 'often erased Africa from their narratives and put the accents on aesthetics' (183).

While the idea of Africa cannot be said to have been temporally static, its Afropolitan or Afropean disavowal does not constitute a sophisticated or nuanced expression of African difference but rather the desire for metropolitan sameness simply because it is powerful. It is difficult to argue with the Afropolitan writer's longing for a utopia that is devoid of an Africa whose 'legacy [is] hard to bear' in Raharimanana words above in emphasising aesthetics rather than ethics in literary production. He reflects Afropean and, consequently, Afropolitan refusal to bear 'the whole continent's pain'. This might explain why Afropolitan and Afropean moral obligation appear to be oriented towards the metropolitan public, its audiences and republic of letters (Casanova 2004) rather than to the minority, primordial or civic publics.

Raharimanana's argument privileging aesthetics over ethics explains the emotional and ideological distance specifically between his generation of Francophone (Afropean) African writers and the older generation. His argument is illuminating also for understanding the moral dissonance between culture and politics as represented in the Afropolitan, who can be seen as the Afropean's Anglophone contemporary as I have suggested previously. It would seem that some contemporary (African) writers have set their faces against any serious social commitment in their work or public lives. It can also be reasonably argued that because such writers do not seem to feel a moral or ethical duty to the continent, Africa is merely raw material for a cultural production targeted at the metropolitan public.

The neologism 'Afropean' is the Francophone equivalent expression for Anglophone 'Afropolitan' despite trends in Francophone African Literary Studies suggesting that the former is merely a word, which captures the dual African and European identity of French-speaking African writers and transcends both (Van Deventer 2014, 64–65; Nimis 2014, 48–49). Nimis further differentiates the idea of the Afropean from the Afropolitan by arguing that the first concept is less 'universalising' than the second (2014, 48–49). However, I make an intervention here to argue that both concepts share an equal weight in existential and psychic alienation from the idea of Africa. They both emphasize a transnationalism that is more invested in globalization and divorced from the history of social, economic and political inequality and lack of human agency, which led to that globalization.

Afropolitan or Afropean efforts at a generational re-interpretation of what contemporary African Literature's character ought to be are premature, I argue. According to Cazenave and Celerier and with specific reference to the Francophone context, '[f]rom the mid-1980s on, African Writers, especially, those living outside the continent, objected to the systemic notion of the African Writer as strictly *engagé* and searched for more individually creative avenues' (2011, 26). In my view such an over-emphasis on aesthetics without the mediation of ethics or a progressive politics is arguably the symptom of an insidious and imperialising past, whose continuing existential and neo-colonial effects new writers seem to ignore. They seem to want to celebrate an African utopia that is either non-existent or still in the future.

Scholars like Simon Gikandi consider Afropolitanism to be a positive mode of intellection and self-apprehension, through which 'a younger generation of Africans – and scholars of Africa – is beginning to question [the] idiom [of Afro-pessimism] and to recover alternative narratives of African identity in search of a hermeneutics of redemption' (9). I argue that such redemption can only be assured on the theoretical level through a materialist account of postcoloniality (Parry 2004) in relation to the colonial. Such an account should take full cognizance of the history that has gone to shape the identity that is described by the term Afropolitan, or even Afropean, and the imperialist and hegemonic consequences of that history.

New African identities, I conclude, ought not to be simply described and analysed as the result of an ahistorical and triumphant globalization or internalized on the experiential level as such. This, in my view, is what most contemporary African writers are doing. The divide between cultural phenomenon and political effect in Afropolitanism, as lived experience and a new form of identity, can only be bridged when contemporary writers, intellectuals or artists acknowledge the burden of history and assume – even if at the symbolic level – a moral responsibility for their uninvited implication in that history. According to Gandhi,

> Postcolonial nation states [and indeed new African writers, Afropolitan and Afropean alike, one might add] are often deluded and unsuccessful in their attempts to disown the burdens of their colonial inheritance. The mere repression of colonial memories is never, in itself, tantamount to a surpassing of or emancipation from the uncomfortable realties of the colonial encounter (1998, 4).

A politically conscious and ideologically sensitive acknowledgment of the past should not restrict artistic or aesthetic freedom of expression as the Afropolitan and Afropean seem to assume but enrich the present by exorcising it of the ghost of the past.

Disclosure statement

No potential conflict of interest was reported by the author.

Notes

1. See Rebecca Fasselt's 2014 interview with Yewande Omotoso, where the latter insists that she 'is not an Afropolitan but of the continent'.
2. For a full discussion of the idea of Afropeanism or Afropean literature, and identity see Allison Van Deventer's "Already Here: Sami Tchak's Afropean Generation" in *Francophone Afropean Literature*, eds. Hitchcott and Thomas 2014.

References

Adesokan, Akin. 2014. "I Am Not an African Writer, Damn You!." *SLIP blog*. Stellenbosch Literary Project, Accessed July 20, 2015. http://slipnet.co.za/view/blog/im-not-an-african-writer-damn-you/.

Bosch Santana, Stephanie. 2013. "Exorcizing Afropolitanism: Binyavanga Wainaina Explains Why 'I am a Pan-Africanist, not an Afropolitan' at ASAUK 2012." *Africa in Words blog* 28 (1), Accessed November 10. http://africainwords.com/2013/02/08/exorcizing-afropolitanism-binyavanga-wainaina-explains-why-i-am-a-pan-africanist-not-an-afropolitan-at-asauk-2012.

Bourdieu, Pierre. 1993. *The Field of Cultural Production: Essays on Art and Literature*, edited and introduced by Randal Johnson. New York: Columbia University Press.

Bosch Santana, Stephanie. 2015. "Exorcizing the Future: Afropolitanism's Spectral Origins." *Journal of African Cultural Studies*. 28 (1): 120–126.

Bratman, Michael E. 2007. *Structures of Agency: Essays*. Oxford: Oxford University Press.

Casanova, Pascale. 2004. *The World Republic of Letters*. Cambridge: Harvard University Press.

Castree, Noel, Alisdair Rogers, and Rob Kitchin. 2013. *A Dictionary of Human Geography*. Oxford: Oxford University Press.

Cazenave, Odile, and Patricia Célérier. 2011. *Contemporary African Francophone Writers and the Burden of Commitment*. Charlottesville: University of Virginia Press.

Cole, Teju. 2011. *Open City*. New York: Random House.

Dabiri, Emma. 2015. "Why I Am (still) Not an Afropolitan." *Journal of African Cultural Studies* 28 (1): 104–108.

Eagleton, Terry. 1983. *London: Literary Theory: An Introduction*. Oxford: Blackwell.

Ede, Amatoritsero. 2015. "Narrative Moment and Self-Anthropolgizing Discourse." *Research in African Literatures* 46 (3): 112–129.

English, James F. 2005. *Economy of Prestige: Prizes Awards, and the Circulation of Cultural Value*. Cambridge: Harvard University Press.

Ekeh, Peter P. 1975. "Colonialism and the Two Publics in Africa: A Theoretical Statement." *Comparative Studies in Society and History* 17 (1): 91–112.

Erll, Astrid. 2011. *Memory in Culture*. London: Palgrave Macmillan.

Eze, Chielozona. 2014. "Rethinking African Culture and Identity: The Afropolitan Model." *Journal of African Cultural Studies* 26 (2): 234–247. Accessed November 5. http://dx.doi.org/10.1080/13696815.2014.894474.

Eze, Chielozona. 2015. "We, Afropolitans." *Journal of African Cultural Studies* 28 (1): 114–119.

Fabre, Michel. 1991. *From Harlem to Paris: Black American Writers in France, 1840–1980*. Urbana: University of Illinois Press.

Fanon, Frantz. 1963. *The Wretched of the Earth*. Translated by Constance Farrington. New York: Grove.

Fasselt, Rebecca. 2014. "'I'm not Afropolitan – I'm of the Continent': A Conversation with Yewande Omotoso." *The Journal of Commonwealth Literature* 1–16.

Gallagher, Susan V. 2001. "Contingencies and Intersections: The Formation of Pedagogical Canons." *Project Muse. Pedagogy* 50 (2): 231–246. http://dx.doi.org/10.1177/0021989414552922.

Gandhi, Leela. 1998. *Postcolonial Theory: A Critical Introduction*. New York: Columbia University Press.

Gates, Henry Louis, Jr. 1985. "Editor's Introduction: Writing, 'Race' and the Difference it Makes." In *"'Race', Writing, and Difference"*, edited by Henry Louis Gates Jr., Chicago: University of Chicago press.*Critical Inquiry* 12 (1): 1–20.

Gehrmann, Susanne. 2015. "Cosmopolitanism with African Roots. Afropolitanism's Ambivalent Mobilities." *Journal of African Cultural Studies* 28 (1): 1–12. Accessed December 8. http://dx.doi.org/10.1080/13696815.2015.1112770.

George, Olakunle. 2003. *Relocating Agency: Modernity and African Letters*. New York: SUNY Press.

Gikandi, Simon. 2011. "On Afropolitanism." In *Negotiating Afropolitanism: Essays on Borders and Spaces in Contemporary African Literature and Folklore*, edited by Jennifer Wawrzinek and J. K. S. Makokha, 9–13. Amsterdam/New York: Rodopi.

Hassan, Salah M. 2013. *"Rethinking Cosmopolitanism: Is 'Afropolitan' the Answer?" Reflections 2012/5*. Amsterdam: Prince Claus Fund.

Hitchcott, Nicki, and Thomas Dominic. 2014. *Francophone Afropean Literatures*. Liverpool: Liverpool University Press.

Huggan, Graham. 2001. *The Postcolonial Exotic: Marketing the Margins*. London: Routledge.

Huggins, Nathan Irvin. 1973. *Harlem Renaissance*. New York: Oxford University Press.

Jahn, Janheinz. 1968. *A History of Neo-African Literature: Writing in Two Continents*. Translated by Oliver Coburn and Ursula Lehrburger. London: Faber.

Jules-Rosette, Bennetta. 1998. *Black Paris: The African Writers' Landscape*. Urbana: University of Illinois Press.

Julien, Eileen. 2006. "The Extroverted African Novel." In *The Novel 1*, edited by Franco Moretti, 667–700. Princeton: Princeton University Press.

July, Robert W. 1967. *The Origins of Modern African Thought: Its Development in West Africa during the Nineteenth and Twentieth Centuries*. New York: F. A. Preager.

Kesteloot, Lilyan. 1974. *Black Writers in French: A Literary History of Negritude*. Translated by Ellen Conroy Kennedy. Philadelphia, PA: Temple University Press.

Mbembe, Achille. 2002. "African Modes of Self-Writing." Translated by Steven Rendall. *Public Culture* 14 (1): 239–273.

Mbembe, Achille. 2007. "Afropolitanism." In *Africa Remix: Contemporary Art of a Continent*, edited by Simon Njami, 26–30. Johannesburg: Johannesburg Art Gallery.

Miller, Christopher L. 1990. *Theories of Africans: Francophone Literature and Anthropology in Africa*. Chicago, IL: University of Chicago Press.

Musila, Grace A. 2015. "Part-Time Africans, Europolitans and 'Africa Lite'." *Journal of African Cultural Studies* 28 (1): 109–113.

Nimis, John. 2014. "Corps sans Titre: Fleshiness and Afropean Identity in Bessora's 53 cm." In *Francophone Afropean Literatures*, edited by Nicki Hitchcott and Dominic Thomas, 48–63. Liverpool: Liverpool University Press.

Nwaubani, Adaobi Tricia. 2014. "African Books for Western Eyes." *The New York Times*, November 28. Accessed December 2. http://www.nytimes.com/2014/11/30/opinion/sunday/african-books-for-western-eyes.html?_r=0.

Parry, Benita. 2004. *Postcolonial Studies: A Materialist Critique*. London: Routledge.

Pierre, Jemima. 2006. "Anthropology and the Race of/for Africa." In *Disciplinary and Interdisciplinary Encounters*, edited by Paul Tiyambe Zeleza. 39–61. Dakar: CODESRIA.

Selasi, Taiye. 2005. "Bye-Bye Babar." *The Lip blog. The Lip Magazine*. Accessed July 7. http://thelip.robertsharp.co.uk/?p=76.

Selasi, Taiye. 2013. *Ghana Must Go*. Toronto: Penguin.

Selasi, Taiye. 2015. "Stop pidgeonholing African Writers." *The Guardian Newspapers*, Accessed July 4. http://www.theguardian.com/books/2015/jul/04/taiye-selasi-stop-pigeonholing-african-writers.

Van Deventer, Allison. 2014. "Already Here: Sami Tchak's Afropean Generation." In *Francophone Afropean Literatures*, edited by Nicki Hitchcott and Dominic Thomas, 64–80. Liverpool: Liverpool University Press.

Wawrzinek, Jennifer, and Makokha, J. K. S. 2011. *Negotiating Afropolitanism: Essays on Borders and Spaces in Contemporary African Literature and Folklore*. Amsterdam/New York: Rodopi.

Williams, Raymond. 1977. *Marxism and Literature*. Oxford: Oxford University Press.

Afropolitanism as critical consciousness: Chimamanda Ngozi Adichie's and Teju Cole's internet presence

Miriam Pahl

Critiques of Afropolitanism that dismiss the concept because of its links to consumerism and commodification assume an unchallenging compliance of those considered as Afropolitans with dominant ideologies of consumption and the rule of capital. Considering Taiye Selasi's article 'Bye-Bye Babar', this seems plausible, but it is also a reductive interpretation that effaces the transformative potential of Afropolitanism. The literary works and online presence in public discourses of writers labelled Afropolitan show that they challenge and revise the present world order in the way that Walter Mignolo and other theorists of decoloniality envisage in their concept of 'critical cosmopolitanism'. Chimamanda Ngozi Adichie and Teju Cole, for example, implement Afropolitanism as a critical assessment of global culture that defies a reduction of the concept simply to its commercial dimension. In their own ways, Adichie and Cole explore the affordances and the limitations of the internet, mobility and globalization.

1. Introduction

> I'm an Afropolitan, a pan-African, an Afro-pessimist, depending on who hates me on any given day. I embrace all those terms. However, labels: they always apply, except when they don't. (Cole in Bady 2015)

These vague words by Teju Cole summarize his position towards present-day identity labels. His statement negotiates a middle ground between the two main positions towards the label 'Afropolitan': one that supports the concept and one that considers it as a celebratory, apolitical and commercially driven phenomenon. Cole might be regarded as self-consciously neutral, or less sympathetically, described as indifferent; but he also expresses a refusal to comprehend these labels as exclusionary, separate categories, preferring to describe them as reconcilable and co-existent. This perception concurs with Cole's larger objective to generate inclusive social thinking and a 'more peaceful internationalism' (Cole in Meyer 2014) through his works, which is ingeniously articulated in one of Cole's Twitter projects, namely 'The Time of the Game'. In 2014, Cole asked his Twitter followers to submit photos of their TV screen showing the final match of the soccer world cup, which he, together with information designers from New York University, assembled into a 'synchronized global view of the World Cup' (Meyer 2014). Thus, Cole acknowledges the different 'non-governmental democracies' of, for example, the screen, the football or the camera. Despite unequal access to the internet and 'multiple uses of screens', these technologies overlap sufficiently to create what he calls 'public time' (a corollary to public space) (Meyer 2014). In effect, his project advocates an 'alternative internationalism', a 'testifying [of Twitter users] to each other's existence' on a global scale. This, as I will develop in the following, is one implementation of Afropolitanism as a form of critical cosmopolitanism which demonstrates that some articulations of the concept can also be politically transformative.

I contend that many African diasporic authors express a globally orientated critical perspective in their literary and cultural works that does not merely praise the possibilities of globalization but more importantly examines persisting power differentials and injustices. Many of these globally positioned authors inhabit a specific location in contemporary society, constituted of their financially enhanced, mobile position and their personal history. Accordingly, 'Afropolitanism' as a concept acknowledges not only a certain position *in* the world, but expresses a certain disposition *towards* the world.[1] Mignolo (2000) and other advocates of the theory of 'decoloniality' distinguish between, on the one hand, cosmopolitan projects that emanate from the interior of Euro-American modernity[2] and seek inclusion through homogenization, and, on the other hand, critical cosmopolitanism that is formed from the 'exteriority of modernity (that is, coloniality)', exterior as the 'borderland', the 'outside that is needed by the inside' (724). Mignolo decries Eurocentric cosmopolitan projects or 'global designs' as he calls them, which draw new lines of exclusion and are 'oblivious to the saying of the people that are supposed to be emancipated' (723). He therefore demands the development of critical cosmopolitan projects that promote 'social organization based on reciprocity, communal (instead of individual) values, the value of wisdom rather than [Eurocentric] epistemology' (742). This distinction is insightful because it theorizes a position from which the current world order of cultural and socio-economic stratifications is challenged and criticized. But it is controversial in its reliance on and perpetuation of a binary of 'inside' and 'outside', a conceptualization of the system of 'modernity' that it tries to overcome.

Chimamanda Ngozi Adichie and Teju Cole have both been raised in Nigeria and have then studied in the USA and live mainly there. Accordingly, from the viewpoint of decolonial theory, they might be 'classified' as 'internal others' of a Euro-American sensibility, having developed a 'double-consciousness [that] lies at the very foundation of border thinking' (Mignolo and Tlostanova 2006, 211).[3] They are positioned, in the language of Mignolo and Tlostanova, 'precisely where the "problem" appears and the solutions are being played out' – at the '"borders" between the color (and gender and sexuality) line and the epistemic line' (214). Mignolo and Tlostanova define critical border thinking and critical cosmopolitanism as an epistemology that is created by those outside the powerful centres, as an orientation that is 'pluri-topic and engendered by the violence of the colonial and imperial differences' (211). Scholars of decolonial theory like Enrique Dussel, Anibal Quijano and Ramón Grosfóguel emphasize the binary between the powerful centre and the abject, silenced periphery; however, these categories are not fully applicable to the experience of these diasporic African writers. Cole and Adichie both describe experiences of racial discrimination in American society,[4] but they also share an enhanced position in terms of mobility and resources, which is amplified in the differently organized virtual world. Social media and the internet, their reach and the new possibilities and limitations they represent, complicate the position of writers like Chimamanda Ngozi Adichie and Teju Cole by adding virtual possibilities of critique and innovation to the physical reality of publishing.

The concept of critical cosmopolitanism as a 'double-consciousness' that is formed at the 'cracks' between privilege and exclusion illuminates the distinctively African experience of the contemporary global society of the writers examined here. It also emphasizes that their positioning allows these writers a critical perspective from which they conceptually deconstruct impermeable social boundaries, hierarchies and power differences. However, Adichie's and Cole's instantiation of Afropolitanism as critical cosmopolitanism in their social media presences also subvert and complicate the underlying binary that decolonial theory assumes. I argue that, in their works, Chimamanda Ngozi Adichie and Teju Cole express a form of critical cosmopolitanism, in that they reintroduce an ambivalence, a multi-layeredness of meanings to the public and online conversations about mobility, globalization and cosmopolitanism from a specifically Afro-centric perspective. Their positioning and their creative works, nevertheless, also challenge and subvert the underlying binary in decolonial theory.

I read this specific locatedness of Afropolitanism in conjunction with these authors' 'extroverted orientation' which, here, takes its cue from a distinction proposed by Eileen Julien. Julien distinguishes between African novels that are oriented inwards, to a national readership, and, contrastingly, the 'extroverted African novel' as a type of narrative produced at the 'cusps of worlds, [...] negotiat[ing] semiotic systems and inscrib[ing] asymmetries of power' (2006, 696). She quotes Pratt to define these novels as a phenomenon of 'the "contact zone," a social and [...] discursive space "where disparate cultures meet, clash, and grapple with each other, often in highly asymmetrical relations of domination and subordination"' (Pratt qtd. in Julien 2006, 684). Although this concept acknowledges the global orientation of these writers, it seems to disregard that their works are also, if differently, successful in the authors' country of origin Nigeria. These works are read and discussed in Euro-American spaces, but also on the African continent. Afropolitan writing, I suggest, constitutes one category of African literature by writers like Chimamanda Ngozi Adichie and Teju Cole who navigate a transnational space in their writings, and engage with issues in their works that resonate on a national and global level since that is their daily reality (as it is for many of their readers). Their works substitute the 'multicultural hybrid' (that has been dominant in postcolonial writing and theory) with complex and dynamic 'patterns of mixing, blending, combining and then falling apart' (Ekotto and Harrow 2015, 8). Multiple affiliations in the social domain remain reversible and keep changing. Adichie and Cole display an African cosmopolitan 'sensibility', which means 'not so much that they are, or present themselves as, socially mobile and multiply affiliated as that they respond to and creatively rework metropolitan demands for cultural otherness in their work' (Huggan 2001, 26). The extraversion that Julien associates with the engagement with global issues is articulated by these writers also in their openness to depart from conventional literary genres.

The opportunities and limitations represented by the internet and the role it plays in contemporary society exemplify my argument. Its infrastructure deconstructs global binaries, but its uses may recreate inequalities in the global society. As one phenomenon of 'thickening globalism' (Nye 2002), the internet's distribution demonstrates the interconnection and interdependence of global social networks. The internet is not accessible to everybody – globalization 'implies neither equity – nor homogenization' (Nye 2002), but it does affect and recreate daily life of those who do have access. Especially the way social media is used in everyday life exemplifies a distinction that, as Mbembe points out in the Chimurenga Chronic (2015), is often confused: 'Internet is a means, it is not the end.' In other words, online activism remains ineffective if it does not overcome the distinction between the virtual and the physical world, a notion that is expressed in Teju Cole's works through his aesthetic articulation of doubt towards the transformative potential of language and literature. Social media offer new modes of connection, interaction and identification in the social world, and, as more and more writers demonstrate, it opens up new horizons for literary practice. For example, Binyavanga Wainaina,[5] a Kenyan writer with a very active Twitter account, published his short story 'I am a Homosexual, Mum' in the blog *Africa is a Country* in order to announce his sexual orientation. His revelation in January 2014 followed Uganda's and Nigeria's introduction of new laws against homosexuality and raised attention on and beyond the continent, with discussions on Twitter, Facebook and other online media. Examining Chimamanda Ngozi Adichie's and Teju Cole's presence online in conjunction with the two meanings of Afropolitanism that will be explained in the following, I want to develop how Afropolitanism might be helpful to analyse these writers' presence in the online and the 'real' world.

2. Afropolitanism

Although the origin of the term 'Afropolitanism' is difficult to trace, it is clear that its discursive uses revolve around two predominant conceptualizations which were first significantly shaped by Achille Mbembe and Taiye Selasi. Mbembe's understanding of the term is expressed in an essay of the same name in which he outlines the movements of people from, within and to Africa (2007). He promotes an image of the world and its peoples as constantly moving and mixing, opposing this to what he calls nativism. Nativism is a bio-racism that, in its mild form, glorifies diversity and, paradoxically, in a more radical version, fights for maintaining cultural and racial purity and tradition. This 'illusion' of purity, Mbembe argues, is the basis for this bio-racism that translates from the individual to the communal or national level into political regulations that allow or disallow people to do what people have always done: Move and find a different life elsewhere. Afropolitanism, as conveyed by Mbembe, acknowledges migration as a natural human phenomenon, re-establishes an 'awareness of the interweaving of the here and there' and undermines national boundaries (28). Chielozona Eze is another scholar who tries to promote an understanding of Afropolitanism as a critical concept. In his summary of Mbembe's position, he emphasizes that Afropolitanism involves a revision of African identity in its abandonment of 'victimhood as a starting point of discourse and self-perception' (240). He emphasizes the possibility that Afropolitanism establishes; to leave behind an oppositional, victimized position that 'Africa' is conventionally assigned to, allowing instead for more nuanced and differentiated subject positions that Afropolitans inhabit.

The concept 'Afropolitanism' has since gained much attention in regard to its second dominant perception: Taiye Selasi coined a popular understanding of 'Afropolitanism' in her essay 'Bye-Bye Babar' (2005) in which she describes the promising situation of 'the newest generation of African emigrants'. Thus, the phenomenon appears as an alternative to 'Afropessimism' and the representation of Africa determined by deprivation and misery, as Simon Gikandi states in the anthology *Negotiating Afropolitanism* (2011, 9) and, instead, focuses on the 'condition of possibility' (10). Selasi in an essay titled 'Taiye Selasi on Discovering her Pride in her African Roots', published in 2013, suggests that 'Bye-Bye Babar' has to be understood as less uncritical and celebratory than it is often interpreted. Her relation to Africa, she says, was in part determined by Western stereotypes and pain and she writes that 'what [she] needed was some other way to know [her]self as African, apart from as heir to [her] parents' hurts'. Accordingly, Selasi's and Mbembe's attempt to re-establish African identity concur in that they try to overcome the victim-position.

The term itself suggests that 'Afropolitanism' is a form of 'cosmopolitanism', and in fact, the critique raised against the two phenomena is comparable. According to Bill Ashcroft, cosmopolitanism forestalls to be a productive concept due to its associations with 'urbanity, sophistication and wealth' – the need for material resources to 'travel freely, to experience and participate in other cultures for long periods' and thus, to be cosmopolitan (Ashcroft 2010, 76). A celebratory excitement with this phenomenon, so the critics argue, obscures the structural differences that disallow major parts of the global society to be 'cosmopolitan'. Conceptualizing cosmopolitanism as a 'state of mind' entails that it is being located in 'an empty space' (Ashcroft 2010, 76). This obscures the subject position of the cosmopolitan and disregards the power hierarchies of global migration and travelling. The experience and reality of refugees and labour migrants, for example, might not be affected by an ideology of empathy, curiosity and tolerance towards strangers.

Translating these points of critique back to Afropolitanism, Brian Bwesigye in the online forum *This is Africa*, for instance, expresses his fear that Afropolitanism develops into a 'new single story', focussing on well-off African emigrants and thereby 'eras[ing] African realities from the literary landscape' – realities of poverty that stand in contrast to those described by Taiye Selasi. The concept is seen as the 'crude cultural commodification' (as Stephanie Bosch Santana (2013) quotes Binyavanga Wainaina saying in her piece published on *Africa in Words*) and appropriation of 'Africa' by capitalist culture, as in the way Graham Huggan theorizes the 'postcolonial exotic'.[6] Emma Dabiri's critique of Afropolitanism on the blog *Africa is a Country* revolves around the pre-eminence of commodification (2014). The assumption is that what is seen as African culture becomes globally commodified, and it is not simultaneously able to change the terms of global power relations. Sandra Ponzanesi examines the same argument in her analysis of *The Postcolonial Cultural Industry* (2014): the fear that difference is transformed 'into a blended and familiar other that meets expectations and can be relegated into neat categories' (43). She objects that 'the fact that they are successfully marketed by transnational entertainment corporations does not necessarily mean that they have become commodity without an edge' (3). This argument might be valid for some articulations of Afropolitanism as well: Although writers like Adichie and Cole inhabit an elite position in society that does not mean that their creative works invariably perpetuate and reinforce structural power differences.

The statement 'The Internet is Afropolitan' that serves as the title for an interview with Achille Mbembe in the Chimurenga Chronic can also be understood in reverse: Afropolitanism 'grew up' online. Susanne Gehrmann develops in her article 'Cosmopolitanism with African Roots' how the controversy around the concept, as well as its quick propagation, is unthinkable without the cyberspace (2015). Most of the discussions about the concept are to be found in online forums and blogs, and many contemporary African writers experiment with online and social media channels and thus certainly also market their literary work. The concept's vigour on the internet distinguishes it from earlier paradigms like pan-Africanism. As will be highlighted in the following, the internet is a crucial factor in the definition of Afropolitanism.

The developments described above suggest that the question should less be to determine whether Afropolitanism is an elitist phenomenon but rather if and how it can also be critical and transformative.[7] Selasi's later essay clarifies that 'Bye-bye Babar' has been largely misunderstood. It should rather be seen as an attempt to depart from Afropessimism and to add an imagination of what might be called an African middle-class experience to the meanings attached to 'Africa' in the global community. This attempt, however, does not 'claim to speak for all' (as Emma Dabiri fears in her blogpost 'Why I am not an Afropolitan' (2014)) and is not supposed to become the 'single story' of Africa. The conversations around the phenomenon demonstrate its multiple layers, and the persisting presence of history in 'success stories' of privilege and mobility. The following discussion will show that Afropolitanism cannot be conceptualized as only an apolitical narrative of transnational consumer lifestyles. Instead, it may be reinvigorated as a helpful concept to describe and analyse an articulation of critical engagement by contemporary African writers with issues of justice and humanity in a globalized world.

3. Chimamanda Ngozi Adichie's *Americanah*

In *Americanah*, Chimamanda Ngozi Adichie makes the main character Ifemelu a blogger and after the publication of the novel, she transfers this fictional blog into the real world (wide web) beyond the novel. The story begins with Ifemelu's visit to a hair salon in Princeton, and, in a series of flashbacks, tells the tales of her coming of age, including her move to America without her boyfriend Obinze, her discouraging experiences searching for a job, and several of her love affairs. These and other experiences are all affected by racial strictures that determine the social relations in the American society depicted in the novel. The blog Adichie creates for Ifemelu inside the novel (as well as its spin-off on the internet) exhibits a strong political and social commitment. It negotiates the hierarchization of cultures and criticizes the white-centredness of the US environment depicted in the novel, and chronicles everyday incidents of racism. Adichie describes her motivation to include the blogging element in her novel thus: 'I wanted this novel to also be social commentary, but I wanted to say it in ways that are different from what one is supposed to say in literary fiction' (Adichie and Rifbjerg 2014). Ifemelu launches the blog 'Raceteenth or Various Observations About American Blacks (Those Formerly Known as Negroes) by a Non-American Black' as an anonymous space to share and talk about her observations. In *Americanah*, the blog is initially only mentioned in passing ('Years later, a blog post would read …' (Adichie 2013, 157)), then it is separated out from the standard text by being printed in a different font and with distinct layout. Finally, it appears online, outside the novel, under the name 'The Small Redemptions of Lagos' (Adichie 2014).

The development of the blog offers a critical perspective on the internet, in that it is represented as relatively liberating, but also with intimidating dynamics. Although the 'internet pretends that it is salvation', as Mbembe contends (Chimurenga Chronic), the development of the blog in the novel depicts that it is also a very fierce and competitive space. Ifemelu becomes aware that, in relation to race, the internet allows her to touch on issues and to express opinions that she feels unable to address in the workshops, the character is shown to run in the novel (Adichie 2013, 389), but it is also a space where insults are expressed without restraints or censorship.

Focusing on the participatory dimension of blog writing, the novel explores how the process of writing is democratized, in the sense that Ifemelu and her readers negotiate topics and values together, but also appropriated by the readers on the internet. Ifemelu is, as Serrena Guarracino shows, 'dispossessed of her own writing' and restricted in her agency as a writer by the readership of her blog as the blog develops into a 'shared space' of 'cultural debate' (2014, 16). The more Ifemelu's readers influence her writing, the more she draws back and allows the blog to develop into an egalitarian space for different voices to speak out. She is excited about the development of the blog; however, readers and their comments also deeply distress her, becoming, 'in her mind, a judgemental angry mob waiting for her' (391). The novel lists the range of responses to the blog-posts – the different ways it is consumed – affirmative and hostile, angry and thrilled (391). As Ponzanesi reminds us, 'audiences are not only critical but also multiple and differentiated' (2014, 47). The fact that Ifemelu is not able to predict which blog posts will be 'successful' (drawing attention and comments) makes clear that the process of meaning making cannot be determined by the blogger, but is to a great extent decided by the recipient. The novel assesses the role of the author, and takes into account 'the critical role of readers and spectators worldwide and their readerly transformations of texts' (Julien 2015, 26). The blog first turns into a site where opinions are created and negotiated, a place of 'dialogic cosmopolitanism' that enables a 'different conceptualization of […] democracy' (Mignolo 2000, 744). But successively, the internet also becomes a sphere that allows for hostile and dehumanizing infringements.

Strikingly, Adichie impedes the role of the reader in the online blog 'The Small Redemptions of Lagos', in that it does not allow readers to comment. In contrast to Ifemelu in the novel, Adichie claims back her authority as the author, seemingly inspired by the fictional experiences of blog writing she explored in the novel. The online blog takes advantage of new audiences that might not be reached by the novel, but curtails the possibility of creating meanings collectively.

Although the experiences depicted in the novel should not be taken as autobiographical information, they do elucidate Adichie's carefully honed public persona. Adichie keeps her private life private and has an eye on how the media portray her.[8] She withdrew a personal article about depression that she had submitted to *The Guardian* earlier, but contrastingly, she has an essay published in *The New York Times* (2015) about her father's kidnapping in Nigeria. Considering these two incidents in conjunction indicates that Adichie deploys an intimate story about her family to explore issues of Nigerian society, but simultaneously, she tries to be in control of publicly available information about her. The story about her father is not a journalistic discussion of kidnappings in Nigeria, but offers insight into the emotional impact of a family member being kidnapped, and thematizes her standing as a writer in Nigerian society. Adichie has become a writer with a celebrity status similar to that of actors and musicians which is a result of her success as a writer, but also of her own 'marketing'. In that respect, the statements she makes about the performer and singer Beyoncé in an interview with *olisa.tv* are equally valid for her own image:

> It's a shame that we live in a world so blindly obsessed by celebrity – an actor or musician talking about a social issue should not be a reason for the press to pay attention to that issue, because they should pay attention to it anyway – but sadly it is what it is. Ours is an age in which celebrities have enormous influence.

The internet and social media (Nwonwu 2015) appear as a space that enhances the possibilities of outreach, while simultaneously it forestalls control of how and where messages and information travel.

In the Chimurenga Chronic interview, Mbembe deliberates:

> the kind of self that emerges in the crucible of these new [internet] technologies, and how these technologies become an extension of ourselves and erase the distance between the human and the object. Human beings are no longer satisfied to simply be human beings.

He develops that, since the internet is 'in the service of the ideology of consumption' the human being has to negotiate subjection to that ideology, too. Adichie's presence online and the publicity around her person demonstrate that this development also affects the position of the author in society. The exploration of the sphere of blogs on the internet mirrors Adichie's own position at the intersection of postcoloniality and postcolonialism, market and critique. Chimamanda Ngozi Adichie has been called 'Afropolitan',[9] a label she resents, 'yet her public persona and her work have been appropriated by the Afropolitan global community', as Serrena Guarracino observes (11). The role of the reader that is explored in the novel seems to play a dominant role here as well, determining the process of meaning making and compromising the authority of the author by imposing a label that Adichie does not agree with.

One blog post in the novel, about the politics of hair, shows how intricately connected culture and consumerism are: After venting her anger about common views of natural and relaxed black hair, Ifemelu lists – and thereby advertises the products she uses for her hair (379).[10] Ifemelu then decides to put up advertisements and even more, she receives 'support' and credits for her blog that become part of her income when her audience grows (388). 'Support. That word made the blog even more apart from her, a separate thing that could thrive or not, sometimes without her and sometimes with her' (387). Her feelings about the development of the blog demonstrate her ambivalent relationship with the fact that 'the "raw and true" writing that had fist prompted her to open the blog has slowly become an exacting job' (Guarracino 2014, 17). The novel explores through the micro-cosmos of the blog the undeniable interrelation between culture and consumerism, a relation that is intensified in the digital sphere.

Besides the reader's determining role, the label Afropolitan, in the predominant consumerist understanding of the term, has probably been imposed on Adichie because of her online presence: Her speeches on Youtube are popular not only in African literature discourses; a feature of her in *Vogue* in March 2015 where she shows readers of the online magazine what she wears every day introduces her to the readership of this fashion magazine, and her appearance in a music video by Beyoncé again addresses an altogether different audience. It is vital to ask if Adichie's work displays African-ness to enhance its value as a commodity in the way that Afropolitanism is accused to do by Wainaina and Dabiri, for example. Adichie demonstrates her critical awareness of market forces in her explorations of social media in the novel and in her careful navigation of her own presence online. Beyond that, Adichie's discussion of women's magazines in *Americanah* indicates that Adichie is politically motivated to appear in its online website: 'It was absurd how women's magazines forced images of small-boned, small-breasted women on the rest of the multi-boned, multi-ethnic world of women to emulate' (223)[11]. Adichie's own mere presence in a women's magazine like *Vogue* offers readers a different body aesthetic and makes the magazine more diverse. This suggests that her works

> relate to the market with a contrapuntal attitude that both endorses and critiques it, embracing instead of removing the dichotomy between postcolonialism as anticolonial critical practice and postcoloniality as the marketability of exoticism in commercial as well as academic terms,

as Guarracino contends (4). In other words, Adichie accepts and strategically uses her specific position in the market to address the challenges of contemporary global society. Instead of perpetuating Euro-American understandings of, for example, race or gender, she openly criticizes policies and cultural practices through these 'mainstream' channels.

Adichie's novel and her presence in online media exemplify how social media writing and the construction of meaning is contested in the dialogue of writers and readers and between the demands of the market and social critique. Writers need to navigate these sometimes opposing influences sensitively, especially in the spaces of social media. There, the distinction between reader and writer becomes less clear, and writing appears in a distinct form, both public and anonymous. Publicness, publicity and the forces of 'mainstream' trends further determine the genre of online writing, linking back to the concept of Afropolitanism. Adichie experiments with social media and the concomitant visibility of authors and bloggers both in her novel and online, and exemplifies how writing and the author's presence in the cyberspace can be a tool for social commentary and transformation, nevertheless, one that needs to be managed carefully.

4. Teju Cole's literary use of Twitter

Teju Cole's biography in itself can be read as a record of cosmopolitanism: He was born in Michigan, USA, and grew up in Lagos, Nigeria. He returned to the USA at the age of 17 and went to college and university there. He currently resides in Brooklyn, but his online presence on Facebook and Twitter attest to his international travels. Cole is highly acclaimed for his books *Open City* (2011a) and *Every Day is for the Thief* (2007), a travel account which was first published as a blog online (Hemon 2014, 77). Although his projects on Twitter are also repeatedly mentioned, little critical attention has been paid to his literary experiments with social media.

In his keynote lecture at the 2015 African Literature Association conference in Bayreuth, Germany, Cole introduces Twitter as an African city in order to demonstrate the internet's importance in revolutionary movements on the African continent like, for example, the Arab spring. He emphasizes the connection, but also the distinction between people marching in the streets and people talking about it on social media. This allusion to the 'confusion of means and ends' that Mbembe also points out runs as a thread through Cole's internet projects. Adichie's publicly accessible social media presences on Facebook and Twitter are operated by her publisher to post news about her. Cole, in contrast, uses Facebook autonomously to point out new articles by or about him, and to offer deliberations about society, recent events and personal anecdotes. Thus, unlike Adichie, he does not appear as a distant celebrity, but creates a kind of intimacy in interaction with the Facebook community. Besides his projects on Twitter, he used the medium similarly, but he has refrained from using Twitter since July 2014.

One of the Twitter projects is the 'small fates' series that Cole was running from 2011 until 2013. According to his website, it was a by-product of his research for a book about Lagos, originating from the brief news sections in Nigerian newspapers. The small fates are 'compressed reports of unusual happenings' that provide a snapshot of human life and experience in Nigeria. Stylistically and content-wise, these 'small fates' are similar to the French 'faits divers', small stories with a 'deranged' causality that were written by Félix Fénéon and published in the French newspaper *Le Matin* around 1906.[12] On Twitter, Cole provided several hundred small fates as 'complete in themselves', out-of-context incidents inspired by Nigerian newspapers, as he explains on his website (Cole 2011d):

> @tejucole 29.12.2011: Love is complicated. With a double-barrelled rifle, Hadezia, in Abuja, widowed herself. (Cole 2011b)
>
> @tejucole 29.12.2011: The Anambra treasury officer, Innocent, who stole N66.5 million in pension funds, insists he was hypnotized. (Cole 2011c)

All incidents are situated in a Nigerian city or village which is mentioned along with the Nigerian state, which evokes familiarity for Nigerian readers, and exposes a clear distance to non-Nigerian readers. Cole distinguishes on his website between reactions to these place names which he expects (and receives) from Nigerian and non-Nigerian readers (Cole 2011d). Some tweets contain a linguistic local reference, 'enriching the irony' for Nigerian readers with local knowledge (Cole 2011d). For non-Nigerian readers, these news stories markedly 'emerge from [a] spatial and historical location of the colonial difference' (Mignolo 2000, 741). Nevertheless, most of them are 'perfectly legible' to any reader, as Cole contends. His concern with non-Nigerian readers – which he elaborates in an interview with Eleanor Wachtel, for example – might suggest that he writes for a largely North American readership; however, his focus there seems to be grounded in the Canadian interview context. The explanations on the website clarify that, firstly, he has a large Nigerian audience, and, secondly, that they belong to his implied audience, too.

The tweets allow for multiple readings, depending on the reader's background, but they emphasize the 'connectors' – the ordinariness of social daily life, the satisfaction readers derive from the irony of the stories – between different social communities, cultures and epistemologies. The small fates evoke a kind of familiarity as they describe everyday life incidents like a grandfather taking care of children, or disputes among married couples, though most times culminating in murder, violence or other gruesome deeds of passion. Cole thus confirms Julien's concept of 'extroverted' African literature as an interpretation of 'Africa' for non-African readers. He builds an alternative archive of life in Nigeria that contributes to our shared social (online) world, making visible a, from a non-African reader perspective, marginalized component of the international community. However, the 'introvertedness' of the tweets and the way they address Nigerian readers complicate Julien's model because it does not account for this orientation. For these Nigerian recipients, Cole reaffirms their culture, a 'Nigerian modernity, full of conflict, tragedies, and narrow escapes'. Unlike the other articles in French newspapers that are about 'big people', the *faits divers*, and also the small fates, 'are stories about little people made big by publicity or the press' (Jullien 2009, 66). Cole acknowledges 'ordinary people' with these tweets, and establishes new solidarities amongst Nigerians and beyond national borders. Cole describes his motivation thus:

> The idea is not to show that Lagos, or Abuja, or Owerri, are worse than New York, or worse than Paris. Rather, it's a modest goal: to show that what happens in the rest of the world happens in Nigeria too, with a little craziness all our own mixed in. (Cole homepage)

One aspect of the 'little craziness' Cole refers to might be the magical mode of knowing that is implicated in many tweets. Hypnosis, *juju* and witchcraft are casually, in a matter-of-fact tone, intermingled with realist descriptions of human interaction. Thus, Cole acknowledges and revalorizes a mode of knowing that is conventionally relegated to an inferior position in societies that are dominated by rational and logical thinking, in Nigerian but even more beyond. In this kind of news, magic and mystical beliefs that are otherwise dismissed as superstition are represented as valuable alternatives to the conventions of rationality. Cole thus advocates an 'epistemic diversality', which Mignolo considers as the necessary basis for 'political and ethical cosmopolitan projects' (743).

Cole's reference to a 'modest goal' implies that he is hesitant about the effects of (internet) literature. This links the small fates to an analysis of *Open City* by Vermeulen (2013). Vermeulen contends that Cole's novel 'responds to the prevalent critique that cosmopolitanism is unable to effect change beyond the domain of culture' (42). This seems equally valid for the small fates series, and is even extended in another Twitter project that Cole carried out: His '7 Short Stories about Drones', a contribution to the debate on drones and the legal and moral implications of their deployment that more explicitly exhibits Cole's political commitment. Cole tweeted these in January 2013, at almost the same time that his essay 'A Reader's War' on US President Barack Obama's foreign policy and his conduct in the 'global war on terror' was published in *The New Yorker* magazine (Cole 2013a). This simultaneity illustrates his motivation to use Twitter in the first place, as a strategy to establish new audiences:

> Maybe it's just a generational thing where I don't think that print media has to be the be-all and end-all. A lot of the people I want to be read by, a lot of the people I want to speak to, are not people who have subscriptions to *The New Yorker* or *The New York Times*, so it's important for me to speak to them in this way also. (NPR 2014)

Although his readerships on Twitter and in *The New Yorker* are probably different, they might still be constituted by people with similar interests. Cole experiments with different genres and media, departing from conventional literary ways and thus expresses resignation towards the power of literature to effect change. He points to an article about drones in the final tweet of the series (Cole 2013b), reminding of 'the need to supplement [literature's] aesthetic performance with a more materially effective program' (Vermeulen 2013, 44).

> @tejucole 14.01.2013: 1. Mrs Dalloway said she would buy the flowers herself. Pity. A signature strike leveled the florist's. (Cole 2013c)
>
> @tejucole 14.01.2013: 2. Call me Ishmael. I was a young man of military age. I was immolated at my wedding. My parents are inconsolable. (Cole 2013d)
>
> @tejucole 14.01.2013: 3. Stately, plump Buck Mulligan came from the stairhead, bearing a bowl of lather. A bomb whistled in. Blood on the walls. Fire from heaven. (Cole 2013e)

The 'seven short stories' are modified first sentences of seven classics of 'world literature', interrupted by a drone strike.[13] Thus, each of these first sentences alludes to the full novel which it uses as its origin, only to subvert the story that could have been, through the newly written brutal ending caused by the 'unmanned aerial device'. Stylistically, the tweets are similar to the small fates – concise and unsentimental, 'exuding a dark humor and a dark wit' (Jullien 2009, 66). Although literature may be assumed to make the reader aware of power divisions and inequalities in the real world, Vermeulen regards this 'dry, nearly affectless' tone that also dominates in *Open City* as signalling 'the insuffiency [sic] of such merely imaginative exercises' (45). Cole does not strain for effects or try to provoke pity for human lives in distant war areas in a sensationalist way. The way he summons these lives simultaneously seems to doubt its own effectiveness, raising the question if this summoning leads anywhere.

A consideration of the impression of these tweets needs to take into account the medium of Twitter, a place where one often finds 'unpolished' language and news lines. Cole himself says that 'it's really weird to see them sprinkled into a Twitter stream full of Justin Bieber and cat videos' (Interview Zhang). Even without recognizing the literary origins of the tweets – and this may be the case for anybody but members of the educated class – the carefully crafted language and sentence structures stand out. The tweets replicate the 'haiku esthetic – [...] the reader is struck by the poetic force of these miniature narratives that suggest so much while saying so little' (Jullien 2009, 68). The shortness of the tweets reinforces this effect and increases the weight of each word. By contrasting daily life business like buying flowers or celebrating a wedding with the sudden impact of the drone, the tweets amplify their intensity. Cole deploys a dry, technical register that only implicitly alludes to and circles around death – the reader is asked to engage, to make the connection and to complete the picture. The tweets imitate the register that is used by news media and the government (which Cole criticizes in the essay) and masks the violence inflicted on human individuals ('levelled', 'immolated').

Taking all seven tweets together, the set refers to a canon of 'world literature' and represents what might be called 'global modern civilization' and its cultural achievements. The novels, as a whole, stand for moral progress and tolerance towards difference and complexity. Cole collates the set of global society's high art with the 'war on terror', metonymically represented by the drones. He boldly eradicates the main characters of a fraction of the global cultural heritage, juxtaposing these noble and praised achievements with a contrastive product of globalization. Enforcing the irony between what this global society praises itself for, and the killing of civilians that is also an integral part of it (as the essay by Cole and the report point out that Cole refers to in his last tweet), he makes a highly critical statement of what globalization means.

Simultaneously, Cole expresses resignation towards literature itself in this project. He imagines how Barack Obama's 'keeping the country safe' ('A Reader's War') could ultimately turn back on itself, and thereby questions the moral progress that the novels attest to. Considering the limited effect that these tweets might have, these doubts seem justified: The short stories' literary astuteness might bypass most recipients on Twitter, and be understood only by educated readers who are not different from the subscribers of *The New Yorker* that Cole mentions in the quotation above. Thus, even though the medium of Twitter reaches new audiences more easily, the literary manoeuvre of this project is mainly self-referential. Beyond this, despite its critical stance against Euro-American domination in the global society, the tweets also inhabit a Eurocentric perspective. The novels originate mainly from Europe and the USA, reaffirming a Eurocentric conception of 'valuable' literature.

In his '7 short stories' as well as the essay 'A Reader's War', Cole contemplates the value of literature for society and connects this to a critique of the cost of lives that the US government accepts in the war on terror. The tweets, in their unsentimental tone, create space and demand time to consider how drone strikes in war areas annihilate human lives. Like in the small fates, Cole interrogates the medium of literature, experimenting with unconventional channels and trying to reach new audiences. He does not rely on conventional media like the novel, engaging instead in a 'more minimal, aesthetic program' (Vermeulen 2013, 55).

5. Conclusion

The presence of Adichie and Cole on the internet exemplifies what one might classify as the diverse layers of Afropolitanism. Other than online presences like 'The Afropolitan' magazine, the Afropolitan shop or even Taiye Selasi's social media presence which embody a celebratory version of Afropolitanism, Adichie and Cole introduce a more critical and innovative element to the cyberspace. These two writers challenge and deconstruct power differentials, evoking transnational spaces that are largely devoid of the stratifications of the real world. Adichie and Cole thus extend Julien's concept of 'extrovertedness', demonstrating that their concern with global issues is also 'introverted' and Afro-centred. Their literary works allow for multiple readings for an 'external' and 'internal' readership.

In the blog featured in *Americanah*, and continued outside the borders of the novel, and in her presence in social media, Adichie explores new forms of publicness and publicity that accompany the internet and social media. She also devotes attention to the close relation between culture and consumption, one that is also a major point of critique towards the concept of Afropolitanism. The novel's exploration of social media writing illuminates how Adichie carefully and strategically navigates her own presence online and the publicity associated with her position as a writer. The connection between culture and consumption is represented as an entanglement that may subject the writer and his writing, but which can also be used strategically.

Teju Cole refrains from this public positioning and rather invests in critical experimentation with social media. He focuses on exploring the potential of language and literature in digital spaces, trying to be 'just to the others out there whose lives we do not think about' by 'telling their stories' (Zhang 2013). He articulates cosmopolitanism as an ideology of empathy and tolerance; nevertheless, he also negotiates the limitations associated with literature, independent of the medium or genre that is used for distribution.

Both Adichie and Cole are concerned with the question of readership. Adichie negotiates the modified role of readers, moving from a fictional US context in the novel to predominantly Nigerian implied readers of the blog that is continued outside the novel. Cole reverses this movement, writing for and about Nigerians in the 'small fates' but inhabiting a Eurocentric position in the 'Seven Short Stories about Drones'.

It is undeniable that many writers who are labelled Afropolitan – like the two examined here – inhabit a privileged subject position and enjoy global mobility, which, nevertheless, proves less relevant in the space where the phenomenon is most active: The internet. The writers demonstrate a strong political engagement in their works, challenging dominant ideologies of capitalism, cultural hierarchies and globalization. The way they implement Afropolitanism in social media cannot be reduced to – but neither separated from – its commercial dimension that many critics of the phenomenon emphasize. The way these writers examine power differentials of globalization shows that something that is commercially successful can still be critical and transformative.

Disclosure statement

No potential conflict of interest was reported by the authors.

Notes

1. My understanding of the concept concurs with that of Chielona Eze, who defines Afropolitanism as an ethical principle in his articles 'Transcultural Affinity: Thoughts on the Emergent Cosmopolitan Imagination in South Africa' (2015) and 'Rethinking African Culture and Identity: the Afropolitan Model' (2014). Like Walter Mignolo, Eze distances his interpretation from the cosmopolitanism that was envisioned by Immanuel Kant.
2. Scholars of decoloniality define the interplay of modernity and coloniality as the dominant power matrix structuring all dimensions of society along hierarchical lines: Economy, history, knowledge, knowledge production and epistemology, language, gender, religion, race and ethnicity each mark a site of modern, and thereby also colonial difference (Grosfuguel 'Transmodernity' 2011, 6).
3. Teju Cole describes his position in American society in an interview with Wachtel (2012), saying: 'I think because I grew up in Nigeria […] I have the foolish bravery of the outsider in thinking I can come in here and write about this city.' He also refers to himself as an 'alien'.
4. Cole describes experiences of racial discrimination in an interview with Eleanor Wachtel. Following the publication of Americanah in 2013, racial discrimination in the USA from a Nigerian perspective is a predominant topic in interviews with Adichie. See, for example, Barber (2013).
5. Wainaina, in his plenary address, 'I am a Pan-Africanist, not an Afropolitan', delivered at the 2012 African Studies Association of the UK (ASAUK) conference, according to Stephanie Bosch Santana's account presented in her essay for the blog *Africa in Words* (2013), clearly rejects the term and concept at that time, but offers a different opinion in an interview with Binyavanga Wainaina and Gemma Solés

(2014). There, he refers to Mbembe's idea of Afropolitanism as 'a different idea than the one that got picked up as a sort of commodity'.

6. According to Huggan, the postcolonial exotic marks the intersection between the regimes of value of postcolonialism (anti-colonial, working towards the dissolution of imperial epistemologies and institutional structures) and postcoloniality (closely tied to capitalist markets, capitalizes on the circulation of ideas about cultural otherness) (28).
7. Teju Cole refers to this in an interview with Aaron Bady:

> The discourse around Afropolitanism foregrounds questions of class in ways the 'I'm not Afropolitan' crowd don't want to deal with and in ways the 'I'm Afropolitan' crowd are often too blithe about. Collectively, we could do better. The phenomena described – Afropolitanism, pan-Africanism – are real, and interesting, and discomfiting, and for very many of us, no matter how we squeal, the shoe fits. (http://post45.research.yale.edu/2015/01/interview-teju-cole/, 16 September 2015)

8. Adichie talks about this incident at length in an interview with Chiagoze Fred Nwonwu for *olisa.tv*, saying that she 'would never have agreed' to the captions of the article which made her feel 'sensationalising and cheap' (Nwonwu 2015).
9. See, for example, 'Chimamanda Ngozi Adichie: The Afropolitan Anthropologist' (http://afrolibrarians.com/2013/12/12/chimamanda-ngozi-adichie-the-afropolitan-anthropologist/; accessed 8 May 2015).
10. For an introduction into the politics of hair, see Shirley Anne Tate's *Black Beauty: Aesthetics, Stylization, Politics* (2009).
11. Women's magazines are similarly assessed in a situation where Ifemelu and Curt sift a range of magazines for ethnic representation of women (375).
12. Teju Cole acknowledges this inspiration on his website www.tejucole.com.
13. Teju Cole uses *Mrs Dalloway* (1925) by Virginia Woolf, *Moby Dick* (1851) by Herman Melville, *Ulysses* (1922) by James Joyce, *Invisible Man* (1952) by Ralph Ellison, *The Trial* (written 1914, published 1925) by Franz Kafka, *Things Fall Apart* (1958) by Chinua Achebe and *The Stranger* (1942) by Albert Camus.

References

Adichie, Chimamanda Ngozi. 2013. *Americanah*. Nairobi: Kwani Trust.

Adichie, Chimamanda Ngozi. 2014. "The Small Redemptions of Lagos." Accessed August 12, 2015. http://americanahblog.com/.

Adichie, Chimamanda Ngozi. 2015. "Chimamanda Ngozi Adichie: My Father's Kidnapping." *The New York Times*, May 30. Accessed November 7, 2015. http://www.nytimes.com/2015/05/31/opinion/sunday/chimamanda-ngozi-adichie-my-fathers-kidnapping.html?_r=0.

Adichie, Chimamanda Ngozi, and Synne Rifbjerg. 2014. "Americanah International Author's Stage." May 20. Accessed November 13, 2015. https://www.youtube.com/watch?v=b8r-dP9NqX8.

Ashcroft, Bill. 2010. "The Transnation." In *Rerouting the Postcolonial New Directions for the New Millennium*, edited by Janet Wilson, Cristina Sandru, and Sarah Welsh, 72–85. Oxon: Routledge.

Bady, Aaron. 2015. "Interview: Teju Cole Post45." Accessed January 20, 2015. http://post45.research.yale.edu/2015/01/interview-teju-cole/.

Barber, John. 2013. "New Novel Shows That Chimamanda Ngozi Adichie Gets the Race Thing." *The Globe and Mail*, September 6. http://www.theglobeandmail.com/arts/books-and-media/new-novel-shows-that-chimamanda-ngozi-adichie-gets-the-race-thing/article12423909/.

Bosch Santana, Stephanie. 2013. "Exorcizing Afropolitanism: Binyavanga Wainaina Explains Why 'I am a Pan-Africanist, Not an Afropolitan' at ASAUK 2012." February 8. Accessed August 12, 2015. http://africainwords.com/2013/02/08/exorcizing-afropolitanism-binyavanga-wainaina-explains-why-i-ama-pan-africanist-not-an-afropolitan-at-asauk-2012/.

Cole, Teju. 2007. *Every Day Is for the Thief.* Abuja: Cassava Republic.

Cole, Teju. 2011a. *Open City.* New York: Random House.

Cole, Teju. [tejucole]. 2011b. "Love is Complicated. With a Double-Barreled Rifle, Hadezia, in Abuja, Widowed Herself." [Tweet]. December 29. Accessed November 17, 2015. https://twitter.com/tejucole/status/152643430244298753.

Cole, Teju. [tejucole]. 2011c. "The Anambra Treasury Officer, Innocent, Who Stole N66.5 Million in Pension Funds, Insists He was Hypnotized." [Tweet]. December 29. Accessed November 17, 2015. https://twitter.com/tejucole/status/152367134050230272.

Cole, Teju. 2011d. "Small Fates." Accessed November 7, 2015. http://www.tejucole.com/small-fates/.

Cole, Teju. 2013a. "A Reader's War." *The New Yorker*, February 10. Accessed November 7, 2015. http://www.newyorker.com/books/page-turner/a-readers-war.

Cole, Teju. [tejucole]. 2013b. "Everything We Know So Far about Drone Strikes: http://t.co/FW0pNdsC" [Tweet]. January 14. Accessed November 17, 2015. https://twitter.com/tejucole/status/290870451956236288.

Cole, Teju. [tejucole]. 2013c. "1. Mrs Dalloway Said She Would Buy the Flowers Herself. Pity. A Signature Strike Leveled the Florist's." [Tweet]. January 14. Accessed November 17, 2015. https://twitter.com/tejucole/status/290867008776597504.

Cole, Teju. [tejucole]. 2013d. "2. Call Me Ishmael. I Was a Young Man of Military Age. I Was Immolated at My Wedding. My Parents are Inconsolable." [Tweet]. January 14. Accessed November 17, 2015. https://twitter.com/tejucole/status/290867500151881728.

Cole, Teju. [tejucole]. 2013e. "3. Stately, Plump Buck Mulligan Came from the Stairhead, Bearing a Bowl of Lather. A Bomb Whistled in. Blood on the Walls. Fire from Heaven." [Tweet]. January 14. Accessed November 17, 2015. https://twitter.com/tejucole/status/290868089879416832.

Cole, Teju. 2014. "The Time of the Game." Accessed November 7, 2015. http://timeofthegame.o-c-r.org/.

Dabiri, Emma. 2014. "Why I Am Not an Afropolitan." January 21. Accessed November 7, 2015. http://africaisacountry.com/why-i-am-not-an-afropolitan.

Ekotto, Frieda, and Kenneth Harrow, eds. 2015. *Rethinking African Cultural Production*. Bloomington: Indiana University Press.

Eze, Chielozona. 2014. "Rethinking African Culture and Identity: The Afropolitan Model." *Journal of African Cultural Studies* 26 (2): 234–247.

Eze, Chielozona. 2015. "Transcultural Affinity: Thoughts on the Emergent Cosmopolitan Imagination in South Africa." *Journal of African Cultural Studies* 27 (2): 216–228.

Gehrmann, Susanne. 2015. "Cosmopolitanism with African Roots. Afropolitanism's Ambivalent Mobilities." *Journal of African Cultural Studies*. Accessed November 17, 2015. http://www.tandfonline.com/doi/pdf/10.1080/13696815.2015.1112770.

Gikandi, Simon. 2011. "Foreword: On Afropolitanism." In *Negotiating Afropolitanism: Essays on Borders and Spaces in Contemporary African Literature and Folklore*, edited by Wawrzinek Jennifer, and J. K. S. Makokha, 9-12. Internationale Forschungen Zur Allgemeinen Und Vergleichenden Literaturwissenschaft 146. Amsterdam, New York: Rodopi.

Grosfuguel, Ramon. 2011. "Decolonizing Post-colonial Studies and Paradigms of Political-Economy: Transmodernity, Decolonial Thinking, and Global Coloniality." *Transmodernity: Journal of Peripheral Cultural Production of the Luso-Hispanic World* 1 (1). http://escholarship.org/uc/item/21k6t3fq.

Guarracino, Serena. 2014. "Writing 'So Raw and True': Blogging in Chimamanda Ngozi Adichie's Americanah." *Between* 4 (8): 1–27.

Hemon, Aleksandar. 2014. "Teju Cole (Interview)." *Bomb* 127: 72–77.

Huggan, Graham. 2001. *The Postcolonial Exotic: Marketing the Margins*. London: Routledge.

Julien, Eileen. 2006. "The Extroverted African Novel." In *The Novel Vol. 1 History, Geography, and Culture*, edited by Franco Moretti, 667–700. Princeton, NJ: Princeton University Press.

Julien, Eileen. 2015. "The Critical Present – Where is African Literature?" In *Rethinking African Cultural Production*, edited by Frieda Ekotto and Kenneth Harrow, 17–28. Bloomington: Indiana University Press.

Jullien, Dominique. 2009. "Anecdotes, Faits Divers , and the Literary." *SubStance* 38 (1): 66–76.

Mbembe, Achille. 2007. "Afropolitanism." In *Africa Remix: Contemporary Art of a Continent*, edited by S. Niami and L. Duran, 26–29. Johannesburg: Jacana Media.

Mbembe, Achille, and Bregtje van der Haak. 2015. "The Internet Is Afropolitan." *The Chimurenga Chronic* New Cartographies. March 17. Accessed August 12, 2015. http://chimurengachronic.co.za/the-internet-is-afropolitan/.

Meyer, Robinson. 2014. "When the World Watches the World Cup, What Does That Look Like?" *The Atlantic*, July 15. Accessed June 1, 2015. http://www.theatlantic.com/technology/archive/2014/07/when-the-world-watches-the-world-cup-what-does-it-look-like/374461/.

Mignolo, Walter. 2000. "The Many Faces of Cosmo-Polis: Border Thinking and Critical Cosmopolitanism." *Public Culture* 12 (3): 721–748.

Mignolo, Walter D., and Madina V. Tlostanova. 2006. "Theorizing from the Borders Shifting to Geo- and Body-Politics of Knowledge." *European Journal of Social Theory* 9 (2): 205–221.

NPR. 2014. "Teju Cole Writes A Story A Tweet At A Time." January 16. Accessed November 7, 2015. http://www.npr.org/2014/01/16/262473432/forget-the-new-yorker-storyteller-turns-to-twitter.

Nwonwu, Chiagoze Fred. 2015. "Exclusive Interview: Chimamanda Ngozi Adichie." *Olisa.tv*, March 12. Accessed November 6, 2015. http://www.olisa.tv/2015/03/12/exclusive-interviewchimamanda-ngozi-adichie-pt-1/.

Nye, Joseph. 2002. "Globalism Versus Globalization." *The Globalist*, April 15. Accessed September 30, 2015. http://www.theglobalist.com/globalism-versus-globalization/.

Ponzanesi, Sandra. 2014. *The Postcolonial Cultural Industry*. New York: Palgrave Macmillan.

Selasi, Taiye. 2005. "Bye-Bye Babar." *The LIP Magazine*, March 3. Accessed August 12, 2015. http://thelip.robertsharp.co.uk/?p=76.

Selasi, Taiye. 2013. "Taiye Selasi on Discovering Her Pride in Her African Roots." *The Guardian*, March 22. Accessed July 9, 2015. http://www.theguardian.com/books/2013/mar/22/taiye-selasi-afropolitan-memoir.

Tate, Shirley Anne. 2009. *Black Beauty: Aesthetics, Stylization, Politics*. Surrey: Ashgate.

Vermeulen, Pieter. 2013. "Flights of Memory: Teju Cole's 'Open City' and the Limits of Aesthetic Cosmopolitanism." *Journal of Modern Literature* 37 (1): 40–57.

Wachtel, Eleanor. 2012. "'Open City' with Novelist Teju Cole." Writers and Company, November 18. Accessed November 6, 2015. http://www.cbc.ca/player/play/2305408699.

Wainaina, Binyavanga. 2013. "I Am a Homosexual, Mum." Africa Is a Country, January 19. Accessed July 6, 2015. http://africasacountry.com/i-am-a-homosexual-mum/.

Wainaina, Binyavanga, and Gemma, Solés. 2014. "Wainaina on Afropolitanism." April 4, 2014. Accessed November 7, 2015. http://www.urbanafrica.net/urban-voices/wainaina-afropolitanism/.

Zhang, Sarah. 2013. "Teju Cole on the 'Empathy Gap' and Tweeting Drone Strikes." Mother Jones, March 6. Accessed November 6, 2015. http://www.motherjones.com/media/2013/03/teju-cole-interview-twitter-drones-small-fates.

Exorcizing the future: Afropolitanism's spectral origins

Stephanie Bosch Santana

Afropolitanism is a term that has risen over and over again in recent popular and critical discourse despite efforts by many African writers and cultural critics to lay it to rest. Its haunting effect is a result, in part, of its unclear and disparate origins coupled with the absence of known originals such as Binyavanga Wainaina's plenary address, 'I am a Pan-Africanist, not an Afropolitan,' delivered at the 2012 African Studies Association of the UK (ASAUK) conference – of which no recording exists. When, in a 2013 essay for the blog *Africa in Words*, I described Wainaina's critique as an attempted 'exorcism' of the term, I had little idea that it would be the first of many similar attempts or that spectres of such lost 'origins' would only fuel Afropolitanism's momentum and continual return.

One source of this portmanteau (created out of the words 'African' and 'cosmopolitanism') is usually traced to an article by Taiye Selasi titled 'Bye-Bye Babar,' published in *The LIP Magazine* in March 2005. Selasi uses the term primarily to designate Africans living, and often born outside of, the continent. She writes:

> Like so many African young people working and living in cities around the globe, they belong to no single geography, but feel at home in many. They (read: we) are Afropolitans – the newest generation of African emigrants, coming soon or collected already at a law firm/chem lab/jazz lounge near you.[1]

Achille Mbembe popularized this term in academic discourse with his 2005 essay 'Afropolitanism,' published in February 2005 in English in *Africa Remix* and in French in *Africultures* magazine at the end of the same year. In this essay, Mbembe defines Afropolitanism as 'an aesthetic and particular poetic of the world' that is founded, in part, on an awareness of 'the presence of the elsewhere in the here and vice versa' (28). His interest is not only in Selasi's global Africans but also the world in Africa. According to Mbembe, 'cultural mixing' or 'the interweaving of worlds' has long been an African 'way of belonging to the world' – whether one resides on the continent or not (28).

In an expanded and little-cited version of this essay in *Sortir de la grande nuit*, published in 2010 and not yet translated into English, Mbembe fleshes out his conception of Afropolitanism as a new aesthetic sensibility, particularly through references to African literature.[2] He outlines two striking 'moments' of Afropolitanism. The first, 'properly postcolonial' moment differs significantly from previous paradigms such as Négritude (222, my translation). Drawing attention to Yambo Ouologuem's *Devoir de Violence* and Sony Labou Tansi's *L'Autre Monde*, Mbembe suggests that this new aesthetic moves beyond 'the fetishization of origins' and the relationship between the self and the Other or the self and the world to the more significant problems of 'self-explication' and the 'after-life' (222–223). It is a 'turbulent', transgressive writing born of suffering and violation. The second moment of Afropolitanism, with which we are more familiar, pertains to 'the entrance of Africa into a new age of dispersion and circulation' (224). The question becomes one of creating new 'mobile' forms of the real through erasure, substitution, deletion, and recreation (224–225).

That this rich essay has remained mostly inaccessible to English-language readers helps to explain the clear *décalage* between discussions of Afropolitanism in Francophone and Anglophone spheres. It is within this latter, decidedly separate, domain that we must read Wainaina's 2012 lecture. In it, he argued that Afropolitanism was a phenomenon increasingly 'product-driven', design-focused, and potentially 'funded by the West'. In the Afropolitan's world, travel was easy and people were fluid. To see Wainaina's point, one needed only to look at the way magazines, designers, and business executives had seized the term for their own purposes. On the homepage of *Afropolitan* magazine, based out of South Africa, essays on the legacy of the ANC sat alongside articles on 'Fashion Conscious Carpeting … so much more than just good looks!' as well as ads for 'Samsonite B-Lite Fresh' suitcases.[3] There was also an Afropolitan Shop, which featured kente-accented laptop bags amongst a host of other products from African designers. Touting the principle of 'Trade Not Aid,' the Afropolitan Shop defined Afropolitanism as 'a sensibility, a culture and a worldview'.[4] Here, I could see how easily style and 'worldview' became conflated, how not only products, but also people and identities were commoditized. It was hard not to miss a similar effect in Selasi's description of stylish Africans 'coming soon or collected already' in a Euro-American metropolitan centre 'near you'.

Wainaina's lecture (at least, as it is represented in my *Africa in Words* post) has gained a good deal of attention and criticism, most of which has been related to Wainaina's critique of Afropolitanism rather than his assertion to be a Pan-Africanist or his connection of these terms to the production of particular kinds of literature on the continent and in the African diaspora. In light of this, it is worth reiterating the literary dimensions of Wainaina's argument. Specifically, Wainaina suggested that Afropolitanism extends its commodity-driven mentality to literature by treating texts as 'singular products'. He pointed to a particular kind of Afropolitan African novel and short story that is often produced – one that may touch upon social and economic issues on the continent but ultimately is written for an audience of 'fellow Afropolitans'.[5] In contrast to these Afropolitan forms, Wainaina depicted a new pan-African literature that travels via digital platforms like Twitter and Wattpad. This genre-bending 'digital pulp', Wainaina argued, is having a revolutionary effect on African literary production. The online medium encourages process-based forms that are shared with audiences as they are written. Although some might call pulp fiction 'trashy' or 'escapist', Wainaina emphasized its ability to reach and excite readers on the continent as well as to critique social reality. We do not pay enough attention, Wainaina suggested, to literature that truly 'transports' us. The new African writing that Wainaina described focuses on the future rather than the past. It is of mixed genres and founded on an ethos of transgression. Perhaps most importantly, it is mobile. It may even fit within the parameters of the aesthetic sensibility that Mbembe calls Afropolitanism.

'Afropolitaine, sûrement pas'[6]

Following Wainaina, a number of writers and academics, including Yewande Omotoso, Emma Dabiri, and Marta Tveit, have also declared that they are *not* Afropolitans. Most recently, Chimamanda Adichie, when asked if she feels herself to be an Afropolitan, replied:

> Je suis fatiguée de ce mot. Je suis africaine. Il y a deux choses qui me paraissent curieuses : d'abord les Africains sont-ils donc tellement en dehors de l'histoire générale de l'humanité qu'ils doivent être

désignés par un mot particulier quand ils voyagent ou se trouvent dans les capitales du mondeLa deuxième chose, c'est que l'histoire (malheureusement pas assez connue) montre que le cosmopolitisme ne date pas d'hier : de nombreux rois africains de la côte Ouest envoyaient leurs enfants étudier en Europe. Bien plus tard, la génération de mon père a beaucoup voyagé, il y a eu de nombreuses vagues de gens revenus dans les années soixante, et qui n'ont cessé de bouger. Ils se définissent comme Africains.

I am tired of this word. I am African. There are two things that seem curious to me: first are Africans so outside of the general history of humanity that they must be designated by a particular word when they travel or are found in the capitals of the world? The second thing, is that history (sadly not well known) shows that cosmopolitanism doesn't date from yesterday: many African kings from the West coast sent their children to study in Europe. And much later, the generation of my father traveled a lot, there have been numerous waves of people coming back in the 1960's, and who have not stopped moving. They define themselves as Africans.[7]

Adichie's description of a long history of African cosmopolitanism and of continual dispersal and return echoes Mbembe's theorizations of Afropolitanism. And notably, like Mbembe's reflections in *Sortir de la grande nuit*, Adichie's words in the above interview have reached Anglophone audiences only through partial translations. Similarly, in a 2014 interview with Gemma Solés (aimed at a Spanish-speaking audience), Wainaina says that Mbembe's Afropolitanism is 'a different idea than the one that got picked up as a sort of commodity'. Wainaina describes cosmopolitanism in Africa, where many urbanites speak five languages, as 'not a shocking thing … it's a thing that is very, very old and enduring'. Much of the issue, in other words, is to do with the term Afropolitan itself. While Mbembe, Adichie, and Wainaina all agree that there is a long-standing form of African cosmopolitanism, Adichie and Wainaina argue that we do not need new names for these enduring practices and identities, but rather a return to older ones – 'African' *tout court* and 'Pan-African,' respectively.

In contrast, Mbembe argues that a new term is necessary 'if we want to revive intellectual life in Africa' ('Afropolitanism' 29). Mbembe warns that pan-Africanism has become 'institutionalized and ossified' and can slip easily and dangerously into nativism (26). Further, unlike Négritude, Afropolitanism no longer focuses on the tension between self and other but rather 'the problem of *self-explication*' ('*la problématique de l' auto-explication*') (Mbembe, *Sortir* 222). Indeed, self-explication was Selasi's original intention in her now infamous 'Bye-Bye Babar' essay, which she says was read by no more than a handful of people in its first several years of publication. In an interview with Aaron Bady in the April 2015 issue of *Transition* magazine, Selasi explains, 'I'd been describing "de-territorialized brown people". I wasn't writing from a position of power; I was writing from a position of pain' (158). Selasi, who is British-born of Nigerian parents and grew up in the USA, describes how she never fit easily into any identity category. Not American, not African, not British, not even Nigerian when in Nigeria: 'Always "you're not".' When she moved to the UK in 2005, Selasi found she shared this experience with more than a few others:

'Afropolitan' came from that stranded place. Not from a utopian vision at all. I was saying, to myself foremost, there are more than six of us. There is an African diaspora, not the original one; there is a new one, a smaller one … I thought: I am going to give us an identity. All six of us. And that's what I did. There was no great … (laughs) I wasn't imagining a superhero costume. (160)

Selasi's 'rhetorical strategy' has changed in recent years – perhaps as a result of the flurry of attention to 'Bye-Bye Babar' – and in her 2013 lecture, 'African Literature Doesn't Exist,' Selasi takes a different tack. She explains:

once you've emptied something you've given yourself the space to refill it, to reflect on what should go inside. In saying 'African Literature Doesn't Exist' I was simply trying to empty the container, to ask then: now that it's empty, what should we put inside? (Bady 156)

Across these two essays, Selasi's approach constitutes its own kind of exorcism. Her summoning of the term 'Afropolitan' reflects an earlier understanding of exorcism (c. 1400) as the invocation of spirits, while her later strategy is more in line with our modern understanding of it as to 'call up evil spirits to drive them out'.[8] Of course, the problem with exorcism as an epistemology is that it 'is a way of not wanting to know what everyone alive knows without learning and without knowing, namely, that the dead can often be more powerful than the living' (Derrida 60).

And so, despite the many exorcisms it has been subject to, Afropolitanism remains a haunted and haunting term. Afropolitanism makes a fitting spectre, for it is always in excess of itself. Like the spectre, it is 'a paradoxical incorporation, the becoming-body, a certain phenomenal and carnal form of the spirit ... neither soul nor body, and both one and the other' (Derrida 5). This surfeit of meaning is at the heart of Afropolitanism as Mbembe defines it. With Afropolitanism:

> We move to a writing of surplus or excess. Reality (be it about race, the past, tradition, or better yet, power) not only appears as what exists and can be represented or portrayed. It is equally that which covers, envelops and exceeds the real. (*Sortir* 223)[9]

As ghost, Afropolitanism lingers, for to banish it, it must also be evoked. Wainaina's address was titled after all, 'I'm a Pan-Africanist, *not* an Afropolitan.'

A new pan-Africanism?

In contrast to the sustained debate that Wainaina's critique of Afropolitanism has generated, the pan-African dimension of Wainaina's speech has received little attention. This is not entirely surprising. In *Pan-Africanism and the Politics of African Citizenship and Identity*, published in 2013, Toyin Falola and Kwame Essien give an 'academic post-mortem' of pan-Africanism as an area of study and discourse. While it served as a powerful ideological weapon in the first half of the twentieth-century, Falola and Essien argue that its 'one-dimensional' focus on race and racism 'could not sustain Pan-Africanism after the demise of colonialism, segregation, and apartheid', leading to its steady eclipsing by diaspora studies (1).

Nevertheless, at ASAUK, Wainaina suggested that pan-Africanism is 'something noble to dream about that is bigger', and in his interview last year with Solés, Wainaina reiterated, 'the idea of a kind of pan-African – I'm a pan-Africanist – of a pan-African movement to open borders, to trade, think, imagine freely across the continent is something that's very deeply important'. In its emphasis on more informal networks of exchange rather than a cohesive political ideology, this pan-Africanism resembles what George Shepperson describes as small 'p' pan-Africanism or 'cultural pan-Africanism'.[10]

Wainaina's pan-Africanism is decidedly continent-centric, and it is Afropolitanism's perceived 'immunity' to Africa that Wainaina critiques most vigorously:

> What immunity is, you have a credit rating in America. What immunity is, you have a green card ... You become this kind of internationalized class of people ... But you're completely immune in reality to the continent ... Leaving America and coming back here [to Kenya] was a very deliberate act ... I'd been lying to myself in that African Afropolitan way that you can build an African literary institution out of New York. Which you can't. (qtd. in Solés)

In addition to Wainaina, other Africa-based writers and writers' groups have declared themselves to be pan-Africanists, too. *Chimurenga* magazine, for example, describes itself as 'a pan African publication' that 'provides an innovative platform for free ideas and political reflection by Africans about Africa'.[11] Similarly, *Jalada Africa*, a new online 'pan-African writers' collective', aims to level the literary playing field by 'making it as easy as possible for any member to publish anything or execute any literary project as quickly and effectively as possible.[12] Malawian writer Shadreck Chikoti, founder and director of Pan African Publishers, also identifies as a pan-

Africanist. Selected by the *Africa39* project as one of 'the most promising 39 authors under the age of 40 from Sub-Saharan Africa and the diaspora', Chikoti explains that for him, 'to be a pan-Africanist is to be someone who wants to contribute to the discourse of the future of Africa' (personal interview). He notes that this is a different form of pan-Africanism than that of the 1960's, which he describes as 'a kind of protest movement against the West'. Rather, he argues, 'The problems that Africa is facing are not necessarily from external forces. Many of them are also from within.' Chikoti has travelled across the continent and to Europe for various writers' workshops, but when I asked him what he thought of Afropolitanism, he said it was not something he thought much about because he had not really heard of it.

As Chikoti's definition of pan-Africanism makes clear, what is at stake here is not just names, but futures. Chikoti imagines one such future in his forthcoming novel *Azotus the Kingdom*, set in an intentionally ambiguous African territory in the year 2559. Based on this concept, he also launched a writing workshop and anthology project called 'Imagine Africa 500,' which invites writers from across the continent to submit stories that envision the African continent 500 years in the future. In fact, all of the 'pan-African' publications mentioned above have strong connections to afrofuturism which, via the genres of science fiction and fantasy, is a rapidly growing literary movement on the continent.

Of these projects, *Chimurenga* magazine's latest endeavour, the *Chimurenga Chronic*, plays most self-reflexively with the connection between pan-Africanism and afrofuturism. The *Chronic* is designed as 'a fictional pan African newspaper … backdated to the week of May 18–24 [2008], the period marked by the outbreak of so-called xenophobic violence in South Africa'.[13] The editors describe the newspaper, which is often only associated with 'the news and newness' as a 'low-tech time-travel machine' that both creates and navigates multiple temporalities. In other words, the *Chronic* uses the time-machine as a double entendre: it not only allows one to travel in time but also 'produces time'. In returning to the xenophobic violence in South Africa in that week in May, the *Chronic* creates numerous, competing timelines rather than a final account of events.

> The issue's editorial, written as a poem titled 'Whose House Is This?', asks:
> Is the newspaper a time machine?
> Have all the images been exhausted?
> Have all the words been disinfected?
> If all news is old news how do we go forward?
> …
> Forget tomorrow.
> Sun Ra said: Linktime has officially ended.
> We'll work on the other side …
> We'll bring them here somehow
> through either isotope
> internal linkteleportation
> transmolecularisation …
> Maybe newspapers should be written by aliens?' (10)

Here, the word 'alien' slips between registers. It belongs at once to the lexicon of science fiction – a genre directly referenced in the lines that quote Sun Ra's film *Space is the Place* – as well to the dehumanizing language of government bureaucracy that categorizes people who belong as 'citizens' and those who do not as 'aliens'. In other words, the kind of language that undergirds, if not sanctions, the 'us versus them' mentality that culminated in violence against foreign nationals in May 2008. In asking whether or not newspapers should be 'written by aliens', the *Chronic*'s editors gesture to the dual aims of their project: to publish a newspaper that gives voice to those who were victims of the attacks and also to use the newspaper as a means to 'work on the other side of time', as Sun Ra suggests, in order to 'reviv[e] the old dream of Pan Africanism' (Edjabe).

The *Chronic*'s vision of a pan-African future, however, is not unaware of the many walls, boundaries, and other impediments to movement. In the March 2013 issue, for example, we find a map of migration post-mortem: the circuitous routes that the bodies of migrants must take as they try to find their way home after death. If an Afropolitan space, as Wainaina once described it, is one of fluid and easy travel, the *Chronic* gestures to the barriers that prevent passage in this world, even when one has already travelled into the next.

Chikoti's vision of the African future in *Azotus the Kingdom* also warns of the proliferation of new borderlines. While Wainaina touted the possibilities for pan-African literary exchange that new digital technologies afford, Chikoti's account is more sobering. Under Azotus's seemingly benign regime, each citizen, or 'occupant', lives in his or her own house alone and never interacts with the outside world except through his or her 'technology curtain'. This new device, as its name suggests, is imagined as a disruptive and fragmenting force, one that ultimately drives people apart from one another. By contrast, print culture in Chikoti's novel is an obsolete and forbidden technology that becomes a site for resistance and subversion. It is only through books pilfered from the central library that his protagonist, Kamoto, learns of sex, race, religion, and of a place called 'Africa.'

A final haunting, then: in Chikoti's novel, an old man appears to Kamoto in his dreams, inspiring him to escape from Azotus's kingdom. As the novel progresses, it becomes clear that this man – imprisoned on an island, breaking rocks all day in the sun – is Nelson Mandela. Given the most recent spate of xenophobic violence in South Africa in April 2015, how much longer will such visions of a new pan-Africanism be rooted in the Rainbow Nation and its struggle for freedom? Mbembe also theorized Johannesburg as the premier Afropolitan centre. It seems that whatever the name of the future one envisions – Pan-African, Afropolitan, or something else entirely – addressing the spectre of old and new divisions will be one of its tests.

A new beginning

It is somewhat ironic that in *Sortir de la grande nuit* Mbembe describes Afropolitanism as an aesthetic that moves beyond the problematic of origins, given that, in Anglophone circles at least, Afropolitanism has been subject to such an extended search for its own. A search that, more often than not, seems to move us further and further away from the artistic and literary practices that might necessitate such a term in the first place. Perhaps sensing this, Binyavanga Wainaina excluded the mention of either pan-Africanism or Afropolitanism from his recent plenary address at the 2015 African Literature Association conference in Bayreuth, Germany. The content of this speech was actually quite similar to that of his ASAUK lecture in its concern with fostering future intra-African networks of literary exchange, particularly via new digital platforms. I cannot help but think that Wainaina had learned something from the previous 'exorcism'. Perhaps by refusing to name the ghost, it could finally be set free.

Disclosure statement

No potential conflict of interest was reported by the author.

Notes

1. http://thelip.robertsharp.co.uk/?p=76

2. For a rare account of this text in English see Karera.
3. This description refers to the magazine's homepage from February 2013. http://www.afropolitan.co.za
4. http://www.theafropolitanshop.com/pages/about-us
5. Since Wainaina's address, the term 'Afropolitan narrative' and/or 'Afropolitan novel' has been used in popular and scholarly discourse. For example, at the Africa Writes festival held at the British Library in 2013, Paul Gilroy chaired a panel titled, 'Fantasy or Reality? Afropolitan Narratives of the twenty-first century.'
6. 'Nigeria – Chimamanda Ngozi Adichie : 'Africaine oui, Afropolitaine, sûrement pas' *Le Point Afrique* 5 Feb. 2015.
7. All translations in this essay, apart from those of Mbembe's 'Afropolitanism' as it appears in *Africa Remix*, are by the author.
8. http://www.etymonline.com/index.php?term=exorcise&allowed_in_frame=0
9. 'L'on passe à une écriture du surplus ou encore de l'excédent. La réalité (qu'il s'agisse de la race, du passé, de la tradition ou mieux encore du pouvoir) n'apparait pas seulement comme ce qui existe et est passible de représentation, de figuration. Elle est également ce qui recouvre, envelope et excède l'existant.'
10. '"Pan-Africanism" with a capital letter is a clearly recognizable movement… On the other hand, "pan-Africanism" with a small letter is not a clearly recognizable movement, with single nucleus such as the nonagenarian DuBois [sic]… It is rather a group of movements, many very ephemeral. The cultural element often predominates' (Shepperson 346). This is a distinction that Tsitsi Jaji helpfully reprises in *Africa in Stereo* in relationship to African diasporic music, including *Chimurenga* magazine's Pan-African Space Station.
11. http://www.chimurenga.co.za/chimurenga-magazine
12. http://jalada.org/about/
13. http://www.chimurenganewsroom.org.za/?page_id=2

References

Chikoti, Shadreck. Personal Interview, April 2014.

Chikoti, Shadreck. 2015. *Azotus the Kingdom*. Blantyre, Malawi: Malawi Writers Union.

Falola, Toyin, and Kwame Essien, eds. 2013. *Pan-Africanism and the Politics of African Citizenship and Identity*. New York: Routledge.

Fasselt, Rebecca. 2014. "'I'm Not Afropolitan – I'm of the Continent: A Conversation with Yewande Omotoso." *The Journal of Commonwealth Literature*.

Karera, Axelle. 2013. "Writing Africa into the World and Writing the World from Africa: Mbembe's Politics of Dis-enclosure." *Critical Philosophy of Race* 1.2: 228–241.

Mbembe, Achille. 2005. "Afropolitanism." Translated by Laurent Chauvet. In *Africa Remix: Contemporary Art of a Continent*, edited by Njami Simon and Lucy Durán, 26–30. Ostfildern, Germany: Hatje Cantz Publishers.

Mbembe, Achille. 2013. *Sortir de la grande nuit: Essai sur l'Afrique décolonisée*. Paris: La Découverte/ Poche.

Selasi, Taiye. 2005. "Bye-Bye Babar." *LIP.* The LIP Magazine, March 3.

Solés, Gemma. 2014. "Wainaina on Afropolitanism." *UrbanAfrica.Net*, April 4. Video. http://www.urbanafrica.net/urban-voices/wainaina-afropolitanism/

'Why I am (still) not an Afropolitan'

Emma Dabiri

During the northern summer of 2013, I was invited to take part in a discussion 'Fantasy or reality? Afropolitan Narratives of the 21st Century' that formed part of the annual *Africa Writes* Festival. Doing the research for that piece (widely available now on the internet, and hosted on *Africa is a Country*'s website), there was scant literature on Afropolitanism. Being invited to revisit my arguments for a panel at the African Literature Association Conference in Bayreuth in the summer of 2015, it is striking to see how the voices of dissent have swelled in volume and noise, compared to the earlier celebratory accounts of Afropolitanism.

In my earlier piece my interest was in Afropolitanism's collusion with consumerism. I wrote there of my desire to position myself 'with a more radical, counter-cultural movement', and to reinvest Afropolitanism (if we are to keep the term) with progressive activism.

In an era such as ours, characterized by the chilling commodification of all walks of life – including the commodification of dissent – we should be especially vigilant about any movement that embraces commodification to the extent that Afropolitanism does.

In her eloquent piece 'Exorcizing Afropolitanism' Stephanie Bosch Santana (2013) outlined Binyavanga Wainaina's 'attempt to rid African literary and cultural studies of the ghost of Afropolitanism', in her account of his plenary lecture at the *African Studies Association UK (ASAUK)* conference in Leeds in 2012. Wainaina's presentation was entitled 'I am a Pan-Africanist, not an Afropolitan', and Bosch Santana explores the way in which Afropolitanism has become 'a phenomenon increasingly product driven, design focused, and potentially funded by the West'. She recognizes that style, in and of itself, is not really the issue, but fears rather that it is 'the attempt to begin with style, and then infuse it with substantive political consciousness that is problematic'.

In a response to 'Exorcizing Afropolitanism' Salami (2013) (founder of MsAfropolitan web site http://www.msafropolitan.com/) argues that Bosch Santana is taking umbrage at African agency. She frames the debate as a choice between African victimization and Afropolitanism, asking ironically: '[H]ow dare Africans not simply be victims, but also shapers of globalisation and all its inherent contestations? How dare we market our cultures as well as our political transformations?'

First of all I would argue that our options are not reduced to one or the other (nor does Bosch Santana suggest they are). Moreover, the rapacious consumerism of the African elites claimed to make up the ranks of the Afropolitans is well documented. In such a context 'the marketing of African cultures and political transformations' sounds alarming. Frantz Fanon's prophetic words once again resonate. In his foreword to the 2004 reissue of the *Wretched of the Earth*, Homi Bhaba asks 'what might be saved from Fanon's ethics and politics of decolonization to help us reflect on contemporary manifestations of globalization' (2004, xi). Bhaba reminds us that the economic landscape engineered by the International Monetary Fund and the World Bank continues to support the compartmentalized societies identified by Fanon. No matter how much wealth exists in pockets, 'a dual economy is not a developed economy' (xii). It is largely in the pockets of the mobile Afropolitan class that much of the wealth is held. What I want to ask is this: In what way does Afropolitanism go about challenging the enduring problematics of duality and compartmentalized society, identified by Fanon as one of the major stumbling blocks to African post-colonial independence?

Is such duality challenged by the small group of Africans who are in a position to be able to 'market their cultures' in the way Salami describes? Salami herself admits that Afropolitanism possibly goes 'overboard in commodifying African culture'. This should not be a throw-away comment. It is a cause for concern. The centrality of capitalism and the importance of commodification are confirmed when one keys the term 'Afropolitan' into web search engines such as Google. What such a search yields are mainly online shops and aspirational luxury lifestyle magazines. There is a great deal of African-y stuff: jewellery, art and ankara toys. These items are recognizable from Fanon too: 'The bourgeoisie's idea of a national economy is one based on what we can call local products. Grandiloquent speeches are made about local crafts' (2004, 99). With the exception of a few well-positioned individuals of African origin, who now have a larger market to whom they can 'sell' this image of Africa, who really are the beneficiaries of this branded Afropolitanism?

Gilroy has argued that commodity culture has resulted in a sacrifice – to the service of corporate interests – of much of what was wonderful about black cultures (2004). Afropolitanism can be seen as the one of the latest manifestations of such a planetary commerce in blackness. It seems as though, having consumed so much of black American culture, there is now a demand for more authentic, more virgin, black cultures to be consumed. Demand turns to the continent where fresh resources are ready to be extracted.

It is no surprise that many producers of Western media are enthusiastic about and supportive of Afropolitanism. To quote Fanon again: 'In its decadent aspect the national bourgeoisie, gets considerable help from the Western bourgeoisie who happen to be tourists enamoured with exoticism.'

I suggest that Afropolitanism is the handmaiden of the 'Africa Rising' narrative and I suspect its championing by the Western media runs the risk of leading us ever further astray from the 'disreputable, angry places', noted by Gilroy, 'where the political interests of racialised minorities might be identified and worked upon without being encumbered by an affected liberal innocence' (2004, 18–19). The danger of Afropolitanism becoming the voice of Africa can be likened to the criticisms levelled against second-wave feminists who failed to identify their privilege as white and middle class, while claiming to speak for all women. Because while we may all be Africans, there is a huge gap between my African experience and that of my father's houseboys.

We are now well versed in the danger of the single story. While Afropolitanism may appear to offer an alternative to the single story, we do not want to run the danger of this becoming the dominant narrative for African success. The traditional Afro-pessimistic narratives, while obsessed with poverty, denied the poor any voice. While Afropolitanism may go some way in redressing the balance concerning Africans speaking for themselves, the problem lies in the fact that we still do not hear the narratives of Africans who are *not* privileged.

The problem is not that Afropolitans are privileged per se – rather it is that at a time when poverty remains endemic for millions, the narratives of a privileged few telling us how great everything is, how much opportunity and potential is available, may drown out the voices of a majority who remain denied basic life chances.

While Afropolitans talk and talk about what it means to be young, cool, and African, are many of them concerned with addressing the world beyond their own social realities, to the issues that concern other Africans? Ogbechi (2008) reminds us that, despite the international lifestyle enjoyed by the Afropolitan, *most* Africans have almost absolute immobility in a contemporary global world that works very hard to keep Africans in their place on the African continent. He points out there is no immigration policy anywhere in the Western world that welcomes Africans, while a major bias against African global mobility abounds in international media. Migrants attempting to cross the Mediterranean Sea share chilling parallels with the Afropolitan: like the Afropolitan these Africans, too, cross-continents, but in contrast to the Afropolitan narrative centred on Africa *rising*, these African's are drowning. Meanwhile, the Afropolitan comes and goes, continent hopping at leisure.

In a recent *Guardian* interview, Taiye Selasi, who popularized the term in her 2005 essay 'ByeBye Babar or What is an Afropolitan?', presents an image of an Instagram-friendly Africa. Her interpretation of Afropolitanism goes beyond being 'open to difference' – part of the Afropolitan assemblage as conceived of by Mbembe (as cited in Makhetha, 2007) – to something resembling producing African versions of American or European cities. Afropolitanism, it appears here, is grounded in the ability to engage in the same pastimes one could expect to enjoy in a Western capital.

In Burkina Faso she danced until 5 am in a western-themed club and watched movies at a feminist film festival. Adama, her charming host, is an 'Afropolitan of the highest order', by virtue of his Viennese wife, and the fact he is studying German at the Goethe Institute. To her, Togo was a seaside treat: which she likens to Malibu with *motorini*, and later she gushes about hanging out on the beach with hundreds of super-cool Togolese hipsters.

Such an itinerary would be acceptable to any self-respecting inhabitant of hipster capitals Hackney or Williamsburg, and it is wonderful that you can now have the Hipster Africa Experience, but I fail to see how this represents anything particularly progressive. It seems again that African progress is measured by the extent to which it can reproduce a Western lifestyle, now without having physically to be in the West. This does not appear to signal any particular departure from the elites' enduring love affair with achieving the lifestyles of their former masters. When I first wrote the 'Why I am not an Afropolitan' piece, I argued that Afropolitanism's enduring insights: vacating the seduction of pernicious racialized thinking, the recognition of African identities as fluid, and the notion that the African past is characterized by mixing, blending, and superimposing, were seemingly increasingly sidelined. Furthermore, the Afropolitanism we were presented with at that time failed to demonstrate Mdembe's articulation of the Afropolitan space, wherein the very concept of the 'traditional' in the African context was taken to task. However, one can observe some interesting developments over the passage of time since then. Firstly, as noted, the critiques of Afropolitanism in its shiniest form have proliferated. In addition, conversations about the Afropolitan as eponymous literary figure are every day more in evidence. Nevertheless, despite novels such as Chimamanda Ngozi Adicihie's *Americanah* which has, at its centre, stories of Nigerian migration, being saddled with the Afropolitan label, Adicihie herself was quick to dismiss such associations. It would appear that migration alone does not an Afropolitan make:

> 'I'm not an Afropolitian. I'm African, happily so,' she says. 'I'm comfortable in the world, and it's not that unusual. Many Africans are happily African and don't think they need a new term.' ("New Novel" 2013)

More recently at the 2015 Pen World Voices Festival in New York (see http://worldvoices.pen.org/2015-on-africa for the programme), Adichie presented her idea of a continental African internationality. This is a powerful concept in many ways, not least for the work it does in presenting Africa as a diverse continent, rather than the undifferentiated monolith perceived of in some parts of the Western imagination. Moreover, African internationality goes beyond merely challenging the Western imagination, by decentring it. Adichie speaks about becoming less interested in the way the West sees Africa, and increasingly concerned by how Africa sees itself. Accordingly it becomes more interesting to think about how a Kenyan sees a Nigerian than how an American might. In such a reconfiguration, cosmopolitanism need no longer be articulated vis-à-vis relations between Africa and the West. Rather we get the sense of a contemporary Pan-Africanism, in contrast to Afropolitanism; a Pan-Africanism that does not seek legitimacy via detours through our Anglo-American 'superiors', but instead fosters a continental internationality.

Such an idea is echoed in the sentiments of Barbadian-Nigerian author Yewande Omotosu whose family emigrated to South Africa when she was 12. Like Adichie, she states, despite her internationality: 'I am not an Afropolitan, I'm of the continent' (Fasselt 2014).

Most tellingly, in regard to the distance many now seek to put between themselves and the term, was a recent Afropolitan event held in Brooklyn New York, hosting a role call of prominent Afropolitans, entitled *After Afropolitanism* (http://cccadi.org/12/exhibition-after-afropolitan/). The choice of name alone demonstrates the extent to which the challenges levelled at the term have become impossible for the Afropolitan set to ignore. The organizers queried 'why some celebrate the term, while others despise it?' But to challenge is not to despise. Similarly reductive responses have summarized my own position in 'Why I am not an Afropolitan' as:

> Binyavanga Wainaina, Achille Mbembe, Frantz Fanon: good. Taiye Selasi's consumerism: bad. (Bady 2015)

The organizers of *After Afropolitan* ask what comes next, after Afropolitanism? Has the term become so bankrupt that it is no longer useable? Must the term now be vacated? Or might we recentralize African *fluidity*, rather than international, aspirational lifestyles, within the Afropolitan assemblage? It is worth considering the generative potential of engaging fluidity in debates around xenophobia, ethnic violence, and homophobia for Africa – for the entire world! The deconstruction of the fixed identities inherited from the colonial era could prove a powerful panacea to many of the continent's ills (for a fuller development of this approach, see Chielozona Eze (2015) in this same journal). Perhaps the increased presence of the Afropolitan as a literary figure will progressively engender more creative articulations of what Afropolitan can and might mean – after all, literature provides the ideal space for such transformative processes to occur.

Nonetheless, in its current manifestation, Afropolitanism is an increasingly contested category, and the word may be irreparably tarnished. While the lifestyles and aspirations of those who might have once confidently employed the term have not changed much, there is little chance of their version of Afropolitanism being ever again seen as the master narrative for African progress, or the single story of African success. While our provocations have seen to that, perhaps they will go even further, contributing to the development of a new Afropolitan narrative. One hopes for such a new narrative: one that might yet unlock the terms' liberatory potential which, to date, remains largely dormant.

Disclosure statement

No potential conflict of interest was reported by the author.

References

Bady, A. 2015. *Interview: Teju Cole « Post45*. Post45.research.yale.edu, January 19. Accessed August 10. http://post45.research.yale.edu/2015/01/interview-teju-cole/.

Bosch Santana, S. 2013. *Exorcizing Afropolitanism: Binyavanga Wainaina Explains Why "I Am a Pan-Africanist, Not an Afropolitan" at ASAUK 2012.* Africainwords.com. Accessed August 10, 2015. http://africainwords.com/2013/02/08/exorcizing-afropolitanism-binyavanga-wainaina-explains-why-i-am-a-pan-africanist-not-an-afropolitan-at-asauk-2012/.

Eze, C. 2015. "We, Afropolitans." *Journal of African Cultural Studies*, 28(1): 114–119.

Fanon, F., and R. Philcox. 2004. *The Wretched of the Earth.* New York: Grove Press.

Fasselt, R. 2014. "'I'm Not Afropolitan – I'm of the Continent': A Conversation with Yewande Omotoso." *The Journal of Commonwealth Literature* 50 (2): 231–246.

Gilroy, P. 2004. *After Empire.* London: Routledge.

Makhetha, T. 2007. *Africa Remix.* Johannesburg: Johannesburg Art Gallery.

"New Novel Shows That Chimamanda Ngozi Adichie Gets the Race Thing." 2013. *The Globe and Mail.* Accessed September 16, 2015. http://www.theglobeandmail.com/arts/books-and-media/new-novel-shows-that-chimamanda-ngozi-adichie-gets-the-race-thing/article12423909/.

Ogbechie, S. 2008. *AACHRONYM: "Afropolitanism": Africa Without Africans (II).* Aachronym.blogspot.co.uk. Accessed August 10, 2015. http://aachronym.blogspot.co.uk/2008/04/afropolitanism-more-africa-without.html.

Salami, M. 2013. *Can Africans Have Multiple Subcultures? A Response to "Exorcising Afropolitanism".* MsAfropolitan. Accessed August 10, 2015. http://www.msafropolitan.com/2013/04/can-africans-have-multiple-subcultures-a-response-to-exorcising-afropolitanism.html.

Part-Time Africans, Europolitans and 'Africa lite'

Grace A. Musila

I once attended an inaugural lecture at an African University where the colleague introducing the professor emphasized that this professor's work was of such excellence and renown that he could no longer be considered an African scholar; he was now a global scholar. When he stepped onto the podium to speak, the professor – newly promoted to global glory – did not dispute this ostensible complement. This comment has remained with me since that moment, about a decade ago. It puzzled me then, and it still does now, because I had always taken it for granted that this particular professor was *both* African *and* global. Thinking about it afterwards, I realized that these colleagues were wrestling with the same demons that some African writers have wrestled with for decades now, in their refusal to be termed 'African' writers, because, among other reasons, the tag 'African' comes with a cloud of assumptions about the quality and content of their writing. It is not uncommon to hear writers protest that they are just 'writers' not African writers. Presumably then, a similar set of anxieties was at play for the colleague introducing the professor. Apparently, and unknown to me, a scholar could not be presumed global *while* African. They had to 'transcend' their Africanness – at least in name – and become an unmarked 'global' philosopher; even if the focus of their scholarship remained decidedly African. While I understand – and emphathise with – the strategic anxieties about labelling, it has always surprised me that these writers chose to distance themselves from the tag 'African' rather than challenge the assumptions attached to the name. There is, to me, an implicit sense of surrender and defeat in opting out of an identity instead of contributing to the dismantling of these associations, and reloading it with more accurate associations. The irony of these modes of surrender to an apparently unmarked 'globality' is one that Nobel Prize winning writer and scholar, Toni Morrison, has eloquently unpacked. In a 2001 interview, asked what her readers should make of her choice to describe herself as a Black woman novelist, Morrison explained:

> I think it was an attempt on my part to refuse to be given the status of honorary white male writer. … People compliment ethnic writers by saying or implying that they are as good as mainstream writers, and whereas I understood the compliment, I thought it would be better for me, in the 1960s and early 70s to establish once and for all that all three of those things come to play: I am Black, I am a woman and I am a writer, and they go together.

In our case then, a rejection of the tag 'African', while articulating protest against narrow pigeonholing of African cultural production, simultaneously betrays aspiration to a form of cultural passing, reminiscent of, but far less transgressive than, racial passing.

I start with this anecdote about the 'global' professor, because similar anxieties are at play in conceptions of Afropolitanism. It seems to me that, in its pairing of African and cosmopolitan, this concept is haunted by anxieties about the 'African' on its own not being deemed cosmopolitan enough; and the cosmopolitan on its own suggesting the erasure or over-integration of the African into a cosmopolitanism which does not fully reference difference. In some sense then, Afropolitanism seems to be about embracing just enough of Africa to retain a certain flavour that sets one apart from the norm – presumably Euro-American – but not so much as to be *too* 'African'. Like Coke Lite or a lite beer, Afropolitanism seems to promise Africa lite: Africa *sans* the 'unhealthy' or 'intoxicating' baggage of Africa.

This set of comments is an attempt to think through some aspects of the debate on Afropolitanism. I have chosen a deliberately provocative title, with only half-cheeky intent; for, as my reflections indicate, at the core of the term Afropolitanism are particular anxieties about Africa and perceptions of the continent. These thoughts are largely in conversation with Achille Mbembe and Taiye Selasi's ideas on Afropolitanism. According to Achille Mbembe (2007), the three major politico-intellectual paradigms in Africa for much of the twentieth century – anticolonial nationalism, African socialisms and pan-Africanism – have largely 'become institutionalized and ossified to such a degree that, today, they no longer make it possible to analyse transformations in process with the slightest bit of credibility' (2007, 26). Mbembe sees Afropolitanism as a particular form of 'broadmindedness', anchored in Africa's histories of flows, both outwards and inwards. At the same time, Afropolitanism places an accent on some African cities and African migrants, both continental and beyond. In his description, Afropolitans emerge as migrants who 'can express themselves in more than one language [and] measure up against not the village next door, but the world at large' (2007, 29). Mbembe's celebration of Johannesburg as the ultimate Afropolitan city which 'feeds on multiple racial legacies, a vibrant economy, a liberal democracy, a culture of consumerism that partakes directly of the flows of globalisation; [and a city] where an ethic of tolerance is being created' (2007, 29) underscores the embeddedness of Afropolitanism in global capital and its attendant consumer cultures, urban cultures, as well as a deep-seated investedness in connectivity to the so-called global metropolis. While this paints a rosy picture of connectivity, heterogeneous blends of cultures and an ethos of tolerance, the unasked question remains: what about those excluded from these circuits of consumption and access, as is the case for a majority of Johannesburg's residents? Given the fact that the dynamics emphasized by Mbembe – global connectivity and migrancy – already resonated with the preceding politico-intellectual philosophies he describes as ossified, the one distinct feature that stands out in his version of Afropolitanism is a particular accent on consumer cultures, as well as tuning into the wavelengths of the world beyond Africa – and more specifically, the Global North.

In this piece, I explore my dis-ease with the promises of Afropolitanism, as a concept which, as Simon Gikandi (2011) rightly notes is rich in conceptual and ideological promise, in countering certain forms of Afropessimism; but seems also to be a concept that was expected to run before it had been allowed to crawl and find its feet. This partly opened up the term to extensive appropriation, commoditization and association with conspicuous consumption, with an African flavour. The perspectives offered in this reflection are in part inspired by Tejumola Olaniyan's ideas on what he calls 'tests of belonging' in African literature; of which he considers the ideological test as better able to weather the storm of the postglobal age; at a time when the key challenge remains the problem of social inequality that has historically been mapped onto a racial grid and Blackness (Olaniyan 2015). This remains a major crisis, both globally, and in Africa, where Blackness continues to coincide with multiple marginalities and heavily discounted futures for millions of Black people and, broadly, people of colour across the world.

The anxieties about Africa outlined above would be dismissible if they were evident only in some definitions of the term 'Afropolitan'. But these anxieties seem to lie at the core of some conceptions of the term. If we look at one of the most cited essays on the subject – 'Bye Bye Babar' – Taiye Selasi (2005) writes that somewhere between the 1980s and 2001, 'the general image of Africans in the West transmorphed from goofy to gorgeous'. Here, Selasi seems to celebrate cultural integration and, in some ways, cultural passing. Later in the essay, she underlines the difficulty of growing up while painfully aware of '"being from" a blighted place, of having surnames linked to countries which are linked to lack, corruption'; and all the while remaining haunted by a feeling of shame 'for not knowing more about our parents' culture and being ashamed of those cultures for not being more "advanced"' (Selasi 2005).

These anxieties about Africa mark Afropolitanism as another mode of integration into a mainstream that appears to remain uneasy with cultural difference, hence the need to tone it down, or what Rob Nixon, in a different context, terms 'botox out' (2011, 184) its wrinkles, and only leave enough of this difference for strategic exoticism, and marketability. In some ways, Afropolitanism is yet another trendy term involved in botoxing out the wrinkles of various struggles of accepting cultural difference as it comes.

I am also intrigued by the range of anxieties that haunt Afropolitanism and its implicit boundaries: Which Africans qualify, who is excluded, and why? In a 1998 interview about her novel, *Paradise* – a story about a utopian all-Black town in 1950s America – Toni Morrison (1998) says that part of her inspiration for her novel came from the realization that 'All paradises, all utopias are designed by who is not there, by the people who are not allowed in.' While Morrison is interested in Black communities' attempts to create all-black utopias at a certain point in US history, her comments nonetheless resonate for me, when I think about Afropolitanism. I am intrigued by who is excluded from the term, despite Mbembe and Selasi's enthusiastic emphasis on flows, fluidity and rejection of boundedness as defining features of Afopolitanism. The urban dictionary describes an Afropolitan as 'an African educated in the US or Europe and spends significant amounts of time in those parts of the world'. This entry further indicates that such people have 'a global perspective on issues'. For Taiye Selasi, 'what distinguishes Afropolitans is a willingness to complicate Africa – namely, to engage with, critique, and celebrate the parts of Africa that mean the most to them' (2005). While Selasi's fiction remarkably achieves this mission of complicating our understanding of Africa and Africans, her essay on Afropolitanism is far less self-reflexive. In some ways, going by these two definitions, we get the sense that the term references people of African descent who are globally mobile. But does this include all globally mobile Africans? Is a Somali shopkeeper in a South African township Afropolitan in the same way as Taiye Selasi? In a similar vein, going by these definitions, I have a sense of characters who qualify as Afropolitan in contemporary fiction. Fola and Kweku Sai's children in Taiye Selasi's *Ghana Must Go* are perhaps Afropolitans, but I get stuck on whether Josef Woldemariam, in Dinaw Mengestu's *How to Read Air* is also Afropolitan, despite decades spent in the USA, and having arrived there from Ethiopia via Sudan and Europe, and having developed a sharp grasp of the cultural logics of these places. My suspicion is that he is not *quite* Afropolitan. In some unstated senses then, the term Afropolitanism seems to come with a certain glow of access, affluence and mobility in the global north that signals particular class and cultural inflections which would therefore not be extended to Brian Chikwava's migrants in *Harare North* surviving on the fringes of London, or the many African migrants who attempt the Mediterranean passage into Europe. Afropolitanism then, seems to reference a particular kind of affluent mobility in the global north, as opposed to all global mobility. Most worryingly, as Emma Dabiri (2015) writes elsewhere in this journal,

> the problem is not that Afropolitans are privileged per se – rather it is that at a time when poverty remains endemic for millions, the narratives of a privileged few telling us how great everything is, how much opportunity and potential is available, may drown out the voices of a majority who remain denied basic life chances.

This risk of drowning out the voices of the majority who remain on the margins of the stylish Afropolitan script is a concern that informed writer Brian Bwesigye (2013) discontent about novelist Helon Habila's critique of NoViolet Bulawayo's *We Need New Names* as poverty porn. While I differ in some ways with Bwesigye's reading of Habila's review, I nonetheless share his concern about the risk of the stories of a majority of the continent's people being silenced, in our pursuit of the Afropolitan single story, to borrow Emma Dabiri's (2014) use of Chimamamanda Ngozi Adichie's phrase. Ironically, despite its celebration of broadmindedness, thanks to its embeddedness in Euro-American affluence and cultural normativity, Afropolitanism, hardly embraces similar forms of mobility and cultural eloquence when these Africans are in, say, China or Saudi Arabia, or indeed, within Africa itself.

My personal unease with the term lies in its easy comfort and uncritical embrace of consumer cultures and an equally uncritical embrace of selective, successful global mobility and cultural literacy in the global North. To echo Emma Dabiri's eloquent critique in her 2014 essay, 'Afropolitanism is too polite, corporate, glossy' (Dabiri 2014). As she further notes, citing Okwunodu Ogbechi (2008) Afropolitanism's emphasis on international travel renders it an ultra-elite concept, in a world where 'most Africans have almost absolute immobility in a contemporary world that works very hard to keep Africans in their place on the African continent' (Dabiri 2014). In such a context, the stylish aura of the term – and the wonderful lives Selasi describes in her essay – belies the layers of friction that haunt people of African descent in Europe and North America. In practice, even for those people and characters who 'qualify' to be deemed Afropolitan, we know that the world is far from warm, fuzzy and welcoming to people of African descent. In fact, we know that no matter how much affluence and cultural mastery an African can command, no matter how successfully we distance ourselves from the Africa of corruption, wars and poverty, the world will always have a qualified welcome for us. The recent trend of police shootings and civilian attacks on Black people in the USA is a sobering reminder of this reality.

Ironically, the fate of Kweku Sai, the successful cardiologist in Selasi's *Ghana Must Go* (2013) powerfully underlines precisely this qualified welcome; when in the blink of the eye, he finds an entire lifetime of hard work, ambition and moral integrity wiped out by racial prejudice. To some degree then, Afropolitanism signals a particular location in the world, significantly marked by a toned down Africanness; hence the need for a new term that combines African and cosmopolitan. Why the need to qualify one's cosmopolitanism? The very necessity of qualifying Africans' being in the world only makes sense when we assume that, ordinarily, Africans are *not* of the world. I am yet to hear of Europeans terming themselves Europolitans, or Americans as Ameropolitans. Perhaps cosmopolitanism is already assumed to be part of these categories? If this is the case, then in qualifying our belonging to the world, Africans effectively reiterate our non-belonging; our qualified access to a cosmopolitan identity as already marked in particular normative grammars that single us out as wanting – in both senses of the term.

References

Bwesigye, B. 2013. Is Afropolitanism Africa's New Single Story? Reading Helon Habila's Review of "We Need New Names" by Brian Bwesigye – Aster(ix) Journal. [online] Aster(ix) Journal. Accessed March 2015. http://asterixjournal.com/afropolitanism-africas-new-single-story-reading-helon-habilas-review-need-new-names-brian-bwesigye/

Dabiri, Emma. 2014. "Why I am not an Afropolitan." Accessed June 2014. http://africasacountry.com/2014/01/why-im-not-an-afropolitan/

Dabiri, Emma. 2015. "Why I am (still) not an Afropolitan". *Journal of African Cultural Studies* 28 (1): 104–108.

Gikandi, Simon. 2011. "On Afropolitanism." In *Negotiating Afropolitanism: Essays on Borders and Spaces in Contemporary African Literature and Folklore*, edited by Jennifer Wawrzinek and J. K. S. Makokha, 9–11. Rodopi: Amsterdam.
Mbembe, Achille. 2007. "Afropolitanism." In *Africa Remix: Contemporary Art of a Continent*, edited by Simon Njami and Lucy Duran, 26–29. Johannesburg: Jacana Media.
Morrison, Toni. Online NewsHour interview, March 9, 1998
Nixon, R. 2011. *Slow Violence and the Environmentalism of the Poor*. Cambridge, MA: Harvard University Press.
Ogbechi, Okwunodu. 2008. "'Afropolitanism': Africa Without Africans." Accessed August 20, 2015. http://aachronym.blogspot.co.uk/2008/04/afropolitanism-more-africa-without.html
Olaniyan, Tejumola. 2015. "African Literature in the Postglobal Age – The Major Tests of Belonging." ALA Conference, Bayreuth.
Selasi, Taiye. 2005. "ByeBye Babar." Accessed March 2014. http://thelip.robertsharp.co.uk/?p=76
Selasi, Taiye. 2013. *Ghana Must Go*. Penguin: London.

'We, Afropolitans'

Chielozona Eze

Open cities – open world

The term Afropolitanism is troubling. It is difficult to think of it without thinking of some people of African descent who seem to evade the responsibility that comes with being African today. Are Afropolitans the African versions of western trust fund kids? Are they privileged snobs who carry one or more international passports and jet from one global city (in Africa) to another (in the West)? Ishtiyaq Shukri (2015) rightly points out part of the baggage that comes with the term. He highlights the association between the concept and *The Afropolitan* magazine.[1] As he charges, *The Afropolitan* magazine comes with its own set of advice on how to reduce travel stress with an essential travel list:

> a well-packed suitcase, toys for the kids, updated music and reading devices and a range of RESCUE products for gentle stress relief – a list so far removed from the experiences of African migrants being brutally attacked by xenophobic mobs in South Africa and drowning in their thousands in the Mediterranean, as to be obscene.[2]

I am in sympathy with those who are cynical about Afropolitanism, understood as a market ploy, or associated with well to do Africans who can afford to travel the world and be at home in African and western cities. It seems, though, that the concept points to a fundamental shift in conceptions of African identity, especially in the twenty-first century, a shift that highlights the fluidity in African self-perception and visions of the world. It is on this basis that I interpreted the term within the context of cosmopolitanism (Eze 2014). What I mean is that one cannot understand Afropolitanism without understanding cosmopolitanism, whose idea it replicates in an intellectual mimetic gesture.

The lifestyle magazine, *The Afropolitan*, is just what it is: a lifestyle, fashion magazine. It has very little to do with the philosophically and, potentially, morally rich concept, introduced by Taiye Selasi (2005), and reaffirmed by Mbembe (2007), and which I sought to ground philosophically (Eze 2014). Perhaps, the magazine has as much in common with the concept as yet another magazine, *The Cosmopolitan*, does with the Greek idea of world citizen, *cosmopolites*. To be sure, cosmopolitanism is derived from the Greek words *kosmos* (world) and polites (citizen); hence *kosmopolites* means a citizen of the world. Based on this inspiration, we provisionally define the Afropolitan (*Afro polites*) as one who, on the strength of birth or affinity, can call any place in Africa his or her place, while at the same time being open to the world. According to Selasi (2005):

> There is at least one place on the African continent to which we tie our sense of self: be it a nation-state (Ethiopia), a city (Ibadan), or an auntie' kitchen. Then there's the G8 city or two (or three) that we know like the backs of our hands ... We are Afropolitans: not citizens, but Africans of the world[3]

What underscores Selasi's conception of the Afropolitan is the absence of fixity to a location on the one hand, and a marked mobility between Africa and the West, on the other. While I agree with the idea of mobility and the 'subtle tensions in between' national, racial and cultural belongings, it is important to note that this mobility does not have to be exclusively between Africa and the West. It can be between one African city and another, or even within an African city. I will return to this further on. In the following section I trace versions of this figure in recent fiction from and about movement in Africa. The goal is to highlight the widening arc of African self-perception, one that goes beyond the conventional postcolonial notions.

In Teju Cole's *Open City*, Julius the protagonist stands out for his openness to the world. Characteristic of his relation to New York is his mobility. In the first part of the novel, we see him walking on the streets of New York. His walks turn into global journeys as he travels to Europe. This mobility is richly symbolic of his self-perception as a global citizen and a person with an open mind. Julius's encounters and conversations with people from different ethnic and racial backgrounds both in the USA and Europe are characterized by an attitude devoid of prejudice. He never judges people based on his expectations of them. To the contrary, he lets himself be informed by his encounter with them. His aesthetics and ethics issue from the same attitude of openness. He never dismisses western music or architecture as Eurocentric. Nor do these western cultural products replace his appreciation of those of Africa. His love for Gustav Mahler never displaced his enjoyment of Fela Kuti. The fact that he is biracial, while being an integral part of his being, is secondary to his openness.

Julius is reminiscent of another literary figure, Refentše in Phaswane Mpe's *Welcome to Our Hillbrow* (2011). Mpe sketches a map of Hillbrow in *Welcome* so that with the novella in the hand you can walk from one end of Hillbrow to another without losing your way. Refentše walks through the city, and his walk eventually ends in heaven from where he gains a greater perspective on reality. His walk from one end of the city to the other fulfils at least one important function: he encounters different people, including blacks from other African nations, the *Makwerekweres*. Refilwe, Refentše's former girlfriend, travels to Oxford for further studies. She takes a 'five minutes' walk from the Headington Hill Campus of the University ... ' (104). Given that ample attention is devoted to Refentse's and Refilwe's time on the streets of Hillbrow and Oxford, and that they are transformed thereby, we are alerted to the fact that they are the ones who need to go through the school of social drama with which Mpe indicts his society for their bigotry. It is therefore fair to argue that walking (spatial mobility) is the motif that frames the figures' radical openness to reality.[4]

Michel de Certau (1984, 93) imbues those who walk through cities with insights. Walking allows people to see and to master what they see; they navigate the strategies of the city designers, that is, the structures of power. On the street, they encounter others with whom they could enter into conflict and, or, solidarity. What we love about these characters is that they are more interested in expanding their circles of friendship across ethnic and racial lines. In so doing, they stake claims to the cities in which they live, and they also weave connections between their cities and the universe. Indeed, what they have in common is their fundamental openness to others and otherness. Their spatial mobility informs their inner mobility and their readiness to negotiate reality. Theirs is what I have already identified as 'transcultural affinity' (Eze 2015). They seek to relate more than they search for difference and exclusion. I identify them as Afropolitans because they lay claim to Africa and the world in a flexible gesture of unbounded humanity.

Why do we need new names?

We are Africans, why do we need new concepts to explain ourselves?[5] Should it not suffice that we simply identify ourselves as cosmopolitans, just as Asians or Europeans might? Given African history, we allow ourselves the freedom to inflect cosmopolitanism the way we have done to reflect a fundamental ideological and perceptual shift in African self-inscription. Part of the African history we speak about is captured in NoViolet Bulawayo's novel, *We Need No Names* (2013). In one of the key scenes in the novel, Darling and her fellow urchins are in Budapest, stealing guavas from an elderly white couple's orchard. A gang of freedom fighters arrives, chanting:

> Kill the Boer, the farmer, the *khiwa*!
> Strike fear in the heart of the white man!
> White man, you have no place here, go back, go home!
> Africa for Africans, Africa for Africans!
> Kill the Boer, the farmer, the *khiwa*! (113)

The thugs refer to themselves as the 'Sons of the soil' (120), and soon, they begin to beat up the white couple. It is at this point that one of the kids, still in the guava tree, asks: 'What is exactly an African?' (121). It is relevant in this context that the question was asked by one displaced person about another, suffering undue pain. That question is an important moral and existential interjection in the narrative; it challenges the nationalist's narrow definition of identity and its moral implications.[6] We realize that the question is not gratuitous when Sbho, unable to contain the humiliation meted out to the white couple, begins to cry. Bastard challenges her: 'What, are you crying for the white people? Are they your relatives?' Bastard's question assumes that empathy belongs only within one's family, that is, as blacks, they should not imagine the pain of the white couple. However, Sbho's answer undercuts Bastard's assumption: 'They are people, you asshole' (122). Can we dismiss Sbho's response as that of a child, who does not know history? But is the action of the Sons of the soil the appropriate response to history?

The Garveyean slogan 'Africa for Africans', which formed the foundational premise of African resistance to colonialism and imperialism, had as its ideal the liberation of Africa from political oppression. It seems, however, to have sustained (epistemic) violence in the postcolony because its premise is the exclusion of the other. Solidarity is defined by blood and soil; Sbho's revelation of her affinity with the white couple directly negates that nativist idea, and opens new vistas for conceiving new ways of being. Her identification with the white couple and the question about identity go to the heart of the title of the novel and of our concern as Afropolitans. We need new names not because we are new – we are not; rather, we need new names because we have new stories to tell about our world. These stories acknowledge those of our ancestors, but seek to expand them in order to contain our extended arc of existence. Unlike most of our ancestors, we have white husbands/wives, Asian brothers/sisters – and all of this takes place on the African continent. Our new stories create and expand our spaces for these relatives. We tell new stories because we believe with Fanon (1968, 206) that 'each generation must, out of relative obscurity, discover its mission, fulfill it, or betray it'.

Afropolitanism: a new ethics of being

We call ourselves Afropolitans, well aware of the misunderstandings in the genealogy of the concept. We are not interested in denying any perceived privilege owing to our birth or status. We move around the world; we are able to be in at least two global cities in a year, and we encounter people from different ethnic, racial and cultural backgrounds. But the truth is that spatial mobility is only symptomatic of our interior mobility. Indeed, what really counts is this interior mobility, that is, how negotiable our relation to the world is. One does not need to have crossed geographical boundaries to be Afropolitan; one only needs to cross the psychic boundaries erected by nativism, autochthony, heritage and other mythologies of authenticity. This, as I hinted in the introductory part, is where I seek to go beyond Selasi's arguably elitist definition of Afropolitanism. All this does not make us rootless. We love where we come from. But that place is an open city, open to others. We are not trees that are condemned to a place. Our roots are in our hearts; we take them wherever we go, and remain committed to openness, which is the premise of our humanistic stance.

We are Afropolitans not because we move from one city to another, but because we are capable of occupying several cultural spaces and relations from which we define who we are. Our self-definition does not seek to exclude; rather it seeks to include. Because we consider the question, 'What is the African?' seriously, we take Darling and her fellow displaced residents of Paradise as true Afropolitans, and Sbho as our ethical lighthouse. Our moral compass, that is, our idea of what is good or bad, permissible or not, issues from the same source out of which she derived the inspiration to perceive the white couple primarily as humans that deserve her empathy, not exclusively as historical enemies. She saw in them fellow Africans who should not have been subjected to torture because of their skin colour or even privilege. Certainly, Sbho would not ignore the past instances of oppression, but her gesture of solidarity would seek to invite the white couple to be part of the solution to Zimbabwean problems as Africans that they are.

The Afropolitan is one who stakes moral claims to Africa and the world, and conversely admits that others can lay the same claim to Africa. The Afropolitan believes that being African is not reductive to colour, heritage or autochthony; rather being African is expansive. Whoever has lived on the continent long enough to identify with it is African; out of this flow all other conceivable forms of relationships. We are all Africans, and we believe that to be is to relate. The more expansive our spheres of relations are, the deeper is our humanity.

We, Afropolitans, believe in the ever expanding universe in which we are the centres; we are the centres of the world because in each of us there is a space big enough to contain apparent contradictions and oddities: We are not half this or half that; we are this *and* that. We are Igbo and Yoruba and Efik and Xhosa; we are black and white and brown. We are at home in Enugu, Lagos, Johannesburg, Bayreuth, Nairobi or Chicago. We are fitted not just with double consciousness; we possess multiple-consciousness, for we perceive the world from multiple perspectives. The talking drum moves our hearts as much as cello does our souls. We are not afraid to engage the world, and we do so, not by defining others but by encountering them. We are more interested in human flourishing than in parading our heritage. Indeed, any aspect of our heritage that does not contribute to the happiness of all is subjected to a ruthless interrogation. We do not mind what colour our next door neighbours are; we mind that they are good neighbours. We do not care which heritage or colour our president is (one can think here of President Guy Scott of Zambia); we care that he or she is a good president, one who is interested in human flourishing in society. For those of us who survived colonization, apartheid, racism, wars or military dictatorships there is every reason to love the world: nothing worse can ever happen to us. There is no excuse for bitterness and hate. We therefore spread the joy of living. In the strong belief that to be is to relate, we conceive our relation in the following paradigms:

Universal narrative: To be Afropolitan means to admit the simple fact that one's culture or society is composed with strands from other societies and cultures. Afropolitans acknowledge that their society comprised (or should comprise) people from diverse ethnicities, and their cultures can no longer be understood in purist categories. They thus assemble a universal narrative with registers from these diverse backgrounds.

What, by the way, is a universal narrative? It is not to be understood in the spirit of the Enlightenment as an essence that applies to all peoples at all times. Rather, it is the fundamental relationality of everything; it is the idea expressed in the Igbo proverb: *Ife kwulu, ife akwudebe ya* – where one thing stands, something else stands beside it. Universality in this regard means that you cannot consider a particular thing to the exclusion of others. An idea has meaning only in relation to other ideas. So do humans. I am human because I relate to other humans. Others affirm me; they provide the context within which my story has meaning. In this context, you are who you are not because you are opposed to someone else. This is true in every African society of today, the Africa in which socio-historical contexts have shifted. To be Igbo today is fundamentally different from being Igbo in the times *Things Fall Apart* was set. To be Igbo today already takes for granted the probable presence of a person of Yoruba, Efik, Xhosa or German ancestry in Igbo society. They, too, have right to be part of that society. They can define themselves the way they deem fit.

Finding beauty in otherness: The issue therefore is no longer how different we are from others, but rather what we can learn from them, from what we have in common with them. This implies a conscious effort to affirm something in others and to seek to relate to them. Let it be the starting point of encounter. The first question Afropolitans ask when they encounter other people is: what do I (or can I) have in common with this person? The next question is: what is beautiful or admirable in this other? The third is: what can I learn from this person? By the time they have answered all these questions, the issue of how they are different from that person would have taken care of itself. Difference becomes merely a reference point of individuality and respect rather than a point of exclusion of the other. A person with a different sexual orientation than ours is just a person with a different sexual orientation. The person with white skin colour is just a person with white skin colour. This, of course, does not blind us to the privileges that that colour carries in certain societies. In this regard, the Afropolitan is keenly aware of history not from the perspective of vengeance but from that of fairness. In matters of history, the Afropolitan distinguishes between lust for vengeance and search for fairness. We could be for the latter; we abhor the former. There is, indeed, no option for us, given our disposition to the world. We believe in Benjamin's (1968) angel of history; we never rest until fairness is restored to all. The angel of fairness is always open-minded.

Disclosure statement

No potential conflict of interest was reported by the author.

Notes

1. *The Afropolitan* is a South African fashion magazine: http://www.afropolitan.co.za/
2. We understand Shukri's interjection within the context of his refusal to be tagged. There is, of course, the risk of Afropolitanism becoming a fashion tag.
3. Theoretically. Selasi's idea builds upon Appiah's 1997 essay 'Cosmopolitan Patriots,' which he expanded in *Cosmopolitanism: Ethics in a World of Strangers* (2006). My reflection owes a lot to the latter.
4. I am grateful to a reviewer for this important observation. It is also true that not all walks or walkers lead to openness.
5. I derived the inspiration for this section from Grace A. Musila's question as to why we need to redefine who we are. See Grace A. Musila 'Part-Time Africans, Europolitans and "Africa Lite"' in this same issue.
6. I use the term moral in its broader sense of the distinction between right and wrong, proper and improper. I will later use the term ethics or ethical to designate not only a set of moral principles, but people in relation to others.

References

Appiah, Kwame Anthony. 1997. "Cosmopolitan Patriots." *Critical Inquiry* 23 (3): Front Lines/Border Posts: 617–639.

Appiah, Kwame Anthony. 2006. *Cosmopolitanism: Ethics in a World of Strangers*. New York: W.W. Norton.

Benjamin, Walter. 1968. *Illuminations: Essays and Reflections*. New York: Schocken Books.

Bulawayo, NoViolet. 2013. *We Need New Names*. New York: Little Brown.
de Certeau, Michel. 1984. *The Practice of Everyday Life*. Berkeley: University of California Press.
Cole, Teju. 2011. *Open City*. New York: Random House.
Eze, Chielozona. 2014. "Rethinking African Culture and Identity: The Afropolitan Model." *Journal of African Cultural Studies* 26 (2): 234–247.
Eze, Chielozona. 2015. "Transcultural Affinity: Thoughts on the Emergent Cosmopolitan Imagination in South Africa." *Journal of African Cultural Studies* 27 (2): 216–228.
Fanon, Frantz. 1968. *The Wretched of the Earth*. New York: Grove Press.
Mbembe, Achille. 2007. "Afropolitanism." In *Africa Remix: Contemporary Art of a Continent*, edited by Njami Simon and Lucy Durán, 26–30. Johannesburg: Johannesburg Art Gallery.
Mpe, Phaswane. 2011. *Welcome to Our Hillbrow*. Athens: Ohio University Press.
Musila, Grace A. 2015. "Part-Time Africans, Europolitans and 'Africa Lite'." *Journal of African Cultural Studies* 28 (1): 109–113.
Selasi, Taiye. 2005. 'ByeBye Babar.' Accessed May 20, 2013. http://thelip.robertsharp.co.uk/?p=76.
Shukri, Ishtiyaq. 2015. 'Why I Asked for My Work to be Withdrawn from the Inaugural FT/OppenheimerFunds Emerging Voices Awards.' http://africasacountry.com/why-i-asked-for-my-work-to-be-withdrawn-from-the-inaugural-financial-timesoppenheimerfunds-emerging-voices-awards-2015-by-ishtiyaq-shukri/.

Being-in-the-world: the Afropolitan Moroccan author's worldview in the new millennium

Valérie K. Orlando

In the last decade, many contemporary African authors of French expression from both North and sub-Saharan Africa have posited perspectives in their novels that reveal a global cosmopolitanism that uniquely defines African literature in the twenty-first century. Moroccan authors writing in French such as Youssouf Amine Elalamy and Fouad Laroui, among others, promote a way of being African in the world that disassociates the author from the literary tropes of earlier decades. They no longer dwell on the angst of the postcolonial condition, the traumas rooted in tensions between modernity and traditionalism, the sociocultural and economic divisions between North and sub-Saharan Africa, poverty and despair. Moroccan authors promote an 'Afropolitanism' in their works that connotes movement forward, to engage in *becoming* something other than the pessimistic stereotypes associated with Morocco as well as the African continent.

Au cours de la dernière décennie, de nombreux auteurs africains contemporainsd'expression française du Maghreb et de l'Afrique sub-saharienne proposent des perspectives dans leurs romans qui révèlent un cosmopolitisme global qui définit de façon unique la littérature africaine du XXIe siècle. Les auteurs marocains écrivant en français comme Youssouf Amine Elalamy et Fouad Laroui, entre autres, soutiennent une manière d'être africaine dans le monde qui dissocie l'auteur des tropes littéraires des décennies précédentes. Ils se centrent moins sur les sujets tels que l'angoisse de la condition postcoloniale, les traumatismes socioculturels enracinés dans les tensions entre la modernité et le traditionalisme, les divisions socioculturelles et économiques entre le Maghreb et l'Afrique subsaharienne, la pauvreté et le désespoir. Les auteurs marocains promeuvent un « Afropolitanisme » dans leurs œuvres qui évoque un mouvement vers l'avant pour engager autres choses que les stéréotypes pessimistes associés au Maroc ainsi qu'au continent africain.

In the last decade, many contemporary African authors of French expression from both North and sub-Saharan Africa have posited perspectives in their novels that reveal a global cosmopolitanism that uniquely defines African literature in the twenty-first century. Authors writing in French, such as Salim Bachi (France/Algeria), Calixthe Beyala (Cameroon), Youssouf Amine Elalamy (Morocco), Fouad Laroui (Morocco), Alain Mabanchou (Congo), Marie Ndiaye (France/ Senegal), and Abdourahman Waberi (Djibouti) among others,[1] promote a 'way of being African in the world' that disassociates the author from the tropes of before: the angst of the post-colonial condition, the traumas rooted in tensions between modernity and traditionalism, the sociocultural and economic divisions between North and sub-Saharan Africa, poverty and despair (Gikandi 2011, 9). Evan Maina Mwangi states in *Africa Writes Back to Self: Metafiction,*

Gender, Sexuality that new, engaging twenty-first-century African writing from the continent and the diaspora 'is neither a "writing back" to Europe nor an endorsement of Euro-American neocolonialism. It is first and foremost about self-perception' (2009, 3).

Writing for, as well as to and of, the African self is the principal characteristic of Afropolitan authors who are conceptualizing new tropes for African literature in the twenty-first century. Afropolitanism, as defined by the founder of the term, Cameroonian Achille Mbembe, serves three functions. First, it politically articulates the transnational migration of the contemporary African author (who lives between the continent and his/her adopted space, usually in Europe). Unlike in the past, authors' movement transnationally does not represent loss, a giving-up of selfhood for emigration, but rather a means to forge affiliations and 'modes of knowledge' (Gikandi 2011, 10).[2] Second, Afropolitan authors articulate a space that is defined by the multiculturality and the ethnically diverse experiences as second, third, and even fourth generation émigrés writing in the West. Third, the term inspires authors to ponder philosophically what it means to be African (racially, culturally, socially, economically) as s/he seeks to establish a phenomenologically grounded *being-in-the-world*. Here, being-in-the-world is conceptualized in terms of Heidegger's notion of *Dasein*: 'an understanding of existence – as an understanding of the being of all beings of a character other than its own' (Heidegger 1962, 33). This being is understood as connected and formulated by a *being-already-alongside* with others. Being-in-the-world, as explains Heidegger, 'is not just a fixed staring at something that is purely present-at-hand ... [it is] *fascinated by* the world with which it is concerned' (1962, 88).[3] This fascination leads to 'intercultural scenarios' in which 'two sign systems come into contact' (Nwosu 2011, 13). The contact allows for a 'new mode of being', or a third way of being that is 'generated from two cultural-ideological signifying fields', those of self and other (2011, 23).

According to Achille Mbembe, Afropolitanism offers a theoretical framework that disassociates itself from past literary moments which, today, have little relevance for global societies. Mbembe clarifies that the three previous, significant literary movements after decolonization – anti-colonial nationalism, African socialism, pan-Africanism – no longer qualify as helpful frameworks through which to study the position of authors who live between continents, cultures, and modes of creativity. Rather, these three literary movements of the past have 'ossified [and] blocked all forms of renewal of cultural criticism and artistic and philosophical creativity [while they also have] decrease[d] our capacity to contribute to contemporary reflection on culture and democracy' (1).

Following Mbembe's definition of Afropolitanism (2008), Africa is open to new interpretations by the African author that are very different from the more essentialist-based earlier twentieth-century concepts of Negritude and pan-Africanism:

> Afropolitanism is not the same thing as Pan-Africanism or Negritude. Afropolitanism is a stylistic, an aesthetic and a certain poetics of the world. It is a manner of being in the world which refuses, on principle, any form of victim identity – which does not mean that it is not conscious of the injustices and the violence which the law of the world inflicted on this continent and its people. It is also a political and cultural position with respect to the nation, to race and to the question of difference in general. Insofar as our States are pure fabrications (recent ones at that), they have, strictly speaking, nothing in their essence which should make us worship them – this does not mean that one is indifferent to their fate. (Mbembe 2008, 2)[4]

Mbembe further emphasizes that divisions with respect to race and geographical divides should not partition Africa. Rather he acquiesces to the idea that:

> all sorts of people have a link with, or simply something to do with Africa – something that gives them the right *ipso facto* to lay claim to 'African citizenship'. There are naturally, those called Negroes. They were born and live in African states, making up the nationals. *Yet if Negro-Africans form the*

> *majority of the population in Africa, they are neither the sole inhabitants nor the sole producers of art and culture of the continent.* (Mbembe 2008, 1)[5]

In many respects, Achille Mbembe in the 2000s argues for a *creolization* of African thought as well as literary and cultural theory much like his contemporaries Patrick Chamoiseau, Raphaël Confiant, and Jean Barnabé did for the Caribbean in 1989 when they wrote and published *Eloge de la Créolité.* Their call for a rethinking of the Caribbean novel as linking continents, philosophies, and views irrespective of language, ethnicity, or colonial history is now a part of francophone literary theory. This early treatise proposing the embrace of the diversity – linguistic and cultural – of the Caribbean, promoted a *Caribbeanness* rooted in 'a braid of histories' (Chamoiseau et al. 1993, 88). The Caribbean author writing in/of and about the region 'had a taste of all kinds of languages, all kinds of idioms' (1993, 88). Emphasizing a plurality in the idea of the One and echoing Edouard Glissant's *Tout-Monde* notion of singularity, Chamoiseau et al. note that 'we, of the Caribbean' are 'at once Europe, Africa, and enriched by Asian contributions, we are also Levantine, Indians, as well as pre-Columbian Americans in some respects. Creoleness is *"the world diffracted but recomposed"*, a maelstrom of signifieds in a single signifier: a Totality' (1993, 88).[6]

In the 2000s, Mbembe's Afropolitan writer also 'embodies both a universalistic dimension and a sensitivity to particular others' (Aboulafia 2001). The writer evokes the totality of being, 'soi-même comme un autre', the self as other, if we rely on Paul Ricoeur's explanation of self-identity as always dependent on recognition of the other's own conception of selfhood. *Oneself as Another*, both the title of Ricoeur's book and its central premise, 'suggest from the outset that the selfhood of oneself implies otherness to such an intimate degree that one cannot be thought of without the other' (1992, 3). The 'Africans of the World', African immigrants, transnationals, émigrés, and exiles, 'citizens of African nations living in the West are automatic Afropolitans' who experience the intra- and extra-continental relationships between self and other (Makokha 2011, 16). They extend their ideas of what it means to be African beyond the borders of 'nativist interpretations of culture and the claim to autochthonous cultures' as seen in earlier paradigms of African cultural production (Makokha 2011, 18). Afropolitanism connotes movement forward and *becoming* something other than the stereotypes associated with the continent as defined by Western, most particularly Euro-American, sociopolitical and economic standards.

> Afropolitanism is the spirit that espouses this 'paradigm of itinerancy, mobility and displacement'. It is the spirit that emanates from those cultural narratives and fictional memories being generated by migrants and their descendants who live in racial minorities across Africa, such as the Asians of Eastern and Southern Africa as well as the immigrants (and their descendants) of African descent currently located in the Diaspora. (Makokha 2011, 19)

African literature in the new millennium has been informed by the global-transnational events of its time: 9/11, the Arab Springs of Egypt, Libya, Tunisia, Morocco, the famines of Ethiopia, the ethnic cleansings of Democratic Republic of Congo, the economic woes of Europe and North America. Therefore, the African author, whether s/he uses French, English, Arabic, Wolof or Ki-Swahili draws his/her sources of reflection from the global interconnections of our era. Whether from sub-Saharan or North Africa, the francophone novel of the new millennium is transnational. Certainly the literary landscape of the Maghreb (Algeria, Morocco, Tunisia) is, today, more than ever, moulded by the movement, displacement, and *placelessness* of Maghrebi authors.[7]

Afropolitan Moroccan literature of French expression in the twenty-first century

Although scholars of the Moroccan novel could cite many contemporary authors as exemplary of those whose themes reflect an Afropolitan sense of being-in-the-world, authors Fouad Laroui and Youssouf Amine Elalamy best characterize contemporary writing from the country. Both authors are examples of the transnational, cosmopolitan writer who writes in-between the continent and elsewhere – Europe, Morocco, and the United States.[8] These authors, in particular, are at the forefront of a new generation of Moroccan author whose oeuvre is not 'rigid of form or governed by conventions of a single genre'. Quite the contrary, their works 'appear as crucibles of interdisciplinary knowledge of all kinds: historical, political, customary, philosophical, sociological' (Kabale 2011, 25). Fouad Laroui lives full-time in Europe but visits Morocco frequently. Youssouf Amine Elalamy (popularly known as YAE) is based in Rabat and travels the world both as an author and visual artist. Elalamy and Laroui are Afropolitan authors and humanists who posit themes that extend beyond the boundaries of Moroccan-centred tropes to engage with some of the most thought-provoking issues of our era.[9] Both writers act as 'guides', *engagés* intellectuals in the true Sartrean sense, as they seek to instruct readers about the sociocultural hurdles of our global age. They offer an Afropolitan, global humanist perspective that interrogates the realities, misconceptions, and challenges facing not only contemporary Moroccans but all of us living as global citizens in the twenty-first century.

Moroccan literature of French expression has followed the same paths as other African literatures in its development. First-generation authors such as Driss Chraïbi, Itzhak D. Knafo, and Mohamed Aziz Lahbabi, writing prose and poetry immediately before, during, and after independence (specifically the years 1954–1966), thematically focused on promoting a strong, nation state as a single source of national identity. Authors of the second generation (1966–1999) established a voice of resistance against what they considered a repressive political regime. Poets Abdellatif Laâbi and Abraham Serfaty, founders of the literary magazine *Souffles*, challenged the monarchy and paid with prison time. Authors, poets, and philosophers Abdelkébir Khatibi, Mohamed Aloui, Abdallah Bensmain, Noureddine Bousfiha, to name only a few, used the pen to explore new forms of sociocultural and political alienation in their societies. In the 1980s Moroccan women began writing in impressive numbers, challenging what had been a predominately masculine realm. Works by Halima Ben Haddou, Farida Elhany, and Badia Hadj Nasser set the tone for later authors Souad Bahéchar, Touria Oulehri, Siham Benchekroun, and Rita El Khayat, writing in the 1990s–2000s.[10]

At no other time in Moroccan literary history has writing in French been so prolific.[11] Moroccan scholar Abdallah Alaoui Mdarhri suggests in his study of Moroccan literature from 1950–2003 that the 'nouvelle génération' of authors writing in the twenty-first century has distinguished itself by breaking with the national discourse of the early post-independence era in order to link the marginalized, contemporary individual with the 'devenir' – the becoming – of his/her contemporary society (Mdarhri 2006, 10). Even as Moroccan writing in French entered the 1990s, it reflected the shifting tides of the sociocultural and political climate at the end of King Hassan II's reign. Several years before Hassan II's death in 1999, Moroccan writing revealed a country on the verge of significant transformations that included looking outside its borders to engage with the ever-increasing globalization of our era. Author Touria Oulehri thinks that sociopolitical transitions in the 1990s also impacted the way Moroccans, in general, and authors specifically, felt about themselves, individualism, and the possibility of a more open society.[12] Autobiographical introspection became a means also through which to critique the state and societal norms as evidenced in novels such as Siham Benchekroun's *Oser Vivre!* ('Dare to live', 2002), now in its third edition. Although the author's work is seemingly autobiographical, predominately using the first person 'je' (I) to tell her story, she also reveals an 'elle' (she), who confronts the collective hypocrisy the author believes is inherent in Moroccan society. Benchekroun emphasizes that the larger community mandates that a woman sacrifice her identity and her independence for the sake of her family and the patriarchal status quo. Her novel considers the overarching sociocultural transitions that began at the end of the 1990s. The political debates of the late 1990s that eventually fostered government reforms of the *Moudawana* (or Family Code) in 2004 are the backdrop to the author's story.[13] Benchekroun's (2002) novel announced the later political reforms instigated by King Mohammed VI in 2004 that ultimately emancipated women legally in many areas of the law. She also condemns the daily societal encumbrances faced by women in a hyper-patriarcal society: 'Au Maroc, la rue n'appartenait pas aux femmes, la nuit n'appartenait pas aux femmes. Les seuls espaces de détente devaient être privés pour être féminins ou n'être que féminins pour supporter les femmes' (In Morocco, the street didn't belong to women, the night didn't belong to women. The only spaces in which to relax had to be private to be feminine or could only be feminine to sustain women) (Benchekroun 2002, 197).

The fields of post-colonial studies and cultural studies, new to English departments in the Moroccan university system, have also influenced French and Arabic literature departments by encouraging interest in the diverse contemporary literatures of Morocco. Although still limited in number, Moroccan students of French expression pursuing their university studies in literature today read Touria Oulehri, Bahaa Trabelsi, Rida Lamrini, and Abdellah Taïa in addition to the canonical authors Driss Chraïbi, Tahar Ben Jelloun, and Edmond Amran El-Maleh. Rachid Chraïbi, chief editor at Marsam Editions, stresses that no theme or debate is too sensitive for the francophone novel. He takes pride in the fact that the novels he publishes 'reflètent la société' (reflect society) and that they constantly enrich debates in politics and influence socio-cultural mores in and outside of the classroom and the nation.[14]

Moroccan authors of French expression repeatedly enter the realm of the 'unsaid' and the 'unsayable' – the *non-dit* – of subjects often deemed a few years before to be too controversial to tackle in novels. Explorations of uncharted waters, by both men and women, have opened up discussion of subjects that continually push the borders of sociocultural convention. Authors, such as the openly gay Rachid O. and Abdellah Taïa, '[donnent] un coup de pied au ventre mou de la littérature marocaine' (kick the soft stomach of Moroccan literature), declares a journalist in a special issue of *TelQuel: Le Maroc tel qu'il est*, the daring, leftist weekly news magazine written exclusively in French. Abdellah Taïa, one of Morocco's most outspoken gay francophone authors, constantly emphasizes that thanks to the French language he was able to emerge somewhat from self-censorship: 'Je n'ai jamais fait un "coming out" à proprement parler. C'est juste qu'en écrivant, je ne pouvais pas faire l'impasse sur cet aspect de ma personnalité' (I never 'came out' in the true sense. With writing, I could not help explore this aspect of my personality) ('Retrospective' 2006, 27). *TelQuel*'s special edition, *Le Best of TelQuel 2006*, declares Taïa to be one of the 50 young, vibrant trailblazers who 'feront le Maroc de demain ... Incha'Allah' (will make the Morocco of tomorrow ... God willing) (Benchemsi 2006, 39). The men and women highlighted in this feature story were, at the time, all between the ages of 21 and 35. They represent the Moroccan hopes and dreams of tomorrow as they shape today's society in the arts, media, business, science, and technology. The article suggests that Abdellah Taïa, who lives both in France and Morocco, like all who are featured, 'bouscul[e] les idées, les vieux, la religion, le confort de l'hypocrisie' (shake up ideas, old people, religion, the comfort of hypocrisy) so that Moroccans will realize that 'ils sont prisonniers de traditions, créées depuis des millénaires, aujourd'hui dépassées' (that they are prisoners of traditions created centuries ago, and out of date today) (Benchemsi 2006, 54). These authors also turn outward to connect with the socio-economic and political events of our time. Terrorism, the Arab Spring, the collapse of Western economies, and the impact of that collapse on Africa, are all subjects of contemporary writing.

Transnational and cosmopolitan: the works of Youssouf A. Elalamy and Fouad Laroui

Elalamy and Laroui's version of being-in-the-world as Afropolitan authors is cast in the mould of Edward Said's notion of 'worldliness' as described in *Humanism and Democratic Criticism*

(2004), the last tome Said wrote before his death. The worldliness inherently found in the Afropolitan novels of Morocco, in general, exemplifies a new phase of North African writing in French. It is a body of literature whose themes extend beyond the well-known tropes of the postcolonial era: the tensions between former colonizer and colonized, the legacy of the French school system and its imprint on the postcolonial nation, the failed mythology and ideology of decolonized nation states, and the isolation and depravation experienced by Maghrebi immigrant communities in France and elsewhere across Western Europe.[15] The new era of transnational, Afropolitan Maghrebi writing encompasses the sociopolitical and human challenges of our time and tends not to dwell on the historical divisions and events of the past. The millennial francophone Moroccan novel is indicative of a new *littérature-monde* which reflects, as Michel Le Bris and Jean Rouad had defined in their work, *Pour une littérature-monde* (2007):

> a new literature, noisy, busy, colored, bi-racial, which announces the world as it is being born … where cultures from every continent mix and mélange … it's a larger, stronger idea of literature, once again finding its ambition to utter the world, to give a sense to existence, to question the human condition, to drive each one of us to the most inner secret of ourselves. *Littérature-monde* … is the giving birth of a new world. (Le Bris and Rouad 2007, 41)[16]

Indeed the assumptions and proscriptions that, for example, Fouad Laroui makes with respect to the universalisms of human nature put into context what is most interesting about this new generation of globalized, non-nationalist, transnational writing of French expression.

Both Fouad Laroui and Youssouf A. Elalamy are writing to reflect a *Littérature-monde* that encapsulates the spirit of Mbembe's Afropolitan transnationalism. Anthony Appiah's work on transnational authors (2002) also constructs a literary framework through which to consider the contemporary Moroccan author as a 'cosmopolitan patriot' who:

> can entertain the possibility of a world in which everyone is a rooted cosmopolitan, attached to a home of his or her own, with its own cultural particularities, but taking pleasure from the presence of other, different, places that are home to other, different, people. (22)

Youssouf Amine Elalamy's *Oussama, mon amour* (2011)

In February 2011, Youssouf Amine Elalamy, known for his novels in French and Darija (Moroccan colloquial Arabic), published *Oussama, mon amour.* Elalamy uses as subjects the global events and pressing social issues of his time that are of concern to Moroccans as 'citizens of Africa' and the world (Mbembe 2008). His most recent novel dwells on the last moments of a young suicide bomber's existence before he blows himself up in an upscale hotel in the middle of a bustling city (which is never named). The narrative is compelling on many levels in our contemporary era where the political repercussions of 9/11 and the subsequent War on Terror have left their marks on generations to come. As French philosopher Jean Baudrillard pointed out in his article 'L'ésprit du terrorisme', written two months after the 9/11 attacks, 'Terrorism, like viruses, is everywhere'. Since 9/11, there has been 'a world diffusion of terrorism that functions as the shadow of any system of domination, everywhere ready to awaken as a double agent. It inhabits the very heart of the culture that battles it'. Terrorism 'secretly coincides with the internal fracture to the dominant system' (2002, 406). Thus, it is not unique to either the Arab-East or the European-West, and its guise is not always one of religious fundamentalism; a point that Elalamy drives home in his narrative.

In June 2011, during the presentation of his most recent work at the Bibliothèque Nationale de Rabat, Elalamy emphasized that his novel, although published earlier in the year and focusing on the universal idea of terrorism, and not specifically 'intégrisme religieux' (religious fundamentalism) in Morocco, seemed to predict events to come. On 21 April 2011, a young 'intégriste' (Islamic fundamentalist) exploded a bomb in the Argane café in a popular tourist area in

Marrakech. The blast killed 12 people, most of whom were foreigners. Although trying not to allude to terrorism in Morocco as always Islamic and always fundamentalist, Elalamy recognized that if his book had been slated for publication after the blast, it would never have seen the light of day, because, as he notes, 'la littérature est collée aux actualités' (literature is stuck to news events). 'Je ne voulais pas l'image stéreotype du kamikaze qui se filme une dernière fois avant l'acte' (I didn't want the stereotypical image of a suicide bomber who films himself for the last time before the act).[17] Yet, if the novel had been published after the event, YAE would have been seen as profiting from the violence.

Elalamy's novel is complex and told from multiple angles in chapters describing flashbacks that could be from anywhere at any time – characterizing the last moments of a religious fanatic, a Timothy McVey, or a self-promoting Unabomber like Ted Kaczynski. Elalamy told me that essentially he wrote the chapters out of sequence in order to make sure the past and present would fuse in the middle, right at the point of the blast. Chaos becomes an ordered series of events as each protagonist – each piece of the puzzle – tells his/her story: Mstafa (the bomber), Mina the prostitute, and Mstafa's sometime-girlfriend, Mjido, the victim, and Brahim, the bomber's father. Morocco is never identified as the specific place of the events (indeed the city and country are never named), and Mstafa professes no religious convictions propelling him to commit his act, which he carries out alone without affiliations to al-Qaeda or any particular ideology. The overall tone of the narrative attempts to draw on universalisms about human nature and Man's will to self-destruct. The storyline dwells on the idea of 'terror as terror', something of human making, as Baudrillard suggests: 'Terror against terror, there is no more ideology behind this. One is, from this point forward, far beyond ideology and politics. No ideology, no cause – not even the Islamic one – can explain the energy that feeds terror' (Baudrillard 2002, 406). Although Elalamy's novel is meant to pronounce universalisms about terrorism and human nature, Morocco is haunted by bombings in Marrakech in 2011 and in Casablanca in 2003 and 2007. These violent incidents are eerily present between the lines. The Casablanca bombings, committed by the al-Qaeda off-shoot *Safia Jilihadia* group, killed over 45 people and left scores wounded.

Elalamy's novel is not solely about a suicide bomber. The work also universally references the lives of contemporary youth who are disenfranchised, wandering in countless countries with limited prospects. The marginalization of young people is often an overarching theme in his novels, particularly *Les Clandestins* (2000). The universal views found in *Oussama, mon amour* that reflect the author's concern about acts of terrorism again recall Baudrillard's early post-9/11 essay: 'Suicidal terrorism is the terrorism of the have nots' (Baudrillard 2002, 411). Elalamy's protagonist is a young man, poor, destitute, and marginalized, without a future, whose violent act will assure him a few minutes of notoriety before being effaced into obscurity, like so many others. It is not religious fanaticism, but destitution and lack of hope that push Mstafa to take his life and those of others. Death for death's sake in 15 minutes of Andy Warhole fame. The sacrificial death is one of 'brutal irruption' and 'of death live, in real time' and because it is such a brutal 'irruption', it is 'more than real … [it is] symbolic and sacrificial' this, Baudrillard notes, is 'the spirit of terrorism' (2002, 408).

To become one among the 'living dead', impoverished and without hope, is to become a terrorist. Mstafa is like 'la pastèque' (the watermelon), inert, unfeeling, which 'n'a pas de tête, pas d'abdomen, ni de bras; elle n'a pas même un cœur qui bat à l'intérieur … la pastèque n'a rien, seulement un visage enfoui à l'intérieur et qui cache bien son jeu. Le corps de la pastèque est son visage' (has neither head nor stomach nor arms; it doesn't even have a heart inside to beat … the watermelon doesn't have anything, only a face buried inside which hides so well its game. The watermelon's body is its face) (Elalamy 2011, 11). Yet, as Mstafa notes, its insides are spattered so well when blown apart. Before embarking on his mission, Mstafa shaves all the hair off his body. He enters a 'becoming watermelon' an identity that allows him, as he says, to 'quitter ce monde comme j'y suis venu' (leave this world as I entered it), like a newborn (2011, 13).

Oussama, the signatory name in the title of the book, often spelled three different ways in the West depending on what language is used, is a name which is not given to Mstafa by Mina, his girlfriend. Although she does compare him to her fantasy television hero whose eerie resemblance to the real Ousama Bin Laden (in English) and/or Ousama Bin Ladin or Ousama Ben Laden (in French) is subtly suggested, she never identifies him as a suicide bomber:

> Bon, il ne vaut pas mon Oussama, mais bel homme quand même. Disons qu'il y a une petite ressemblance avec le mien, les yeux, le front, et peut-être même la bouche, tiens. En revanche, pas un poil sur le visage. Remarque, qu'est-ce que j'en sais moi, sa barbe il la portrait peut-être ailleurs ....
>
> (Well, he isn't my Oussama, but a fine looking man all the same. There is a slight resemblance with mine, the eyes, the forehead, and maybe the mouth, perhaps. But, not a hair on his face. But, what do I know, maybe he wore his beard before, somewhere else...) (Elalamy 2011, 19)

Mina is a young woman who has decided that prostitution is the only life she can lead in order to live. Mina's fascination with Oussama (of course alluding to Bin Laden) metaphorically calls our attention to Western rhetoric that always links terrorism to Eastern/Arab or Islamicized names. Again, Elalamy plays a paradoxical role of denouncing Islamic terrorism, while also trying to discuss the heinous act as a universal one. Terrorism is a possibility that looms large in disenfranchised and disconnected sectors of all societies today; from Marrakech 2011 to Boston 2013. The author explores the name 'Oussama', even on the cover of his novel, in order to make a point about the Western, negative associations made at the expense of Arab peoples. Terrorism-Bin-Laden-Radical-Islam, we find out in the testimonies of victims, witnesses, and through the confession of the culprit of Elalamy's novel, is moulded from free associations with no merit. Promoting or denouncing Islamic radicalism has no place in the author's prose. The challenges facing young people, Elalamy opines, are due to the lack of social mobility, access to education, and to a voice in society. Such a 'drôle de poisson' (strange fish), Mina remarks, is really the defining characteristic of Mstafa: 'pas du tout méchant comme sur la photo à la télé. Bon, il ne vaut pas mon Oussama, mais bel homme quand même' (not at all mean like in the photo on TV. Well, he's not up to par with my Oussama, but a nice looking man all the same) (2011, 19). This suicide bomber has his own terror to live with and to use. His own death belt, 'cette ceinture' full of explosives 'est [sa] petite guerre à [lui]' (his little own war), and it is also his 'haine' (hate), his cry, and his voice: 'je veux qu'on [m]'entende pour une fois' (I want them to hear me for once) (2011, 31).

And what of the victims? Elalamy shows us that these are also universal archetypes. One suicide bomber affects countless lives. Not only those implicated in the violent blast, but also the families he left behind, as attests Mstafa's father, Brahim, a butcher by trade who avows that he loved his son, but should have shown him more affection (2011, 117).

Elalamy's cover art (Figure 1) is interesting and calls attention to what extent acts of terrorism do affect countless lives – most notably, those of the suicide bomber's fellow citizens. He also underscores the fact that terrorism, as we have seen in the last few years (Sweden, Morocco, USA), most often comes from within, not from some outside force. The hand of Fatima, prominently displayed on Elalamy's cover – a collage of his own making (he is also a visual artist) – melds truncated faces. The faces denote one of a monster overlaid with another whose young eyes seem determinedly steadfast. The hand of Fatima is inscribed with the slogan 'touche pas à mon pays' (don't touch my country), an adaption of the 1980s anti-racism campaign in France 'touch pas à mon pote' (don't touch my pal). Immediately following the 2003 bombings, the Moroccan government placed the hand with the slogan on billboards across Morocco. The meaning evokes a certain brand of nationalism, formed to stand up to undesirables or those considered dangerous to

Figure 1. Cover art by Youssouf Amine Elalamy for his novel, *Oussama, mon amour* (2011).

national sovereignty. This slogan for Elalamy is troubling. In an essay, *Le Journal de YAE*, written immediately after the Casablanca bombings in May 2003 and the ensuing billboards, Elalamy notes in a chapter boldly capitalized with the heading, TOUCHE PAS À TON PAYS

(DON'T TOUCH YOUR COUNTRY), that the slogan has allowed for multiple exclusions and harassment by government officials based on religious association, social status, and political affiliations (Elalamy 2003). For example, he notes, immediately following the 2003 attacks, certain groups (for the most part, conservative Islamic ones) were barred from demonstrations and vigils organized for the victims of the terrorist attacks. Since the first bombings in 2003, Moroccan authorities and political institutions as well as the monarchy and King Mohamed VI have become increasingly hard-line:

> Dès l'instant où l'on accepte de dire *Ma tkich bladi* « Touche pas à *mon* Pays », toutes les dérives sont permises. … Sur le mode du désormais légendaire « Tous ceux qui ne sont pas avec nous sont contre nous » (G.W. Bush au lendemain des attentats du 11 septembre), on nous somme de choisir notre camp. …le « Touche pas à *mon* Pays » s'est vite transformé en un « Touche pas à *ma* marche », tout aussi discriminatoire que le premier.
>
> (The moment where we accept to say *Ma tkich bladi* 'Don't touch my country', all derivatives are allowed. … In the manner now legendary 'all those not with us, are against us' (G.W. Bush in the aftermath of the attacks of September 11), we are cowed into choosing our camp … the 'Don't touch my country' has quickly transformed into a 'hands off my demonstration', just as discriminatory as the first.) (Elalamy 2003, 6)

« Touche pas à mon pays » for Elalamy has become a slogan that, in its nationalism and inward retrenchment to the authoritarian realms of a hard-lined regime, is reminiscent of the despotic era of King Hassan II, known as *Les Années de plomb* (The Lead Years, 1963–1999). During this time, thousands of Moroccans were persecuted, went missing, and were tortured in prison. Elalamy believes that the state is now drawing its map from the crimes it committed in the past, promoting hate, intolerance, suspicion, exclusion, and relegating to the margins many who are protesting for their particular interests and causes. The bombings in Morocco's recent history have created social chaos and scepticism about contemporary incursions by state authority on the rights of the individual. Many of the questions Moroccans are asking themselves with respect to one's right to exercise his/her freedom of speech in the public space verses the state's right to control and maintain surveillance of citizens' free movement in that same space, are similar to the ones debated in the United States and throughout the West. Hence, Elalamy's Mstafa is a protagonist in an Afropolitan narrative that echoes throughout the globe:

> Paniqués, terrorisés, nous [tenons] l'autre à distance. Affolés, déroutés par ces crimes commis par des Marocains contre d'autres Marocains, nous sommes prêts à nous mutiler jusqu'aux parties saines de notre corps. Se peut-il que la passion citoyenne nous ait rendu schizophrènes au point de ne plus nous reconnaître?
>
> (Panicked, terrorized, we keep the other at a distance. Distraught, confused by these crimes committed by Moroccans against other Moroccans, we are ready to maim ourselves; even the healthiest parts of our body. Could it be that civic passion has made us schizophrenic to the point that we no longer recognize ourselves?) (2011, 3)

Elalamy's most recent novel posits the Afropolitan proclivity for questioning the priorities of African nations which have emerged from colonialism but which teeter on the brink (and often succumb to) totalitarianism: 'Those figures of sovereignty whose central project is not the struggle for autonomy but the generalized instrumentalization of human existence and the material destruction of human bodies and populations' (Mbembe 2003, 14). Elalamy's oeuvre also resonates with Western nations which, in order to justify the War on Terror, have forced their citizens to give up what we once thought were inalienable rights to freedom of speech, assembly, and political causes.

Fouad Laroui's *La Femme la plus riche du Yorkshire* (2008)

In novels such as *La Femme la plus riche du Yorkshire* (2008) and the earlier, *Méfiez-vous des parachutistes* (1999), Fouad Laroui demonstrates that today's contemporary Moroccan narrative is universal, linking the individual to the greater, global collective. In *La Femme la plus riche du Yorkshire*, leading protagonist Adam Serghini, from the 'small town of Essaouria' on the Atlantic coast of Morocco, decides to leave his homeland in order to 'see other countries and try to understand the world … understand the world, in all its diversity and its richness, in all its languages, its colours and its sounds. Read it, live it, listen to it breathe, taste it…' (2008, 8). His mission as a humanist–*homme du monde* and self-professed 'ethnologue' (ethnologist) is to capture the essence of what it means to be human without having to define his identity by static conceptions of nation, ethnicity, and class. His being-in-the-world does truly depend on a '*Being-already-alongside* with others'. Laroui's conception of being is one '*fascinated by* the world with which it is concerned' (Heidegger 1962, 88).[18] Adam's fascination with those around him is cultivated by his self-professed role of 'enquêteur' (researcher) as he explains why he decided to travel to England and, subsequently, spend most of his time at the local pub named the Blue Bell. Laroui peppers Adam's French with the occasional English word to denote the cosmopolitan, multilingualism of his Moroccan traveller:

> l'essentiel, son projet secret, c'est qu'il voulait *comprendre l'Anglais*. Fascinant, l'Anglais ! On connaissait le Peul, on subodorait le Soussi, on disséquait le Papou, mais l'*English*? Certes, des préjugés circulaient, des portraits, des croquis tracés sur l'ouï-dire et la mauvaise foi ; on le disait ambigu ou inverti, du côté de Tanger, on le croyait riche à Marrakech, on l'imaginait fou à Essaouira ; mais Adam Serghini voulait du *visu*, du vécu, du humé du furtivement palpé. Il alla donc voir, *in situ*, ne haïssant ni les voyages ni les explorations…Il ne lui avait fallu que quelques jours pour découvrir où se nichent l'âme, la vérité profonde, l'essence de cette ethnie mystérieuse : au pub ! [19]

> (The most important, his secret project, is that he wanted to *understand the English*. Fascinating, the English. One knows the Fulani, one is suspicious of the Soussi, one dissects the Papuan, but the *English*? Certainly, prejudices have circulated, portraits, sketches drawn on hearsay and bad faith … we think of him as ambiguous or introverted in Tangiers, as rich in Marrakech, or we imagine him crazy in Essaouira; but Adam Serghini wanted from firsthand experiences, the freshness of the stealthily palpated. He therefore went to see, *in situ*, not being adverse to trips or explorations … He only needed a few days to discover where the soul, deep truth, the essence of this mysterious ethnicity resided: at the pub!) (Laroui 2008, 10–11)

The plot of *La femme la plus riche du Yorkshire*, if there really is one, centres on Adam Serghini, who is a Moroccan PhD economist, former intern in France, invited to England by an unnamed university in Yorkshire. While wholeheartedly welcomed by his colleagues at the university, applauded for his knowledge and intellect, as well as recognized for his multiculturality (he has studied in France and speaks English), his interaction with the locals, most particularly in the local pub, is much more problematic. Understanding 'l'Anglais' (the Englishman/woman) as well as 'l'Anglais' (English, the language) are synonymously intertwined for the young researcher. Adam reverses Western conceptions about the Arab-Other onto the English-other, collapsing what he knows from earlier contact with the English in Morocco into a master stereotyping narrative of his own making. Yet, not wanting to accept the credo of this stereotype, he decides to travel to ground zero to really understand and form his own conclusions about the English.

Mistaken for being French with an Italian name (Morocco is just too far off the radar to be comprehended by the colourful band of English *petite monde* he frequents), Adam is constantly confronted with his otherness in the land of 'Shakespeare and Hamlet'. When mistaken for being French, he professes 'No, I'm Moroccan', much to the disappointment of the white-Anglos he meets. 'Hein? Comment? *What*? Vous n'êtes pas français?' (What? You aren't French?) is generally uttered in dismay, particularly by women (2008, 29). Adam is constantly caught in the trap of being from nowhere and everywhere. Certainly his name, he remarks in a conversation with a fellow pub buddy, connotes his cosmopolitanism, as a traveller destined to be a *passepart-out* (someone from everywhere and nowhere):

> Adam Serghini … c'est français ça? On dirait un nom italien. – *Not exactly*, lui dit-il, très fier. Adam, c'est dans toutes les langues du monde. Quant à Serghini, ça vient peut-être des rivages phéniciens ou du Nil, ou de la péninsule Arabique, on ne sait pas vraiment, les invasions l'ont fait connaitre un peu partout dans le monde. C'est ainsi – porté par des chameaux – que ce nom est arrivé chez nous, dans notre pays.
>
> (Adam Serghini … that's French? Seems Italian. Not exactly, he responds proudly. Adam is a name in every language of the world. As for Serghini, it comes perhaps from the Phoenician shores of the Nile, or the Arabian peninsula, we're not really sure, the invasions made it known almost everywhere in the world. That's how – brought on the backs of camels – the name arrived here, in your country.) (Laroui 2008, 28)

While realizing that he is not *chez lui* and that 'when in Rome' he had better 'do as the Romans', he nevertheless acknowledges that there are certain misconceptions promoted by the Occidental that he cannot let go and, on the contrary, must dispel. Upon meeting Cordelia, the richest 'Femme' of Yorkshire (owner of several upscale boutiques 'very, *très chics*'), his ire reaches its tipping point (2008, 13). Her Western arrogance, lack of respect for those who are not rich, white, and from the upper echelons of British high society, encourage Adam to begin his work as 'un ethnologue'. He decides to conduct 'une enquête', a study of the village dwellers in order to try to fathom the stereotypes confronting him and others from elsewhere. Cordelia – who Adam renames Cruella – is a metaphor for the colonial past, while also symbolically representing the neocolonial present and the racism, the miscomprehension, and the ignorance of the West; certainly whenever the Arab-African diaspora is the topic du jour. She accuses him of being a 'parasite', as the orientalist-essentializing overtones of her conversation confront him head on: 'L'Arabe est le parasite du chameau' (the Arab is the camel's parasite), she tells him. Adam responds, telling her that he has never seen a camel in his life. Yet, despite this fact, he states, 'cette bestiole [me] colle à la peau dans l'imaginaire de certains Européens' (this animal sticks to [me] in the imaginary of certain Europeans) (Laroui 2008, 133).

Adam, as a cosmopolitan researcher, must take the high road to combat the ignorant and the unschooled. The novel, thus, is not about the formation of a young man from his experiences in Europe, but about the ignorance he confronts in the West rooted in our contemporary, post-9/11 times. In a reversal of the *bildungsroman*, Adam takes it upon himself to change the West before it alters him. As a global humanist he is willing to let some things go – adapting, for example, to bad English food, 'les champignons insipides, cuites à l'eau tiede' (insipid mushrooms boiled in warm water) served up by his hosts at the bed and breakfast where he is staying – but there are issues, larger in scale, that he must challenge. The power of his eloquence and Afropolitan worldview are rooted in strong principles: 'Il n'y a que sur les principes généraux, ce qui transcende les nations et les ethnies, ce qui ne concerne que l'être humain, que je me permets d'avoir un avis. La cruauté, par exemple, est inacceptable' (there are only on general principles, that which transcends nations and ethnicities, that which only concerns the human being, on which I allow myself to have an opinion. Cruelty, for example, is unacceptable) (Laroui 2008, 68).

Adam quickly discovers that the British subjects he visits are staid, fixed in time, and unchanging in their rigidity as well as their capacity to stereotype others. The pub is the place where Adam finds all the answers to what it means to be English. It is the quintessential locus of what being English means to the Moroccan traveller/tourist/ethnologist: 'les pubs qui suintent un doux renoncement à l'Empire et au Commonwealth … c'est là où il faut être' (pubs which ooze a sweet rejection of the Empire and of the Commonwealth … that's where one must be

… that's where you have to be) (Laroui 2008, 12). Adam notes that it is 'in the shadows' of the interior of the Blue Bell where he finds 'his refuge' (2008, 12).

Laroui's novel exemplifies current, Moroccan francophone authors' investment into the *littérature-monde* of our millennium. His is a worldly text, that according to Edward Said, 'allow[s] us to take account not of eternally stable or supernaturally informed values, but rather of the changing … values and human life that are now fully upon us in the new century' (2008, 61). Laroui's Afropolitanism connotes the image of being both inside/outside culture, language, and semantics at the same time. His identity is construed through constant movement and displacement, as he engages with multiple languages and experiences in diverse nations.

Fouad Laouri's protagonist, Adam, reflects the author's own transnational wanderings. The author is a Moroccan economics and physics professor at the University of Amsterdam, where he has lived for the past 15 years, teaching in Dutch and English but writing his novels in French. What is intriguing about *La Femme la plus rich du Yorkshire* is that it is a novel set in Britain, written in French by a Moroccan. Its semi-autobiographical narrative exemplifies a being-in-the-world that is conceptualized in 'placelessness', wherein the protagonist is neither rooted in his homeland nor the host nation. Laroui's novel breaks with traditional francophone Maghrebi novels (spanning an era from the late 1950s to the end of the 1990s) whose themes explored the geographical and psychological tensions of the French-North African context both during and after colonialism. These works include Driss Chraibi's *Les Boucs* (1955), Albert Memmi's *Agar* (1955), Assia Djebar's *La Soif* (1957), and the later Beur,[20] novels contesting the abject parameters of assimilation in France: Mehdi Charef's *Thé au harem d'Archimed* (1983), Leila Houari's, *Zeida de nulle part* (1985) and Azzouz Begag's, *Le Gone du chaâba* (1986). In the global cosmopolitan context, Laroui's narrative is not about the trials and tribulations of exile or the arduous immigrant experience of assimilation in Europe, because Adam Serghini has no intention of staying long in Britain, or anywhere for that matter.

Fouad Laroui's Afropolitan narrative performs two functions as it breaks with past canonical scripts associated with the 'immigrant-in-Europe' trope offered by many postcolonial authors from francophone North Africa writing from the 1950s to the 2000s.[21] First, by setting his character in Britain, the narrative refutes the traditional, immigrant paradigms of North African communities living in French cities, or *les banlieues*, marginalized, ghettoized areas we all know so well as the recognizable backdrops of numerous beur/banlieue novels by authors writing in France such as Mehdi Charef, Azzouz Begag, Soraya Nini, Farida Benghoul, among others. Second, Laroui's novel establishes a space that defines an opening up to the world – a worldly narrative based on one individual's being-in-the-world – as Adam's identity is formed by the transnational experience he lives. In short, he is what he is because of his constant placelessness. Adam's identity is rooted in his ability to 'self-locate' anywhere. His very placelessness gives him agency because he does not have to kowtow to any norms of integration (Ghosh and Sarkar 1995–1996, 106). Adam's *being-in-the-world* is established by being everywhere and nowhere in the world. His community is everyone and no one at the same time. His languages are Arabic, French, and English. He is not 'exiled', but rather *exilic*, to borrow Said's conception of the term evoking displacement – a 'willed homelessness … a good way [to live] … for one who wishes to earn a proper love for the world' (Said 1983, 7).

As Laroui demonstrates, exile in our contemporary times is not always negative, but a venue through which to discover an immense wealth of human possibilities. The author, living between two cultures, discovers a means through which to self-actualize and to explore self-understanding and self-realization through the liberation of exile. This self-actualization for Adam Serghini means that he realizes to what extent the West holds little superior knowledge for him and is, more often than not, full of ignorance. When discussing his origins with Cordelia/Cruella, Adam runs headlong into the limits of exasperation. When she realizes that he is not French, she accuses him of lying her. Her diatribe against the young man is atrocious. In one scene she categorizes Adam in all the possible Arab stereotypes fabricated by the Western world. Cruella screams: '*So you lied to me*!: Tu m'as menti!' (both in English and French in the original): '*Your Prophet was a bad man*' (written in English): 'Il a épousé une gamine de six ans. Votre roi Bourguiba est un tyran. Le Nil n'est pas le plus long fleuve du monde, c'est l'Amazone … Vous ne produisez pas les meilleurs chameaux du monde' (He married a girl of six. Your king Bourguiba is a tyrant. The Nile is not the longest river in the world, it's the Amazon. …You don't produce the best camels in the world) (Laroui 2008, 11).

Laouri's mixing of French and English in the text alludes to his credo that the Moroccan author lives a life of 'l'acrobatie linguistique' (acrobatic linguistics). While the use of French today in Morocco is generally viewed as a choice, every novel Laroui writes does evoke the inherent linguistic conundrums faced by all Maghrebi authors. When using the 'Other's' language, particularly when writing from the Arab world, authors often wonder what Western language they should choose, since most people (both authors and readers) do not have sufficient command of modern standard Arabic to read and write in it. This fact is explored in an essay Laroui wrote in English, entitled *The Curse of the Moroccan Writer*, published by a small press in Morocco in 2011. His essay outlines the diglossic space he and others must negotiate when taking up the pen to write in a Western language (Laroui 2011, 10). The uniqueness of Morocco, or what has become known as *l'exception marocaine* (usually used to describe Morocco's uniqueness in political terms), extends even to the realm of its literary polyglotism. Fouad Laroui's *plurilingue* (plural lingual) notion stems from earlier works by Moroccan author and philosopher Abdelkebir Khatibi, notably *Amour bilingue* (1983 a) and *Maghreb pluriel* (1983 b). In *Maghreb pluriel*, Khatibi remarks that the Maghreb is inherently cosmopolitan and proposes that Moroccan authors use a 'pensée-autre' (another way of thinking) to explore their being-in-the-world; a being that is always situated between three geographical locations, multiple languages, and cultural registers:

> En fait, il n'y a pas de choix. Il faudrait penser le Maghreb tel qu'il est, site topographique entre l'Orient, l'Occident et l'Afrique, et tel qu'il puisse se mondialiser pour son propre compte. D'une certaine manière, ce mouvement est depuis toujours en marche … il faut écouter le Maghreb résonner dans sa pluralité (linguistique, culturelle, politique) … seul le dehors repensé, décentré, subverti, détourné de ses déterminations dominantes, peut nous éloigner des identités et des différences informulées.
>
> (In fact, there is no choice. One must think of the Maghreb as it is, a topographical site between the East, the West and Africa and how it can globally become on its own. In a certain way, this movement has always been happening … We have to listen to the Maghreb resonate in its plurality (linguistically, culturally, politically) … only the outside, rethought, de-centered, subverted, derailed from its dominant determinations, can keep us away from endemic identities and differences.) (Khatibi 1983b, 39)

Fouad Laroui's writing, thus, evokes Khatibi's decentredness, espousing a Moroccan polytransnationalism that extends beyond the Maghreb. He enjoys his 'placelessness' in the world, at the crossroads of East, West, and African, as he engages a new and Other-way of thinking. Laroui explores his version of a *pensée-autre* in *The Curse of the Moroccan Writer*:

> The Moroccan writer, (unlike his counterpart writing in English in the West) … is confronted with … serious problems. To begin with, there is the question of language, more precisely of diglossia. All Arabs, without exception – though to differing degrees – speak one language (their dialect) and write another (Classical Arabic). (2011, 19)

Laouri's study asks the essential question: 'So what's left for the Moroccan writer who insists on taking up the pen? Those who do so in Arabic form an elite who write for an elite', since most Moroccans are not fluent enough in Classical Arabic to write or read novels using it (2011, 19). Using one of the dialects of the Maghreb is not an option, because, again, who will read it and how will his work be marketed outside his home country? Additionally, Laroui notes, Berber, the language of many Moroccans, is just a non-starter: 'I'm Berber. For me, Classical Arabic is just as much a foreign language as French' (2011, 19). The author concludes, noting that: 'The Moroccan writer [therefore] uses the language of the Other or the language of others: either way, it's mission impossible…Eppur, si muove' as he turns to French, English, Spanish, or German to express his prose (2011, 19). This polylinguistic conundrum has shaped Fouad Laroui's, as well as most Moroccan contemporary authors', conception of being-in-the-world. Their Afropolitanism is spawned from the very nature of this multicultural and polylingual space that makes-up the Moroccan author's environment.

Laroui's *La Femme la plus riche du Yorkshire* compels readers to realize that although the Afropolitan author can write in the Other's language, it does not always mean he will really understand the cultural paradigms intertwined with this language. This is the lesson that Adam takes away with him at the end of the novel. In the closing pages, Cordelia, although manipulative and wealthy, cannot escape abandonment by her daughters and Adam's refusal to make love to her. As she weeps in despair, he comforts her, noting the strange picture they make: 'L'Etranger consolant l'Autochtone' (the foreigner consoling the autochthon) (2008, 148). He closes her door and escapes her wrath; metaphorically escaping the Western yoke that has assimilated and effaced Others for centuries.

Adam's being-in-the-world is formed by his refusal to be a doormat or attached to the hostile environment in which Cordelia/Cruella has ensnared him. Although his study of the people of Yorkshire has ended, he still admits that as far as the English are concerned, 'il n'a toujours rien compris' (he still hasn't understood anything) (Laroui 2008, 150). As he sits in a public garden after the incident with Cordelia, he notices that the flowers in the flowerbed in front of him have curiously arranged themselves to say: 'FUCK OFF' (in English in the novel) (2008, 154). When he alerts the nearby gardener about the offensive language, noting that he would like to rearrange the flowers to say something less vulgar, the gardener tells him: 'Si vous le faites, je serai obligé d'appeler la police et vous serez arêté pour vandalisme. On prend ça très au sérieux, en Angleterre. Ce n'est pas le Sahara, ici, où les gens de votre sorte ont arraché toutes les fleurs. On voit le résultat' (If you do that, I'll have to call the police and you'll be arrested for vandalism. We take that very seriously here in Britain. This isn't the Sahara, where people like you pull up flowers. We've seen what that does) (2008, 157). Adam quips back, 'Si je comprends bien, la végétation jouit d'une sorte d'immunité en Angleterre? Elle peut insulter, diffamer, blasphemer' (If I get your meaning, vegetation here in England enjoys immunity? It can insult, defame, and utter blasphemy) (2008, 157). The gardener does not respond and walks away.

Adam notes the incident down in his study and takes the train back to Europe. Later, when those he visits ask him, 'What are the English like?', he answers: 'Ce sont des gens très polis. Quant au reste, je n'en sais rien' (They are polite. As for the rest, I can't tell) (2008, 158). Being unable to tell, or arrive at any definitive conclusions, is the essence of Laroui's novel. The placelessness of the author (and his protagonist) allows him to self-locate anywhere while he enjoys a being-in-the-world that is formed by the freedom of self-actualization and temporality – he is always in the space of *not knowing*. As a contemporary Moroccan, francophone author, who lives both in and outside his home country, Fouad Laouri offers a perspective that encourages readers to 'reflect on the very foundations of our civilization', on our commonalities and also our differences (Zimmerman 2004, 500). His work compels us to formulate ways to compromise in order to live as productive and compassionate citizens of the world. Understanding others, or at least trying to, requires going beyond the barriers of the socioculturally and nationally determined conceptions of identity of oneself and of others. In the new millennium, this is the spirit of Afropolitan Moroccan authors writing in French.

Notes

1. The list is certainly not limited to those authors writing in French. Authors writing in English such as Nigerian Helon Habila, Kenyans M.G. Vassanji and Shailja Patel, Libyan Hisham Matar, Zimbabwean Brian Chikwava, equally can be classed in the Afropolitan camp. See Makokha (2011).
2. Some examples of the most well-known African francophone works of the past which for the first time took to task the disenfranchisement of African immigrants in Europe are: *Les Boucs* (Driss Chraibi, 1955); *Le Docker noir* (Ousmane Sembene, 1950); *Un Nègre à Paris* (Bernard Dadié, 1959).
3. Heidegger's emphasis.
4. My translation.
5. My emphasis and translation.
6. Author's emphasis.
7. Maghrebi authors such as: Salim Bachi (Algeria), Souad Bahéchar (Morocco), Farid Yamina Benguigui (France/Algeria), Boudjellal (Algeria), Hajer Djilani (Tunisia), Youssouf Amine Elalamy (Morocco), Mohamed Leftha (Morocco), Edmond Amran El Maleh (Morocco), Nine Moati (Tunisia), Arussiyya Naluti (Tunisia), Leila Sebbar (Algeria), Abdellah Taia (Morocco), and Fawzia Zouari (Tunisia) have responded to the challenges of the twenty-first century in aesthetically and sociopolitically engaged ways that are remarkably different from those of the past. The themes of these authors represent the current trends, sociocultural and political tensions of the Maghreb in a myriad of manners that extend beyond the scope of this article.
8. Yet there are many more Moroccan authors who could be considered Afropolitan. See Orlando (2009).
9. These national themes are much more social-realist in nature, focusing on poverty, women's emancipation, and enfranchisement in society, corruption, and the tension between Islam and secular politics.
10. For a complete analysis of most of these texts, see Orlando (2009).
11. Authors writing in-country are published by the many small publishing houses in Morocco which specialize in printing novels, poetry, and essays in French. See Orlando (2009).
12. Interview with Touria Oulehri, Rabat, Morocco, 17 January 2007.
13. The *Moudawana* of 2004 basically brought women out of the dark ages as far as granting them rights to divorce and access to the judicial system. There have been several *Moudawanas* in the past, but the 2004 legislation has gone the farthest in granting rights to women under the law.
14. Interview with Rachid Chraïbi, Editor, Marsam Editions, 29 January 2007, Rabat, Morocco.
15. Think of earlier canonical first- and second-generation authors' texts such as Algerian Mouloud Feraoun's *Le Fils du pauvre* (1950), Moroccan Driss Chraïbi's *Le Passé simple* (1954), Mohamed Dib's *L'incendie* (1954), and Khateb Yacine's *Nedjma* (1956) and later, Beur and Banlieue, second-generation novels of authors such as Azzouz Begag, Nina Bouraoui, Mehdi Charef, and so on.
16. 'Une littérature nouvelle, bruyante, colorée, métissée, qui [prononce] le monde en train de naître…où se brass[ent] et se mêl[ent] les cultures de tous les continents… [c'est] une idée plus large, plus forte de la littérature, retrouvant son ambition de dire le monde, de donner un sens à l'existence, d'interroger la condition humaine, de reconduire chacun au plus secret de lui-même. La littérature-monde…[est] l'enfantement d'un monde nouveau' (Le Bris and Rouad 2007, 41).
17. 'Rencontre littéraire', Youssouf A. Elalamy, 7 June 2011, Bibliothèque nationale, Rabat.
18. Author's emphasis.
19. Author's emphasis.
20. Beurs, first generation sons and daughters of Maghrebi immigrants, were the first authors to write in French about their experiences stemming from a bicultural identity. Beur is the word 'Arabe' (in French) said backwards in the code language, *verlan,* popular with youth in France who live predominantly poor, disenfranchised, immigrant *banlieues* (neighborhoods) on the outskirts of large, urban centers.
21. The best examples of these are: Driss Charibi's *Les Boucs* (1955), Mehdi Charef's *Le Harki de Meryem* (1989), and Yamina Benguigui's *Inch'Allah Dimanche* (2001), to name only a few.

References

Aboulafia, Mitchell. 2001. *The Cosmopolitan Self: George Herbert Mead and Continental Philosophy.* Urbana: Illinois University Press.

Appiah, Anthony Kwame. 2002. "Cosmopolitan Patriots." In *For Love of Country?: A New Democracy Forum on the Limits of Patriotism*, edited by Martha Nussbaum, 22–29. New York: Beacon Press.

Baudrillard, Jean. 2002. "L'esprit du terrorisme." *The South Atlantic Quarterly* 101 (2), Spring: 165–202.

Begag, Azouz. 1986. *Le gone du Chaâba*. Paris: Éditions du Seuil, Collection Virgule.

Benchekroun, Siham. 2002. *Oser vivre!* Casablanca: Eddif.
Benchemsi, Ahmed. 2006. "Les 50 qui feront le Maroc de demain." *TelQuel* (Special Issue), Dec.: 39–50.
Benguigui, Yamina. 2001. *Inch' Allah Dimanche*. Paris: Albin Michel.
Chamoiseau, Patrick, Jean Bernabé, and Raphaël Confiant. 1993. *Eloge de la Créolité*. Paris: Gallimard/ Johns Hopkins Press.
Charef, Mehdi. 1983. *Le Thé au harem d'Archi Ahmed*. Paris: Mercure de France.
Chraïbi, Driss. 1955. *Les Boucs*. Paris: Denoël.
Chraïbi, Driss. 1954. *Le Passé simple*. Paris: Denoël.
Dadié, Bernard. 1959. *Un nègre á Paris*. Paris: Présence Africaine.
Djebar, Assia. 1957. *La Soif*. Paris: Julliard.
Dib, Mohamed. 1954. *L'incendie*. Paris: Seuil.
Elalamy, Youssouf Amine. 2000. *Les Clandestins*. Casablanca: Eddif.
Elalamy, Youssouf Amine. 2003. *Le Journal de YAE*. Bordeaux: Hors Champs.
Elalamy, Youssouf Amine. 2011. *Oussama, mon amour*. Casablanca: La croisée des chemins.
Feraoun, Mouloud. 1950. *Le Fils du pauvre*. Le Puy: Les Cahiers du Nouvel Humanisme.
Ghosh, Bishnupriya, and Bhaskar Sarkar. 1995–1996. "The Cinema of Displacement: Towards a Politically Motivated Poetics." *Film Criticism* 20 (1–2), Fall–Winter: 102–113.
Gikandi, Simon. 2011. "On Afropolitanism." In *Negotiating Afropolitanism: Essays on Borders and Spaces in Contemporary African Literature and Folklore*, edited by Jennifer Wawrzinek and J. K.S. Makokha, 9–13. Amsterdam: Rodopi.
Heidegger, Martin. 1962. *Being and Time*. New York: Harper Row.
Houari, Leila. 1985. *Zeida de nulle part*. Paris: L'Harmattan.
Kabale, Sim Kilosho. 2011. "Afropolitanism and Erudition in Francophone African Novels, 1994–2000." In *Negotiating Afropolitanism: Essays on Borders and Spaces in Contemporary African Literature and Folklore*, edited by Jennifer Wawrzinek and J. K. S. Makokha, 26–45. Amersterdam: Rodopi.
Khatibi, Abdelkebir. 1983a. *Amour bilingue*. Montpellier: Fata Morgana.
Khatibi, Abdelkebir. 1983b. *Maghreb Pluriel*. Paris: Denoel.
Laroui, Fouad. 1999. *Méfiez-vous des parachutistes*. Paris: Julliard.
Laroui, Fouad. 2008. *La Femme la plus riche de Yorkshire*. Paris: Julliard.
Laroui, Fouad. 2011. "Les Apories de l'hybridité maghrébine: une étude de *De Tous les Horizons* de Driss Chraïbi." *Contemporary French and Francophone Studies* 15(3), June: 313–320.
Laroui, Fouad. 2011. *The Curse of the Moroccan Writer*. Tangiers: Edition Dhbar Bladna.
Le Bris, Michel, and Jean Rouad. 2007. *Pour une littérature-monde*. Paris: Seuil.
Makokha, J. K. S. 2011. "Introduction: In the Spirit of Afropolitanism." *Negotiating Afropolitanism: Essays on Borders and Spaces in Contemporary African Literature and Folklore*, edited by Jennifer Wawrzinek and J. K. S. Makokha, 13–22. Amsterdam: Rodopi.
Mbembe, Achille. 2003. "Necropolitics." *Public Culture* 15 (1): 11–40.
Mbembe, Achille. 2008. "Afropolitanisme." *Africultures 66* (2006). 14 December. Accessed December 12, 2012. http://www.africultures.com/.
Mdarhri Alaoui, Abdallah. 2006. *Aspects du roman marocain (1950–2003)*. Rabat: Editions Zaouia.
Memmi, Albert. 1955. *Agar*. Paris: Corréa.
Mwangi, Evan Maina. 2009. *Africa Writes Back to Self: Metafiction, Gender, Sexuality*. New York: SUNY Press.
Nwosu, Maik. 2011. *Markets of Memories: Between the Postcolonial and the Transnational*. Trenton: Africa World Press.
Orlando, Valérie. 2009. *Francophone Voices of the 'New' Morocco in Film and Print: (Re)presenting a Society in Transition*. New York: Palgrave Macmillan Press.
"Retrospective: 2006 Les temps forts". 2006. *TelQuel* (December 23–January 5): 20–31.
Ricoeur, Paul. 1992. *Oneself as Another*. University of Chicago Press.
Said, Edward. 1983. *The World the Text and the Critic*. Cambridge, MA: Harvard University Press.
Said, Edward. 2004. *Humanism and Democratic Criticism*. New York: Columbia University Press.
Sembene, Ousmane. 1956. *Le Docker noir*. Paris: Debresse.
Yacine, Kateb. 1956. *Nedjma*. Paris: Seuil.
Zimmerman, Jens. 2004. "Quo Vadis?: Literary Theory Beyond Postmodernism." *Christianity and Literature* 53 (4), Summer: 495–519.

Naija boy remix: Afroexploitation and the new media creative economies of cosmopolitan African youth

Krystal Strong and Shaun Ossei-Owusu

This article examines how young African cultural entrepreneurs harness the economic, technological and creative openings created by globalization with a focus on the Naija Boyz, two Nigerian-born, US-based brothers, who became YouTube sensations via their 'African Remix' genre of hip hop video parodies. With over 20 million views, the videos are situated within four converging movements within contemporary African youth cultural production: the maturation of African hip hop; the specific resurgence of Nigeria as a cultural hub driven by Nollywood and the local hip hop scene; the circulation of new media technologies; and, the formation of an increasingly cosmopolitan, tech-savvy generation of African youth. Using the Naija Boyz' images and lyrics, the YouTube videos are analyzed as critical commentaries of (black) American and African cultural scripts, which interrogate issues of gender, class, citizenship, and inter-/intra-diasporic relations. Moreover, the Naija Boyz are posited as archetypes of a rising generation of African youth, whose intercultural experiences outside of the African continent serve as a form of social capital that constitutes the basis of new (and potentially problematic) creative economies, which expand the presumed boundaries and concerns of African youth cultures.

Introduction

In the opening frames of their debut video 'Crank Dat Naija Boy' (2007), Olatoye and Teju Komolafe, the YouTube sensations better known as the Naija Boyz, bear the normative aesthetic and performative style markers of black American (male) rappers – oversized t-shirts, dark sunglasses, and bling bling around the neck – with a single, type-betraying derivation. Instead of a fitted baseball hat, which would conventionally complete the uniform of the urban black male, a traditional Yoruba *fila* cap crowns their first impression. In a similar act of synchronous familiarization and defamiliarization, the Naija Boyz announce their purpose ('we get dis new remix for you wey we dey call de Naija boy') as they snap their fingers in the well-recognized style of Southern US rappers. Then, in a telling act of cultural translation, the text 'Nigerian Boy' appears across the screen, conceivably, for those viewers unaware that Naija signifies Nigeria and the Naija Boy, its native son. In the next scene, the Naija Boyz first demonstrate their remixed version of the dance routine originally made popular by the black American teenage rapper Soulja Boy,[1] while now wearing full Yoruba attire by the side of a road in an undisclosed location. Though the combination of the initial caption, 'Nigerian Boy', and their traditional outfitting might suggest the video's location in Nigeria, the anomalous presence of American-style homes and street lamps betrays this presumption. The above descriptions sample the clever ways the Naija Boyz play with cultural expectations and narrate the cross-cultural and cross-racial terrain that increasingly constitutes the experiences of a growing number of African youth, who display their cosmopolitanism as a form of social currency derived from intercultural dexterity.

Elsewhere in the 'Crank Dat' video, O' and Teju prophetically boast on the track that 'All too fresh and all too clean/this Naija American Dream/when I crank that Naija Boy/my African people go scream.' Indeed, with over 20 million views of their music videos since 2007, the Naija Boyz can claim to have masterfully mobilized two of the most conspicuous elements of contemporary global youth practices – new media and hip hop cultures. Within their self-designated 'African Remix'[2] genre, the Naija Boyz re-appropriate black American songs and videos with a decidedly 'African' comedic interpretation, offering what can be viewed as parodies and, thus, critical commentaries of (black) American and African cultural tropes. This article examines the conditions of possibility and substance of the Naija Boyz' YouTube videos, with a focus on how their inventive digital creations herald emerging shifts in the production and projection of African culture(s) among youth grappling with the challenges (and openings) created by global social changes. Moreover, by virtue of their location in the 'new' African diasporas of recent emigrants (Okpewho, Davies, and Mazrui 1999; Koser 2003), the cultural entrepreneurialism of the US-based, Nigeria-born Naija Boyz problematizes folk and scholarly assumptions about the boundaries of African youth cultures and their underlying political economy.

The explosive popularity of the Naija Boyz' African Remix videos are understood, here, as a manifestation of four converging movements in contemporary African youth cultures, namely the: (1) expansion of hip hop in Africa, (2) resurgence of Nigeria as a nucleus of African cultural production, (3) increasing accessibility to digital technologies, and (4) formation of a conspicuously cosmopolitan and tech-savvy generation of African youth. While cosmopolitanism is a widely contested set of theories that refers most broadly to projects of 'planetary conviviality' (Mignolo 2002, 721), rooted in alternative ways of thinking about morality, community formation, identity, and civic practice beyond the nation, this article takes up the aesthetic and performative dimensions of cosmopolitanism. We position the intersection of entertainment and technology as a strategic site of cosmopolitan practices, which exemplify the ways African youth reimagine themselves amidst the competing logics of cultural citizenship and estrangement at the core of experiences of the contemporary world.

In the discussion that follows, we explore the socio-cultural conditions enabling the Naija Boyz' YouTube enterprise. Then, using lyrical and visual analysis of the content of their videos,[3] we examine the role of class, gender, and inter-/intra-diaspora relations in their representations as well as the discourse generated by the community of users who consume (and choose to comment on) their YouTube channel. From one perspective, we argue, the videos demonstrate the experimental practices of increasingly mobile African youth actors, who directly participate in the processes of cultural globalization occurring in Africa and the Western hemisphere. Yet, from another, we ask whether the videos represent a form of cultural and economic opportunism that deploys problematic tropes of Africa and black America, which we characterize as 'Afroexploitation', given its evocation of the prickly politics of cultural representation within 1970s black urban cinema.[4] Finally, we situate the African Remix videos in a broader context to consider what the Naija Boyz' ascendance may indicate about the socio-economic possibilities imagined and enacted by African youth via creative industries.

To be sure, discussing any notion of 'African youth culture' is conceptually slippery on multiple fronts. Who constitutes *African* youth is often territorially bound to the African continent in ways that elide the multifaceted and multidirectional nature of diasporic cultural production, and often privilege a site over processes and exchanges in Africa and globally. Moreover, *youth* is already an especially contested and ambiguous social category that varies based on geography, disciplinary perspective, temporal context, and a host of other factors. Perhaps most importantly, due to social and economic marginality, youth status is increasingly flexible and the transition into adulthood indefinitely delayed. Finally, *youth culture* as an analytic term is also difficult to tackle, as it could be understood as a set of values, practices, norms, or belief systems that demarcate a particular group from others or as cultural products (e.g. music, fashion, vocabulary) produced for or by young people. Our discussion of the Naija Boyz' enterprise complements and complicates perspectives on African youth culture by examining the foreseeable as well as counterintuitive ways young Africans participate in the refashioning of cultural identity and discourse in the midst of distinct technological, economic, political, and cultural transformations.

Transnational currents

As a three-decades-old cultural art form and industry, hip hop has emerged from its humble roots in the South Bronx and Jamaica to become a global commodity that has compelled scholars to reconsider globalization, technology, cultural production, and identity (e.g. Rose 1994; Mitchell 2001; Chang 2005). Hip hop also serves as a site for inquiry into the production of contemporary African youth cultures because it has reconfigured the repertoire from which significations of cultural and generational identity are drawn. Not only does hip hop function as a lingua franca through which youth of African descent, among others, situate themselves in relation to global black cultures (Flores 2000; Osumare 2007; Alim, Ibrahim, and Pennycook 2009; Ntarangwi 2009), it also serves as a prominent lens through which African youth articulate (at times in the form of open resistance) the precariousness of their futures, as in the case of the rap-loving 'hooligans' of Dar es Salaam, to cite one example (Perullo 2005). The cultivation of hip hop in Africa follows a path previously tread by other cultural products, such as film, literature, and other music genres within the African diaspora (Hebdige 1987; Monson 2000; Edwards 2001; Wallsten 2005). Nevertheless, it is worth noting that the traction of its regional and national articulations has been overwhelmingly uneven, privileging the locutions of black American artists who occupy a hegemonic position (Gilroy 1993). In recent years, the stylistic evolution and commercial viability of Africa's hip hop scene(s)[5] have increased the recognition of African hip hop as a genre in its own right and, more fundamentally, demonstrated the multidirectionality of the relationship between Africa and African diasporic youth – upon which the practices of emerging artists like the Naija Boyz depend.

To a large extent, discussions of hip hop in Africa have shifted away from early claims that the pioneers of local hip hop industries suffered from copycat-ism,[6] or being excessively referential (and reverential) to the aesthetic and performative scripts of American hip hop. Such gestures are, perhaps, better understood dialogically, as attempts to discursively and performatively engage with Black American hip hop hegemony from the margins. Omoniyi et al., for instance, describe the 'structural affinity' between the stage names of black American and Nigerian artists (e.g. 2Pac and 2Face) as part and parcel of the global currents of popular culture and a reflection of hip hop's function as a community of practice (2009, 6). Moreover, with greater visibility and 'street cred' (credibility) ascribed to African hip hop in recent years, previously uneven exchanges between Africa and Black America are levelling, as localized processes of indigenization and greater mainstream recognition of African artists indicate (Alim, Ibrahim, and Pennycook 2009). African-bred, though residentially absent, hip hop artists have helped raise the profile of African hip hop while reppin' (representing) their homelands, including the likes of Senegalese American Akon, who launched his chart-topping career in the US, and Somali-born K'Naan, whose song 'Wavin' Flag' was the 2010 FIFA World Cup anthem. At the same time, 'homegrown' African hip hop artists hold their own in this regard, due to the refinement of local industries' sound, the establishment of MTV Base in Africa, which has stimulated the circulation of contemporary African music across the continent, and ever-increasing inter-continental collaborations.[7]

The mutually reinforcing home-based and diasporic development of African hip hop suggests that the industry, though still evolving, has finally come of age and succeeded in its efforts to 'discursively carve out a recognizable creative patch' of its own (Omoniyi 2008). Perhaps what is most significant to remember is that, although hip-hop emerged as a subculture that valorized agency and an anti-hegemonic disposition, its movement into the mainstream has made it susceptible at least, and beholden at most, to mercenary impulses. Undoubtedly, capitalism shapes the contours of African youth's agency but it does not necessarily determine social action. As we shall see later in the discussion, hip-hop, along with technological innovation and the concomitant growth of the internet and social media in Sub-Saharan Africa, have helped embolden African youth and provided both ideological and cultural avenues for the articulations of identity and community. To interpret hip hop simply as a commercial enterprise would be a gross, functionalist misunderstanding, but to see the industry as a bastion of unfettered agency would be a misreading as well. As it relates to African youth and hip-hop, a more measured way of thinking about African youth agency, especially the Naija Boyz, would be to situate their action and artistry along the dimensions of economic accumulation, social relationships and networks (e.g. imagined communities), and cultural capital that is specific to both local and national identities.

The Nigerian cultural 'renaissance'

Though the Naija Boyz' African Remix genre is facilitated by the maturation of African hip hop more broadly, their practices must also be situated within the specificities of Nigeria's ongoing cultural renaissance through its booming local hip hop and film industries, which, together, have rebuilt Nigeria's stature as a continental (and diasporic) cultural hegemon. Nigeria's cultural renaissance, if it may be called that, is not an entirely new phenomenon, but rather a revival of an era epitomized by the Second World Black and African Festival of Arts and Culture (FESTAC), which Nigeria hosted in 1977. Through FESTAC, Nigeria articulated a vision of itself as the epicenter of global black nationhood (see Apter 2005) – a claim echoed by some contemporary Nigerian artists. Take, for instance, the 2011 release of Nigerian artist D'Banj's highly anticipated video for the remix of his hit song 'Mr. Endowed'. Featuring American hip hop icon Snoop Dogg on both the song and, significantly, the video, the collaboration acts as a symbolic marker of Nigerian hip hop's arrival as a legitimate force to be recognized by the (black American) hip hop establishment, here, represented by Snoop Dogg, who, in the video, swaps his American passport for a Nigerian one.

Like other African hip hop industries, Nigerian hip hop struggled to develop its identity throughout the 1990s and early 2000s. However, with improved production quality and greater access to digital editing tools, in more recent years, Nigerian hip hop has largely shed the influence of its American stylistic progenitors and developed a peculiarly 'Naija' sound that incorporates pidgin English and other local languages. This development has been a cause for greater continental and global recognition, as Nigerian artists are typically front-runners at African music awards and, in 2011, Naija hip hop was given the distinction of representing African hip hop at the US-based Black Entertainment Television (BET) Hip Hop Awards where Nigerian male and female rappers performed in freestyle 'cyphers'.[8] Moreover, the commercial viability of Nigeria's music industry has engendered alternative local and regional creative economies, which have supplied young people with attractive avenues for social mobility in an unstable global economy.[9]

Any discussion of Nigeria's youth-dominated creative economies must also acknowledge the film industry, which has eclipsed the contemporary Nigerian music industry in scholarly attention.

Though Naija hip hop and Nigeria's film industry,[10] popularly referred to as Nollywood, are separate industries, both draw from similar social, cultural, and economic repertoires and have followed comparable developmental trajectories. Apart from its role as a medium for youth to express the ambivalences of the postcolonial world (Ugor 2009), like the hip hop industry, Nollywood's expansion has been facilitated by shifts in technique, financing, and cultural ethos, which have favored the participation of young people. Scholars elsewhere (e.g. Cocq 2006; Zajc 2009) have documented Nollywood's character as 'low-cost', 'non-institutionalized' and tied to ad hoc training networks for new technologies. For our purposes, the mainstreaming of the Nigerian film industry underscores what might be considered the 'renegade practices' of a contingent of trailblazing young producers-cum-entrepreneurs, who deploy the same unconventional techniques of cultural sampling, guerilla marketing, and informal distribution that made other putatively 'lowbrow' cultures like American hip hop, pulp fiction, and straight-to-DVD films vibrant and profitable.

Just as the Nigerian hip hop industry matured through a process of self-affirming exchanges with its progenitors, Nollywood has also evolved into a genre of culturally resonant films that domesticates and transforms the tropes of other hegemonic film industries with local idioms. The films' embeddedness within local cultures has formed the basis for Nollywood's internationalism and its enablement of national and regional economies (Okome 2007; Akpabio and Mustapha-Lambe 2008). This cultural and economic symbiosis also points to what Adejunmobi (2007) has described as Nollywood's expression of 'the regional popular'. Distinct from the dichotomization within globalization studies between so-called 'homogenizing' and 'resisting' cultures, Adejunmobi locates the regional popular as an alternative circuit that emphasizes 'localized immediacy'.[11] In its dynamic interaction with African publics, so Adejunmobi reasons, Nollywood is transnational in reach and conversant with hegemonic trends, yet still detached from dominant systems of cultural production, neither resisting nor assimilating. In wedding the sonic innovations of the Naija hip hop movement with the visuals of the Nollywood home video industry, the Naija Boyz capitalize upon the cultural and commercial possibilities engendered by both industries.[12] In doing so, they defy the assumed incompatibility between 'local' relevance, global cultures, and commercial goals, and signal the emergence of new publics interested and willing to financially invest in the consumption of 'African' stories that hinge upon Nigeria's cultural particularities.

Traversing the digital divide

Beyond its role in fueling the growth of Nigerian culture industries, new media technologies have played a more diffuse role in youth cultural production. Generally, the proliferation of internet-based technologies and the growing access to social media in Africa and its diaspora(s) have been lauded as evidence of an 'African Renaissance', through which Africans marshal greater control over their own representations (Wall 2009). At almost five times the global average, internet usage in Africa grew by over 3000% from 2000 to 2011 (Stats, Internet World 2012). Yet, unevenness still characterizes the landscape of technological access (Wallsten 1999; Dasgupta et al. 2005; Pick and Azari 2008), particularly among those engaged in cultural production. For instance, in a survey of YouTube videos with content about Africa, Wall (2009) found that, of the videos tagged with the words 'Ghana' and 'Kenya', the few that were produced by self-identified Africans were uploaded from Western locations where posters purported to live. Thus, while YouTube and other sites provide an opening for Africans to be cultural producers, such avenues still privilege those located in or that have access to the infrastructural resources of Western countries, including the Naija Boyz, who are based in the US. Only 13.5% of Africans based in the continent (or 139.9 million people) have regular access to the internet, compared to

36.1% of the rest of the world (Stats, Internet World 2012). These disparities accentuate the gap between Africa and the Rest, as well as economic elites and the poor within the continent and diaspora (Keniston and Kumar 2004), though this may be changing with the ever-increasing participation of African youth in social media networks via mobile phones and cyber cafes (see Burrell 2012).

Bearing these inequities in mind, new technologies have, nevertheless, made global cultures more accessible in Africa, while also increasing the audibility of African cultural products, such as hip hop and film, for global audiences. The proliferation of YouTube and other forms of user-generated media has played an especially prominent role in this process, giving artists and audiences unprecedented levels of agency in their production, consumption, and social interaction.[13] YouTube is perhaps the prototype of online content sharing, particularly among music and technology enthusiasts. Scholars have noted the transformative impact the video has had on music culture (e.g. Watkins 2006; Iton 2008) and YouTube only enhances visual signification within hip hop production. At the same time, the site has given independent artists greater visibility and a low-cost avenue to broaden their audience. This creative agency is one of the most important outcomes of changes within the technological landscape.

These developments are also fundamental to understanding how the Naija Boyz' endeavors relate to the digital practices of African youth, since the internet, especially blogs and social media such as YouTube, Facebook, and Twitter, have created important dialogic spaces that can be said to constitute 'African cyber-communities'. Borrowing from Rheingold's (2000) definition of 'virtual community' and 'fragmegration', Alzouma (2008) suggests that African cyber-communities, which, by definition, transpose imagined common interests from the 'real' to the virtual world, represent the 'fragmegrative' processes of a cultural globalization, in which multiple referents are mobilized in an increasingly flexible and unstable identity construction that involves both fragmenting and integrative dynamics. Similarly, we argue that the globalization of hip hop and technology are a fundamental component of the new identity logics of African (youth) cultures, typified by greater conjunction and disjunction.

Conspicuous cosmopolitanism

Taking seriously the conditions making possible the Naija Boyz' enterprise requires the conceptual repositioning of 'African youth'. In the field of African studies, in particular, attention to the precariousness of young people's social location has grown, most notably in the work on how the young navigate the socio-economic constraints of late capitalism.[14] While useful in recasting African youth as social agents despite their perception as a 'lost generation' (O'Brien 1996), there is the dangerous tendency in the broader discourse on African youth culture to discuss how streams of global culture are domesticated in Africa (i.e. in hip hop), as opposed to ways culture circulates outward. There is also the presumption that African youth are territorially bound and that their experiences and cultural products exist in geographic isolation. These two tendencies are inconsistent with young cultural entrepreneurs like the Naija Boyz.

Though the Naija Boyz assert themselves as 'African youth' and, more fundamentally, legitimate producers of 'African' culture even despite their geographic location outside of Africa, perhaps their social location is better understood as the interstitial spaces referred to as the 'betwixt and between'. Here, betwixt and between signals the work of Victor Turner (1986; also Turner and Bruner 1986), whose concept of liminality has been essential in the analysis of persons situated in the interstices of societies and cultures.[15] In our discussion, the marginal location and creative and re-formative tendencies of such individuals is precisely what positions them to marshal ethnic, national, racial, and pan-African cultures as recipients *and* producers. As we argue, it is their very location 'in-between' that enables them to develop the cosmopolitanism, mobility, and connectivity, which are central to the possibilities currently envisaged by youth connected and connecting to Africa, especially those who are cultural producers. Within scholarly discussions pertaining to African youth, this problematizes the territorial boundedness of 'African culture' and, even, 'African youth', challenging also the disempowering treatment (albeit likely unintended) of young people as only being acted upon by global cultures, as opposed to speaking to – and with – from positions of creative self-assertion. In this sense, the Naija Boyz invite a conceptual broadening of the location and boundaries of African (youth) culture, which are conditioned less upon geographic locality and more upon self-assertive performance.

As the opening discussion of the 'Crank Dat Naija Boy' video notes, inter-cultural (also, interracial) entanglements frame the experiences of the Naija Boyz (hereafter referred to as NB), and form a consistent thread throughout their videos. These entanglements, we argue, map their interstitial location within and between worlds, and constitute what we are calling 'conspicuous cosmopolitanism'. As Clifford (1994) notes in his classic text on diasporas, cosmopolitanisms are fundamental to diasporic discourses, which necessarily articulate the dis/articulation between nationalist, assimilationist, and diasporic ideologies, among others. Indeed, the cosmopolitanism performed by the NB must be situated within the (at times, overlapping) repertoires of black American youth, immigrant, and African diasporic cultures. For instance, the NB's performances of self replay (in remixed fashion) conventional hip hop scripts that link self-value with materialism and perceived envy, usually described as 'hate' by unknown detractors. Later in the 'Crank Dat' video they relay:

> Na broken English I go talk
> Watch me lean and watch me jock
> Jocking all those haterz man
> When I do dat Naija Boy
> It be game ova for dem […]
> You catch me at your Naija party
> Eating some *egusi* stew
> Haterz get mad because I get me some Gucci shoe[16]

With these lyrics, the NB make reference to: 'haters' (envious detractors), whose machinations are overturned by their performance of the Naija Boy; the 'Naija party', or Nigerian social gatherings reproduced in the US, particularly in cities with large Nigerian populations such as Washington DC, Houston, and Atlanta; and, finally, at least one of the causes for the hate levied against them – their material consumption of designer items like Gucci shoes.

We may gather that part of what makes their 'Naija Boy' style worth producing a video about in the first place is the perceived intrinsic value of its forms of speech, physical comportment, and sociality. For even casual consumers of hip hop music, these claims will be familiar forms of self-aggrandizement. Elsewhere, Manthia Diawara refers to this 'parodic reclaiming of the stereotype' as 'homeboy cosmopolitanism', wherein hip hop culture overturns negative media clichés about black urban culture with affirmative self and collective description (2000, 245–246). At the same time, the NB's cosmopolitanism exceeds the prided forms of consumption within hip hop (and, indeed, mainstream American culture), which they signal with the Gucci shoe reference. Here, the 'homeboy' ideal is expanded to include specifically Nigerian markers of attainment, as expressed by a scene where the NB 'spray'[17] money at a party, and a montage of (male) Nigerians who are world-renowned entertainers or athletes. The inclusion of these elements expresses the NB's desired and actual affinity with (black American) hip hop cultures, and asserts the co-presence of their demonstrably prided ethnic particularity.

Still, beyond this conjoining of both (black) American and Nigerian displays of economic excess, the NB also make use of a more subtle form of cosmopolitanism through the satirical manipulation of whiteness. Shortly after the words 'Nigerian Boy' appear in the opening scenes of the video, two young white (presumed) American women are introduced, who are watching the NB perform their signature dance on YouTube. The next time the viewer sees the two women, one is performing the Naija Boy routine, while the other films her doing so. Then, in another sequence, two white men dressed in American-style clothing and *fila* caps, mirroring the NB, attempt to 'crank dat Naija boy' with little rhythm or success. Thereafter, they are joined by the NB who laugh heartily at their efforts in a non-mocking fashion and dance with them.

On the one hand, this unexpected (and narratively unnecessary) tokenization of white people conveys the NB's claims about the cross-cultural desirability of their dance moves, which act as a stand-in for the entire Nigerian cultural repertoire. But, in a less obvious manner, the inclusion of white people suggests that the NB as characters and producers have regular access to white people in the first place, which implies their location outside of Nigeria, where there is only a relatively small expatriate community. Further, white people are the primary comedic defaults throughout their videos, and form one of the bases of their self-differentiation and posed cosmopolitanism.[18] In this manner, the NB display a *conspicuous* cosmopolitanism driven not by an intrinsic liminality, but by the *spectacle* of being 'in-between' and having access to multiple forms of cultural, racial, and national repertoires, which are presented as a form of social capital.[19]

'I'm the true African': Intersections of race, culture, and moral value

In subsequent videos, the issue of cultural in-betweeness – specifically, assimilation – is addressed more substantially, as the NB's on-screen personas and behind-the-scenes production undergo discernible facelifts. Like the original version, the remix of the song 'Kiss Kiss' is most overtly about the divergent paths two men seek to win a woman's heart. But, in the NB's rendering, the peculiar challenges of the new immigrant are tackled. While the African Remix has undergone a subtle form of commercialization with the inclusion of directing and production credits to the real-life NB, the characters themselves are recast as Nigerian immigrants, so 'fresh off the boat' that they eat snow during one scene. The video enters into the politics of assimilation in America by first approaching the issue of xenophobia. In the opening interlude, in which the NB act as radio hosts introducing the remix, a white American offers a racist rant, which reveals that his problem is 'all of you damn Nigerians. If you're not doing 419 scams,[20] you're busy stealing other people's music. Why don't you just go back to Africa?' Then, the NB reference the complementarity of inter and intra-racial aversion with scenes that relate dis/connections within African-black American relations. In arriving in the US, the NB greet an attractive (presumed) black American woman, who scoffs at their advances. Then, in a reactionary attempt at cultural assimilation, they mimic the aesthetics of urban black men by changing from traditional Yoruba attire to baggy jeans and hooded sweatshirts. In another effort at connecting, the NB wave at two (presumed) black American men, who only reluctantly return the greeting. The blind assimilationist path chosen, the NB thereafter channel an exaggerated black urban performative style.

The scenes offer an instructive counterpart to the narrative of cultural pride underlying 'Crank Dat', which glosses over the challenges of finding one's place within American society as a (black) immigrant. This narrative is further complicated by the introduction of gender and sexual politics as O' and Teju attempt to attract the attention of an African beauty, who upsets their gender and cultural expectations. The young woman sings:

> I'm a simple girl from Africa but New York is where I reside,
> So fellows don't you get it?
> Ain't got no time for your games.
> That's right, no I ain't with it,

And you should know I got a Nigerian upbringing.
That African upbringing.
I got paper [money], yo,
And a Cadillac,
With a law degree.
I thank God for that.
African shorty.
The kind you bring home to your Mom, cuz I'm the one you want.

This guarded (yet boastful) response to their advances mobilizes the 'independent woman' tropes of contemporary American society, particularly within the black American community, which have received renewed media interest in recent years concerning the supposed unmarriagability of black women in America.[21] The Nigerian-American woman poses a challenge to the NB, who offer exclamations of surprise to her claims of economic and educational achievement. The two, however, take opposing paths to woo her, which ultimately reinforce the discourses of cultural pride, cosmopolitanism, and economic status from the first video. For instance, Teju continues to mimic hip hop style and flaunts the fact that he has 'different accents' that can be mobilized at will. O' also emphasizes his cultural adeptness but eschews blind cultural assimilationism that fails to appreciate the cultural and *economic* value of African culture. Unlike his brother, he dresses in a professional style (i.e. a tailored blazer, button-down shirt, and slacks), which correlates with his socio-economic claims that, 'I'm king of my village/and my money get my image … I get miles, darling/and US dollar/No be 419 o/I get money proper.'[22]

Though this plotline could be interpreted as arguing that cultural sincerity trumps assimilation, it is hard to ignore the subtle encoding of commonplace criticisms levelled against black American culture, especially by black immigrants. For instance, the rejection of uncritical American cultural assimilation can be re-read as a specific caution against the mimicry of black urban (hip hop) culture and style, in favor of a more professionalized aesthetic in which money ultimately buys one's image and social acceptance. This underlying script is more legible in the 'Single Ladies' remix video based on the song by international superstar Beyoncé, in which the NB jest of luring her away from her equally famed husband, rapper Jay-Z, in the hopes of obtaining a green card. In their efforts to court her, the NB reason:

If you want find husband and make a good children
The kind wey turn to doctor after I go kuku beat them
Choose me, I get good genes and good system
I was raised in Naija as a good Christian (YES O!)
American Baby
Beyoncé, I can be your Jay-Z
We be the same I'm just a darker rapper
I'm the true African
He's a swagger jacker[23]

In this self-satire of the way some immigrants strategically marry citizens of their host country to obtain a green card, the NB, perhaps unintentionally, make a cultural and moral judgment that marrying and procreating with a Nigerian immigrant guarantees the (black) American woman 'good children' that will become doctors given the NB's 'good genes' and 'good' Christian background. This projected future, of course, is in contradistinction to (black) American Jay-Z who, though admittedly 'the same', is not the 'true African' but a 'swagger jacker' (meaning, a charlatan or weak copy).

Incidentally, this discourse on authenticity is not confined to Africa-black America relations, but also the conflation of Nigerian culture with African culture writ large. As Mahon (2000, 480) notes, global cultures are characterized by hybridity, which is often coupled with 'anxiety' about the purity and authenticity of cultures – a conflict that plays out in the NB's production and reception. For instance, though the NB brand is the '*African* Remix', Nigerian, and particularly Yoruba, culture acts as a stand-in for the continent. The NB claim that they are 'Naija Boyz, African Boyz', yet this cultural conflation is not lost on viewers, who offer mixed reactions. For example, one viewer responded positively to 'Crank Dat' by posting on the song's YouTube page, 'I'm not Nigerian but African just the same. Thanks for representing', while another advocated for a country-specific Ghana remix.

Perhaps the most telling exchange relates to a debate in the 'Kiss Kiss' comments on the nationality of the 'Nigerian' love interest (who is actually of Ethiopian ancestry), which devolved into a discussion of race and whether a non-Nigerian should represent a Nigerian.[24] One viewer complained that they 'don't understand WHY [you] use [an] Ethiopian gal', while another offered a somewhat patronizing explanation that 'She's probably saying she is Nigerian for the sake of the video. You must be an American-born Nigerian ... 99% of Africans [would] perceive that she hails from the Horn of Africa ... This is just something we Africans know.' Along that line, the casting prompted the claim that '[Somalis] ain't BLACK', followed by lamentations that the debate was rife with beliefs that 'nothing beautiful or good can come from Africa'. Though it is difficult to state categorically the geographic location, nationality, and ethnicity of consumers of the NB's videos, we might assume from the comments sampled above that they represent an audience, primarily, of people of African descent, with a high percentage of Africans (especially Nigerians and/or recent immigrants) based in Western countries, though also in Africa.

These discourses delve into the complex politics of navigating the terrains of ethnicity, race, and national citizenship. Moreover, they problematize already knotty discussions of what constitutes an African authenticity. These discussions on what constitutes the 'bona fide' African become more complicated when considered alongside the growing accessibility of social media and digital technology, not to mention and the increasingly cosmopolitan proclivities of African youth across the diaspora. While the 'African Remix' genre ultimately aims to culturally affirm 'African' cultures, through the particularities of Yoruba-centered Nigerian experiences, this process is rife with contradictions, fissures, and contestations at the level of production *and* consumption. For all the NB's cosmopolitan swagger, xenophobia and the perhaps unexpected challenges of intra-diasporic relations frustrate its execution.

'Big ups to my African queens': Flipping the hip hop gender script

The 'Lollipop' and 'Black and Yellow' remix videos provide a segue way from concerns with cultural assimilation to a more substantial engagement with gender and sexual politics. Based on rapper Lil' Wayne's chart-topping and sexually explicit song of the same name, the remix posits African food consumption as a form of cultural preservation with the African woman as the praised conduit. The NB state:

> Shawty, I'm a fan of your stew and pounded yam
> Your food is never bland
> That's why I like to eat your *fufu* with my hands [...]
> I said, I like fast food
> But not as much as rice and stew
> McDonalds I go bypass you
> Because *dodo* [fried plantain] is better

On a basic level, the remix retains the prior focus on cultural pride and critiques elements of mainstream American (food) culture. For instance, the NB relay that 'Johnny Just Come',[25] the recent immigrant, regards American food as 'no sweet' (unpalatable), that consuming American food, especially salad, is effectively not eating, and that any potential American love interest should 'prepare to be embarrassed' because, in the manner typical of many African cultures, they consume food by licking their fingers 'like a lollipop'. However, it is worth noting that, in reframing the song as an appreciation of African food culture and women as its custodian, the NB effectively neutralize the sexually explicit scripts in the original text, in which the lollipop metaphor refers not to food consumption practices, but to oral sex acts. This is particularly noteworthy as the hyper-sexualization of hip hop musical content and imagery is a persistent critique of the genre, which the NB evacuate from their re-appropriations, though perhaps re-inscripting a more subtle form of gendering with their correlation of women with domesticity.

Meanwhile, the 'Black and Yellow' remix of American rapper Wiz Khalifa's ode to the US city of Pittsburgh is poignantly re-appropriated to offer the NB's most focused discussion of African women from the perspectives of colorism and racial aversion-desire. Black and yellow, the two colors most popularly associated with the sports teams of Pittsburgh, are rearticulated as the two skin colors used to describe Nigerian women (and, indeed, African diasporic women): *dudu*, dark-skinned, or black; and *ọmọ pupa*, light-skinned, or yellow. The video begins with two white (presumed) American males flipping through an issue of *National Geographic*, which contains a series of pictures of African women bearing tribal marks. The NB, on seeing the young men's confusion about the women who 'look like their faces have been scratched', decide to give them a lesson on 'African Babes'. They begin:

Tribal marks on our face
White boys dey laugh
But that's our taste
We love their skin tone, their wrapper, and their lace […]
Whether Yoruba, Igbo girl, or Hausa
Black or yellow, *dudu* or *omo pupa*
The question remains which one to choose now
So I can pay her bride price, two cows […]
Up in my town, look around, you go see babes
Black or yellow (4x)
Take your pick, thick or thin, two shades
Black or yellow (4x)

Here, the NB offer up simultaneous rebuttals to critiques of African aesthetic norms that do not conform to Euro-American beauty standards, as well as the divisive ethnic and phenotypic differences that so often fracture black and African (diasporic) communities, albeit from the perspective of male sexual and marital preferences.

Then, shifting the focus of their message from their American interlocutors to 'African beauties', they note:

Just got a call from Naija, this just in
Too many dark girls want to pretend that they're light-skinned
She thinks say she fine, cause she dey bleach face
But if you see the side effects, you go be craze
Stay natural like you supposed to do
Whether you be yellow banana or black like your school shoes

In the message to 'dark girls', the NB tackle the complex issue of colorism within African diasporic communities, where skin color preference, shaped by slavery, colonialism, and Euro-American standards, has led to the valuation of lighter-skinned people of color, particularly women, to the extent that skin bleaching is rampant on the African continent as well as the Caribbean (Charles 2003; Glenn 2008). Colorism is especially widespread in African and American popular culture, where lighter-skinned black women are disproportionately favored as features in films and, especially, hip hop videos (Sharpley-Whiting 2008). It is also worth noting that the NB acknowledge the unspoken truth underlying dangerous practices such as skin bleaching: that the attainment of whiteness is often the aim of such practices, even if unconscious.

The NB's engagement with gender and sexuality unsettles conventional perspectives on black women (and the uses of their bodies) in hip hop, whose complicated misogyny is a persistent critique. Here, the 'ho' is replaced by the 'African babe' who functions, not as a sexual object, but a guardian of culture who is meant to 'stay natural' like '[she's] supposed to do'. Yet, with the exception of the young, upwardly mobile woman from the 'Kiss Kiss' video, who is posited as a welcome challenge to the cultural insincerity of the NB as unabashed assimilators, the remaining women featured in subsequent videos are still subject to a less sexually exploitative though similarly insidious form of patriarchy, when compared to the 'video ho' prevailing ideal. Just as the NB domesticate, literally, the sexual politics of the original 'Lollipop' video by reframing the action in culinary terms, the 'Naija Girlz', both seen and unseen, are equally domesticated and relegated to spaces of passivity and reception. Though Nigerian (and presumably all black) women are cautioned against skin bleaching and encouraged to be their natural selves, ultimately, 'Black and Yellow' is about the male gaze of both the outsider (the white male clandestinely desiring that which he fears) and the 'insider', the NB, who have their 'pick' of African Babes. Moreover, it becomes clear that the Naija *Boyz* are the primary agents capable of displaying the forms of intercultural dexterity performed throughout the African Remix videos and not their gender counterparts.

Culture and commerce: Considerations of Afroexploitation

While the above discussion has probed the substance of the NB videos with an emphasis on the narratives of ethnic pride, assimilation, and gender and sexual politics, it is important to underline the political economy of their cultural production, which amplifies the artists' intentions and also provides a useful frame for querying our larger concerns with whether the African Remix videos qualify as a form of 'Afroexploitation' aimed at exploiting African representations for commercial gains. As Kamari Clarke (2007) reminds us, attention to the political economy of African diasporic cultural production is especially critical because the variance in socioeconomic status among diasporans creates problematic differences in the capacity to culturally produce and, thus, shape the imagination of Africa and African identity. The NB are certainly recipients of the privileges of their location in the West as their access to the means of producing such videos allows them to produce discourses about Nigeria and Africa *from outside*.

The film genre of Blaxploitation emerged in the early 1970s at a time when black Americans nurtured and espoused 'black power' while Hollywood began to see the viability of black film consumers. Designed to capture putatively 'honest' and 'authentic' representations of African American urban life, Blaxploitation films often entailed themes of retribution, crime, and (in) justice while having a cast of actors who played roles that often included drug dealers, pimps, corrupt police officers, and politicians. Of course, there was contestation around the genre as some saw it as a positive development that created more opportunities for black filmmakers and actors, whereas others saw it as another manifestation of caricatured and pathologized blackness. Afroexploitation occupies a similarly tenuous relationship within the diaspora.

On the one hand, there have been some positive benefits that include: the success of Nollywood and the concomitant job opportunities that are generated for African artists who would otherwise be confined to precarious local economies; the recognition of a large consumer base for African cultural production; and, the proliferation of independent music, film, and fashion companies that are run by African entrepreneurs and extricated from demands of Western, multinational companies. The rise of the African middle class, which is marked by 'changing lifestyles, greater spending power, more recreational time, the harnessing of technology and a new political assertiveness and cultural self-confidence' has played a key role in conspicuous cosmopolitanism and the positive embrace of African identity that constitutes Afroexploitation (Smith and Lamble

2011). While blacks across the diaspora have championed African identity since the dispersals of the slave trade, this current iteration is marked by distinct socio-cultural and economic phenomena (e.g. globalization, availability of new technologies, neoliberalism) that have made it more profitable to espouse African identity, as demonstrated mostly clearly in the global embrace of Nollywood.

At the same time, there is an underbelly to this positive embrace of African identity. First, as noted by scholars of the diaspora (e.g. Edwards 2001; Gilroy 2002), there is as much difference as there is unity. While, conspicuous cosmopolitans like NB do have access to different insights into the diaspora by virtue of their geographic locations, others do not and either may not have generous readings of their representations of African identity, or see them as caricatures and inauthentic. Moreover, the profit motive, along with the successful formula of promulgating stereotypes of blacks (whether local or internationally) by African-descended people raises the time-old question about the politics of representation, or, more crudely, mimicry for profit.

With the globalization of hip hop and digital technologies as well as the commercially lucrative path paved by the Nigerian film and hip hop industries, young people are capitalizing upon new avenues for the expression and production of re-mixed and re-imagined cultures. Though the African continent continues to be plagued by political and economic instability, the field of culture is one cause for optimism, as African youth, more than ever, are cultivating a spirit of ethnic, national, continental, and/or racial pride through popular culture, even when there is a disconnect between this realm and the social and political sphere. As has been the case with youth cultures that have come before, the African Remix genre interrogates so-called 'high cultures', including mainstream American culture and black American cultural hegemony, through its assertion of ethnic and racial difference, to be sure, but also the experience of in-betweeness. As the push-back from racist xenophobes and reluctant diasporic brethren indicate, the process of navigating gaps between cultures is fraught with contradictions that threaten the acceptability of cultural (re) productions.

Acknowledgements

We are grateful to Olatoye and Teju Komolafe (the Naija Boyz) for granting an interview during the research for this article. An earlier version was presented at the University of Ibadan (Nigeria) Department of Anthropology Interdisciplinary Discourse (July 2011). We wish to thank the participants of the seminar, three anonymous reviewers, and Jason Price and Reggie Royston for helpful comments to previous versions of this article.

Notes

1. The Naija Boyz video was the most popular in a slew of YouTube remixes of the chart-topping single and accompanying dance routine titled 'Crank That (Soulja Boy)', which incorporates a few new moves common in Yoruba dance styles. This remix video, along with others from the Naija Boyz, were of standard music video length—between three and six minutes.
2. The concept of the 'remix' is well known within popular culture. The origins of modern remixing (along with hip hop) are often traced back to Jamaican cultural productions of the late 1960s and early 1970s, with the musical engineering of artists like King Tubby, Errol Thompson, and Lee 'Scratch' Perry (see Hebdige 1987; Maysles 2002). Following precedents set by parodists like 'Weird Al' Yankovic, YouTube remixes, in particular, are a genre in which amateur and professional artists create alternative versions of songs or videos usually while recycling the original instrumentals. With the proliferation of open source practices in recent years, the contemporary era has been characterized as a 'remix culture', which Lessig (2008) defined as a 'read/write' culture in which the boundary between consumer and producer is routinely traversed, such that a fundamental part of cultural consumption is its productive reappropriation in remixed form. More relevant to our discussion, remix music culture has also been

described as a means for the negotiation of (gendered) ethnic identity, as Maira's (1998) discussion of 'Bhangra remix' parties among Indian American youth in New York City illustrates.

3. Readers will find it useful to view the Naija Boyz' videos, alongside our discussion on their African Remix YouTube channel located at: http://www.youtube.com/user/AfricanRemix. Their official website is located at http://www.naijaboyz.com.
4. The concept of 'Afroexploitation' signals the well-known critiques of Blaxploitation film production of the 1970s, known for its aestheticization of an urban black culture that was both hyper-masculine and violently sexist (for useful discussions of the internal contradictions of Blaxploitation representations, see Robinson 1998; Simon 1998), Here, the concept is retooled to examine the politics of self-representation of Africa and African people.
5. It is important to note the diversity of African hip hop in terms of viability and visibility. For instance, the hip hop industries in English-speaking Africa, particularly, Nigeria, Ghana, South Africa, and Kenya often act as stand-ins for African hip hop writ large, while others remain less recognized. This is, no doubt, influenced by their intelligibility within hip hop's Anglocentric landscape.
6. See, for instance, the May 2011 Associated Press article describing the maturation of Naija hip hop from 'mainly imitating' American hip hop to developing a recognizable 'Naija' sound (Ibukun 2011).
7. For example, Nigerian artist 2Face Idibia's single 'I'm So Proud to be African' with Haitian-American Wyclef Jean, South African HHP's collaboration with black American Nas, the popular (though unauthorized) mash-up of Afrobeat king Fela Kuti and black American Jay-Z in a remix to the latter's 'Roc Boys', among others.
8. These unscripted freestyle battles, in which artists extemporaneously rap 'off the dome', or without preparation, are a much-anticipated component of the BET Hip Hop Awards, which remains the largest stage for hip hop music, on its own terms. Selection for participation in these cyphers is regarded as a sign of respect within the hip hop community. In this sense, the participation of Nigerian rappers such as Ice Prince, M.I., Naeto C, and Sasha, among others, along with the acknowledgement of Nigeria as a hip hop regional node, are indications of the growing influence of Nigerian hip hop.
9. Among students in south-western Nigerian universities, for instance, moonlighting as featured performers in school and urban showcases were tactics commonly used to supplement family support.
10. Nigeria's film industry is second only to Bollywood in terms of annual films released (Statistics 2009) and generates over $590.2 million in annual revenue (Akande 2009). Despite the now ubiquitous technical critiques of Nollywood films, its genre conventions, nevertheless, connect with a vast audience within the diaspora, which consumes over 50 million copies per year, excluding pirated copies (Evuleocha 2008; Larkin 2004).
11. For further discussion of localized immediacy, see Forman (2002) on the centrality of local neighborhoods in the territoriality of American hip hop.
12. In yet another indication of the creative space shared by both industries, according to O' and Teju Komolafe, their foray into YouTube music video production was actually intended to be a launching pad for Nollywood filmmaking careers (personal communication, 9 October 2009).
13. In the above-cited article in *The Guardian* on Naija hip hop, the chief executive officer (CEO) of Nigerian record label Chocolate City, Audu Maikori, notes that the internet and social media, in particular, have allowed Nigerian artists to circumvent traditional commercial streams and establish new audiences online.
14. Durham (2000) and de Boeck and Honwana (2005) offer helpful discussions of this scholarly shift.
15. In Turner's original work on the Ndembu of Zambia, it is worth noting that the concept of liminality described the period within rites of passage, during which initiates occupied a socially ambiguous role as neither their previous social status nor the status they were in the process of becoming. However, the concept of liminality has since been productively retooled to describe the experiences of those 'between' other social stages (i.e. youth), cultures, etc.
16. Translations of vernacularized languages are often imprecise. However, for the benefit of readers unfamiliar with Nigerian pidgin English, italicized translations of extended lyrics are offered, hereafter, in footnotes, when appropriate: 'Na broken English I go talk/*I speak broken English*/Watch me lean and watch me jock/*Watch me lean and jock (two dance moves)*/Jocking all those haterz man/When I do dat Naija Boy/*When I do that Naija Boy*/It be game ova for dem […]/*It's over for them (haters)*/You catch me at your Naija party/*You see me at Nigerian parties*/Eating some *egusi* stew/*Eating egusi (local Nigerian) stew*/Haterz get mad because I get me some Gucci shoe/*Haters are mad because I wear Gucci shoes*'.
17. During special occasions, such as weddings, Nigerians 'spray' money on dancers or individuals being celebrated by carefully placing bills on the head of the subject.

18. A common comedic tool throughout the videos is to feature white people doing 'Nigerian' things, even when these sub-plots have nothing to do with the lyrical and visual narratives. In the 'Lollipop' video, a white male is seen eating, with his hands, a Nigerian soup that is apparently so hot that he must pour water over his head. Then, in a jarring documentary-style clip, a black woman, presumably Nigerian, is seen with a wrapper tied around her upper body like a tube dress 'overseeing' (inverse slavery pun intended) a white woman who is also wearing Yoruba-style clothing as she pounds yam.
19. What we are describing here as conspicuous cosmopolitanism also relates to an emerging discourse that has been labeled 'Afropolitanism', or African cosmopolitanism. Understood, in similar terms, as an identity and transnational experience, Afropolitanism is growing as a form of self-identification among African diasporans with physical and cultural ties to African and Western countries. See Wawrzinek and Makokha (2011) for an introduction.
20. 419 scams are named after the article of the Nigerian Criminal Code relating to advance-fee fraud, and popularly refers to forms of fraud, especially cyber fraud, that have come to be associated with Nigeria.
21. Though the pathologies of black America have been located in male–female reproductive relations (or lack thereof) since the Moynihan Report, in recent years, a slew of media investigative reports and self-help literature have tackled the 'problem' of single, educated, and unmarried black women with keen interest.
22. I'm king of my village 'and my money get my image … /*My money gives me status*/I get miles, darling and US dollar/*I have airline miles and US dollars*/No be 419 o I get money proper/*My money was not illegally obtained, it's 'proper'*.
23. 'If you want find husband and make a good children/*If you want to get married and have good children*/ The kind wey turn to doctor after I go kuku beat them/*The kind that will become doctors*/Choose me, I get good genes and good system/*Choose me, I have good genes*/I was raised in Naija as a good Christian (YES O!)/*I was raised in Nigeria as a good Christian*/American Baby/Beyoncé, I can be your Jay-Z/We be the same I'm just a darker rapper/*We (Jay-Z and the NB) are the same, I'm just darker*/I'm the true African/He's a swagger jacker / *He's a copy-cat.*'
24. The NB admit that the featured woman is actually Ethiopian not Nigerian and that, ironically, a white American friend sings the lyrics to her solo (personal communication, 2009).
25. The phrase 'Johnny Just Come', used popularly to describe new African immigrants and their experiences of culture shock, is a contemporary derivative of 'Johnny Just Drop', attributed to Nigerian music icon, Fela Kuti, who released a live album of the same title.

References

Adejunmobi, M. A. 2007. "Nigerian Video Film as Minor Transnational Practice." *Postcolonial Text* 3 (2): 1–16.

Akande, Victor. 2009. "Film Festivals and Nollywood: An Evaluation." *The* Nation, August 27, 2009.

Akpabio, E., and K. Mustapha-Lambe. 2008. "Nollywood Films and the Cultural Imperialism Hypothesis." *Perspectives on Global Development and Technology* 73 (4): 259–270.

Alim, H. S., A. Ibrahim, and A. Pennycook. 2009. *Global Linguistic Flows: Hip Hop Cultures, Youth Identities, and the Politics of Language*. New York: Taylor & Francis.

Alzouma, G. 2008. "Identities in a 'Fragmegrated' World: Black Cyber-Communities and the French Integration System." *African and Black Diaspora: An International Journal* 1 (2): 201–214.

Apter, A. H. 2005. *The Pan-African Nation: Oil and the Spectacle of Culture in Nigeria*. Chicago: University of Chicago Press.

Burrell, Jenna. 2012. *Invisible Users: Youth in the Internet Cafes of Urban Ghana*. Cambridge, MA: MIT Press.

Chang, J. 2005. *Can't Stop Won't Stop: A History of the Hip-Hop Generation*. London: Macmillan.

Charles, C. A. D. 2003. "Skin Bleaching, Self-Hate and Black Identity in Jamaica." *Journal of Black Studies* 33 (6): 711–728.

Clarke, K. 2007. "Transnational Yoruba Revivalism and the Diasporic Politics of Heritage." *American Ethnologist* 34 (4): 721–734.

Clifford, J. 1994. "Diasporas." *Cultural Anthropology* 9 (3): 302–338.

Cocq, E. 2006. "Audiovisual Markets in the Developing World." In *Trends in Audiovisual Markets: Regional Perspectives from the South*, 1–15. Paris: UNESCO.

Dasgupta, S., et al. 2005. "Policy Reform, Economic Growth, and the Digital Divide." *Oxford Development Studies* 33 (2): 229–243.

de Boeck, F. and A. Honwana (eds.). 2005. *Makers and Breakers: Children and Youth in Postcolonial Africa*. Oxford: James Currey, Trenton: Africa World Press, and Dakar: Codesria.

Diawara, M. 2000. *In Search of Africa*. Cambridge, MA: Harvard University Press.

Durham, D. 2000. "Youth and the Social Imagination in Africa: Introduction to Parts 1 and 2." *Anthropological Quarterly* 73 (3): 113–120.

Edwards, B. H. 2001. "The Uses of Diaspora." *Social Text* 66: 45–74.

Evuleocha, S. U. 2008. "Nollywood and the Home Video Revolution: Implications for Marketing Videofilm in Africa." *International Journal of Emerging Markets* 3 (4): 407–417.

Flores, J. 2000. *From Bomba to Hip-Hop: Puerto Rican Culture and Latino Identity*. New York: Columbia University Press.

Forman, M. 2002. *The 'Hood Comes First: Race, Space, and Place in Rap and Hip-Hop*. Middletown: Wesleyan University Press.

Gilroy, P. 1993. *The Black Atlantic: Modernity and Double Consciousness*. Cambridge: Harvard University Press.

Gilroy, P. 2002. *Against Race: Imagining Political Culture Beyond the Color Line*. Cambridge: Harvard University Press.

Glenn, E. N. 2008. "Yearning for Lightness: Transnational Circuits in the Marketing and Consumption of Skin Lighteners." *Gender & Society* 22 (3): 281–302.

Hebdige, D. 1987. *Cutn'Mix: Culture, Identity and Caribbean Music*. London: Routledge.

Ibukun, Y. 2011. "Nigerian Hip-Hop, Long a Copy, Grows into its Own." *The Guardian*. May 4. http://www.guardian.co.uk/world/feedarticle/962818

Internet World Stats. 2009. *Internet Usage Statistics for Africa* 2009 [cited October 1, 2009 2009]. http://www.internetworldstats.com/stats1.htm.:

Iton, R. 2008. *In Search of the Black Fantastic: Politics and Popular Culture in the Post-Civil Rights Era*. New York: Oxford University Press.

Keniston, K., and D. Kumar (eds.). 2004. "The Four Digital Divides." *IT Experience in India: Bridging the Digital Divide*: 11–36.

Koser, K. 2003. *New African Diasporas*. London: Routledge.

Larkin, B. 2004. "Degraded Images, Distorted Sounds: Nigerian Video and the Infrastructure of Piracy." *Public Culture* 16 (2): 289–314.

Lessig, L. 2008. *Remix: Making Art and Commerce Thrive in the Hybrid Economy*. New York: Penguin. doi:

Levinthal, D., ed. 1999. *Blackface*. Santa Fe, NM: Arena.

Mahon, M. 2000. "The Visible Evidence of Cultural Producers." *Annual Review of Anthropology* 29: 467–492.

Martin, M. T. 1995. *Cinemas of the Black Diaspora: Diversity, Dependence, and Oppositionality*. Detroit: Wayne State University Press.

Maira, S. 1998. "Desis Reprazent: Bhangra Remix and Hip Hop in New York City." *Postcolonial Studies* 1 (3): 357–370.

Maysles, P. 2002. "Dubbing the Nation." *Small Axe* 11 (Mar 2002): 91–111.

Mignolo, W. 2002. "The Many Faces of Cosmo-polis: Border Thinking and Critical Cosmopolitanism." *Public Culture* 12 (3): 721–748.

Mitchell, T., ed. 2001. *Global Noise: Rap and Hip Hop Outside the USA*. Middletown, CT: Wesleyan University Press.

Monson, I. T. 2000. *African Diaspora: A Musical Perspective*. New York: Taylor & Francis.

Ntarangwi, M. 2009. *East African Hip Hop: Youth Culture and Globalization*. Urbana and Chicago: University of Illinois Press.

O'Brien, D. B. C. 1996. "A Lost Generation? Youth Identity and State Decay in West Africa." In *Postcolonial Identities in Africa*, edited by R. Werbner and T. Ranger, 55–74. London: Zed Books.

Okome, O. 2007. "Nollywood: Spectatorship, Audience and the Sites of Consumption." *Postcolonial Text* 3 (2): 1–20.

Okpewho, I., C. B. Davies, and A. A. A. Mazrui. 1999. *The African Diaspora: African Origins and New World Identities*. Bloomington: Indiana University Press.

Omoniyi, T. 2008. "So I Choose to Do Am Naija Style." In *Global Linguistic Flows: Hip Hop Cultures, Youth Identities, and the Politics of Language*, edited by H. Samy Alim et. al. New York: Routledge.

Omoniyi, T., S. Scheld, and D. Oni. 2009. "Negotiating Youth Identity in a Transnational Context in Nigeria." *Social Dynamics* 35 (1): 1–18.

Osumare, H. 2007. *The Africanist Aesthetic in Global Hip-Hop: Power Moves*. New York: Palgrave Macmillan.

Perullo, A. 2005. "Hooligans and Heroes: Youth Identity and Hip Hop in Dar es Salaam, Tanzania." *Africa Today* 51 (4): 75–101.
Pick, James B., and Rasool Azari. 2008. "Global Digital Divide: Influence of Socioeconomic, Governmental, and Accessibility Factors on Information Technology." *Information Technology for Development* 14 (2): 91–115.
Rheingold, H. 2000. *Virtual community: Homesteading on the Electronic Frontier*. Cambridge, MA: MIT Press.
Robinson, C. J. 1998. "Blaxploitation and the Misrepresentation of Liberation." *Race Class* 40 (1): 1–12.
Rose, T. 1994. *Black Noise*. Middletown, CT: Wesleyan University Press.
Sharpley-Whiting, T. D. 2008. *Pimps Up, Ho's Down: Hip Hop's Hold on Young Black Women*. New York: New York University Press.
Simon, R. 1998. "The Stigmatization of 'Blaxploitation'." In *Soul: Black Power, Politics, and Pleasure*, edited by M. G. and R. C. Green, 236–249. New York: NYU Press.
Smith, D., and Lamble, L. 2011. "Africa's Burgeoning Middle Class Brings Hope to a Continent." *The Guardian*, December 25. http://www.guardian.co.uk/world/2011/dec/25/africas-middle-class-hope-continent
Statistics, UNESCO Institute of. 2009. *Information Sheet No. 1: Analysis of the UIS International Survey on Feature Film Statistics*. UNESCO Institute of Statistics 2009 [cited September 30, 2009 2009]. http://www.uis.unesco.org/ev.php?ID=7651_201&ID2=DO_TOPIC
Turner, V. 1986. *The Anthropology of Performance*. New York: Performing Arts Journal.
Turner, V., and E. Bruner, eds. 1986. *The Anthropology of Experience*. Urbana, IL: University of Illinois Press.
Ugor, P. U. 2009. Youth Culture and the Struggle for Social Space: The Nigerian Video Films. Thesis (PhD). University of Alberta, Edmonton.
Wall, M. 2009. "Africa on YouTube: Musicians, Tourists, Missionaries and Aid Workers." *International Communication Gazette* 71 (5): 393–407
Wallsten, S. 2005. "Regulation and Internet Use in Developing Countries." *Economic Development and Cultural Change* 53 (2): 501–523.
Watkins, S. 2006. *Hip Hop Matters: Politics, Pop Culture, And the Struggle for the Soul of a Movement*. New York: Beacon Press.
Wawrzinek, J. and K. S. Makokha (eds.). 2011. *Negotiating Afropolitanism: Essays on Borders and Spaces in Contemporary African Literature and Folklore*. Amsterdam: Rodopi.
Zajc, M. 2009. "Nigerian Video Film Cultures." *Anthropological Notebooks* 15 (1): 65–85.

Index

INDEX